THEOCRITUS AND THE INVENTION OF FICTION

The bucolic *Idylls* of Theocritus are the first literature to invent a fully fictional world that is not an image of reality but an alternative to it. They are thereby distinguished from the other *Idylls* and from Hellenistic poetry as a whole. This book examines the bucolic poems in the light of ancient and modern conceptions of fictionality. It explores how access to this fictional world is mediated by form and how this world appears as an object of desire for the characters within it. The argument culminates in a new reading of *Idyll* 7, where Professor Payne discusses the encounter between author and fictional creation in the poem and its importance for the later pastoral tradition. Close readings of Theocritus, Callimachus, Hermesianax, and the *Lament for Bion* are supplemented with parallels from modern fiction and an extended discussion of the heteronymic poetry of Fernando Pessoa.

MARK PAYNE is Assistant Professor of Classics at the University of Chicago.

THEOCRITUS
AND THE
INVENTION OF FICTION

MARK PAYNE
The University of Chicago

CAMBRIDGE UNIVERSITY PRESS
Cambridge, New York, Melbourne, Madrid, Cape Town, Singapore,
São Paulo, Delhi, Dubai, Tokyo

Cambridge University Press
The Edinburgh Building, Cambridge CB2 8RU, UK

Published in the United States of America by Cambridge University Press, New York

www.cambridge.org
Information on this title: www.cambridge.org/9780521124294

© Mark Edward Payne 2007

This publication is in copyright. Subject to statutory exception
and to the provisions of relevant collective licensing agreements,
no reproduction of any part may take place without the written
permission of Cambridge University Press.

First published 2007
This digitally printed version 2009

A catalogue record for this publication is available from the British Library

ISBN 978-0-521-86577-7 Hardback
ISBN 978-0-521-12429-4 Paperback

Cambridge University Press has no responsibility for the persistence or accuracy of
URLs for external or third-party internet websites referred to in this publication, and
does not guarantee that any content on such websites is, or will remain, accurate or
appropriate.

Contents

Preface		*page* vii
Acknowledgments		viii
	Introduction: In the realms of the unreal	1
1	The pleasures of the imaginary	24
2	The presence of the fictional world	49
3	Becoming bucolic	92
4	From fiction to metafiction	114
	Conclusion: The future of a fiction	146
Bibliography		170
Index		181

Preface

I would like to thank all the people who have contributed to this book in the various phases of its development. Special thanks are due to my dissertation advisor Suzanne Saïd, who guided me not just through the dissertation itself, but through all the projects that led up to it, and to the members of my dissertation committee, James Coulter, James Zetzel, David Sider, and Lowell Edmunds, for their many helpful observations and criticisms. I would also like to thank all my colleagues at the University of Chicago for their advice and encouragement.

My fellow graduate students at Columbia University, Francisco Barrenechea, Jackie Elliot, and Sarah Nooter, helped me tremendously as I was getting started with this work, and the participants in my Theocritus and Hellenistic poetry seminars at the University of Chicago contributed just as much as I was nearing the end of it. Thomas Pavel was kind enough to read an early version of the Introduction, and Marco Fantuzzi, in a remarkable act of generosity, to read the entire work in about a week. I am very grateful to them both, and to the two anonymous readers for this Press, who also offered many invaluable suggestions.

Finally, I would like to thank my wife Laura, for everything, and for reminding me why we read fiction in the first place.

Acknowledgments

An earlier version of Chapter 1 appeared as "Ecphrasis and Song in Theocritus' *Idyll* 1," *Greek, Roman, and Byzantine Studies* 42 (2001): 263–87.

An earlier version of part of Chapter 3 appeared as "Narrative technique in Theocritus's *Idyll* 12," *Arethusa* 36 (2003): 37–48.

Introduction: In the realms of the unreal

No, shepherd, nothing doing.[1]

The studies of Theocritus' bucolic poems in this book have grown out of the mixture of puzzlement and curiosity that I felt when I first read them. On the one hand, they seemed to me to lack the pointed vigor of expression that I admired in Greek lyric and tragic poetry. On the other, they were devoid of the attractions of plot and character that make rereading Homer so rewarding. I tried to map the appeal that I nonetheless felt in them onto that of the later pastoral tradition. But here again I found that, despite the resonant names of the later literature – Lycidas, Comatas, Damoetas – their allure did not reside in the kind of verbal magic that attracted me there. In the plainness of their poetic language, they read more like William Carlos Williams than the *Eclogues*, or *L'après-midi d'un faune*. What began to occur to me as a result was that the appeal of the poems did not in fact consist in any of the traditional resources of lyric and narrative poetry but in something rather less concrete, and more difficult to place, which I here call the world of the poems. By this I mean a complex of elements that embraces the physical characteristics of the places the herdsmen inhabit, their nature and behavior as fictional characters, and the positioning of them and their fictional world in relation to the reality of the reader. In each of these areas the bucolic poems manifest themselves as neither making present the world of myth, nor offering an imitation of life. Their world is the first fully fictional world in Western literature, and the pleasures of this fiction are so great that the poems can do without most of what is a source of delight in earlier poetry: vigorous and stimulating language, engaging plots, absorbing characters. Their appeal lies instead in fiction's ability to reveal to us a world that we have not encountered or imagined before.

At this point then I want to distinguish between two kinds of fiction: on the one hand, fictions that are a useful model for understanding the

---

[1] William Carlos Williams' translation of *Idyll* 1.15; Williams (1986–88) II.268.

reality that we ourselves inhabit, and, on the other, fictions that offer an alternative to it. This does not map exactly onto the distinction between realist and fantastic literature. *The Lord of the Rings* and *Star Wars* function just as well as *War and Peace*, or the *Iliad* and *Oedipus Rex* (Aristotle's preferred examples) in the first category, even though they feature non-human characters in a world other than our own. Because their agents are recognizably motivated by factors that determine human action in the real world, these narratives quite easily fulfil the function mimetic theory envisages for fiction as a cognitive tool for understanding and reflecting upon real-world behavior. On the other hand, works that contain human agents in real-world locations, such as the chivalric romance, may be useless as mimetic fiction because of the kinds of character and behavior these agents exhibit, or because they do not engage in activities that would allow us to recognize patterns of real-world possibility and necessity. I have indicated my reasons for not wanting to call such fictions "fantastic," and I am also hesitant to call them "ideal," because of the moral or metaphysical baggage this would saddle them with. I have opted therefore for the less loaded "fully fictional" to describe them.

The distinction between mimetic and fully fictional fictions is a theoretical one. Most fictions offer the reader the opportunity to engage with a world that is, for the duration of the reading, an alternative to reality, while at the same time allowing this reader to reflect upon some aspect of his or her real-world experience by comparing it with the fiction. Instantiations of the extremes do exist, however, and there is a well-known mimetic literature that explores the consequences of preferring its fully fictional sibling. *Don Quixote* and *Madame Bovary*, for example, tell of a self that falls under the spell of such fictions, which do not elucidate reality, but rather dim its allure in comparison with themselves. In Theocritus' time too, this polarization of fiction into mimetic and fully fictional kinds is clearly visible, in the contrast between, on the one hand, dramatic poems that offer small-scale vignettes of everyday life (mime and its literary derivatives) and, on the other, Theocritus' pastoral fiction, dramatic poems that offer an alternative to it. The visibility of this theoretical distinction in the period may well be the result of crises in the status of literary representation brought about by the birth of the Library at Alexandria and the systemization of discursive knowledge this entailed. As well as the polarization of fictional worlds, there is an emergent poetry of fact in the period, whose truth claims rest upon objective witnesses and a marked change in the panegyrical use of myth. Various responses to the suddenly urgent question "What are poets for?" can be discerned, and I shall argue that the fully fictional world of the bucolic poems is not the least of these. By demonstrating so clearly in these poems that a fictional world may occasion our assent to its existence and even our desire to belong to it, even though it manifestly lacks any true being as the presence of myth, history, or even contemporary reality, Theocritus rewrites the agenda for poetic invention, and so makes his bucolic poetry visible as a new possibility for literature. Aligning the emergent genre with the possibility of pure, or absolute, fiction, Theocritus invests its world with the ontological prestige in respect to everyday human reality that had once belonged to myth. Before looking more closely at this valorization of pure fictionality in relation to Theocritus' contemporaries, however, I want first to look briefly at a modern fiction that will help to clarify what I mean by a fully fictional world, and the kind of appeal that is inherent in it.

The Story of the Vivian Girls, in What Is Known as the Realms of the Unreal, of the Glandeco-Angelinian War Storm, Caused by the Child Slave Rebellion, to give it its full title, is, at 15,145 single-spaced typewritten pages, almost certainly the longest work of prose fiction ever created. It was written over the course of several decades by Chicago janitor and dishwasher Henry Darger (1892–1973), and illustrated by him both in the course of its creation and after the manuscript was complete and the author had moved on to other projects.[2] Darger's story is the chronicle of a war waged by the Christian nations of Angelinia, Abbieannia, and Calverinia against the rebel, slave-owning state of Glandelinia and its allies. The primary model is clearly the American Civil War, with children taking the place of African Americans as both the cause of the war and its most important protagonists, but this real-world source in no sense inhibits our recognition that the resultant world is fully fictional in nature. So too, plot structures, objects, and named characters from (among others) Mark Twain, Longfellow, Harriet Beecher Stowe, and the Oz stories of Frank Baum all find their way into the *Realms of the Unreal*, where they become part of the new fictional world.[3] This is not intertextuality – appropriation is not intended to establish a relationship between the new work and the old, any more than the book is intended as a commentary on the Civil War. It is rather what theorists of fiction have called transduction – the process by which characters and

---

[2] The best introductions to Darger's work are Bonesteel (2000) and MacGregor (2002). Both consider Darger under the rubric of outsider artist, Bonesteel emphasizing the artist, MacGregor the outsider. John Ashbery's volume of narrative poetry, *Girls on the Run* (New York: Farrar, Straus, Giroux, 1999), a free fantasy on the adventures of the Vivian Girls, did much to popularize Darger's work in poetry circles, and Jessica Yu's 2004 film, *In the Realms of the Unreal*, has brought it to the attention of a still larger audience.

[3] Bonesteel (2000) 34 gives details of Darger's library, and which parts of it ended up in his own work.

situations can be transported from preexisting fictional worlds into new ones, where they are fully independent of their predecessor.[4]

What is true of Darger's use of literary and historical sources is no less true of his appropriations of contemporary imagery to illustrate his work. Since he never learned to draw, the thousands of figures who populate his world – the little girls, winged dragons, and winged little girls who are the heroines of the story, as well as the adult armies who are their adversaries, and the landscapes of gigantic flowers, trees, birds, and storms where their battles are fought – were not drawn freehand, but created by techniques of collage, tracing, and photographic enlargement that Darger evolved over the course of his life as a means of realizing ever more grand and fantastic compositions. His sources were primarily newspapers and popular magazines, with favorite images retraced time and again to make intricate compositions in which dozens of figures are distributed over a picture plane, at times carefully articulated to give an illusion of naturalistic depth, at times treated as a pure visual surface.[5] His own additions are limited to details of hairstyle and dress in the case of his story's human protagonists, and (male) genitalia when they appear unclothed.[6] More dramatically, the beings known as Blengins, who start out as winged serpents but later appear in human form, have the bodies and faces of little girls, but are adorned with rams' horns and fantastically colored butterfly wings. While the material is appropriated from the real world, its ontological transformation is absolute; all connections to its source are severed, and this sampled material manifests a new, fully fictional creation.

Darger seems to have responded to the presence of this invented world in two ways. Detailed accounts of battles, with casualty lists that supplement them, give the author the air of a journalist reporting on a world that is ontologically independent of the writer even as he reflects on his efforts as its creator: "I have here written as far as I was able, in unusually long details to make the scenes more striking, but even then even I have not succeeded in accomplishing what should have been done, as it is impossible to describe them as they really are."[7] Here the author doubts his successful realization of a world that is independent of him, yet, at other times, his work manifests that world to him with such intensity that its very presence appears proof of its independence. It is a remarkable feature of his large-scale compositions that, of the dozens of figures they contain, almost

---

[4] See Dolezel (1998) 199–226.   [5] On the sources, see Bonesteel (2000) 29.
[6] Cf. MacGregor (2002) 520–37 on the "fantasy phallus" in the artwork. Whatever its origins in Darger's creative personality, its addition explicitly marks the independence of fictional image from real-world source.
[7] Citation from *In the Realms of the Unreal* in Bonesteel (2000) 44.

all are oriented towards the viewer, and many make eye contact with their observer from within the fictional picture space they occupy.[8] Their gaze denies the ontological boundary that separates their world from ours, as if we could simply walk out of our own world and into the fictional world of *In the Realms of the Unreal*. In a scene that rivals the metafictional gusto of the most daring postmodern novel, Darger's characters within the fiction comment upon this aspect of the way they are portrayed in its illustrations. At one point in the story its protagonists, the Vivian Girls, come across some old books that contain a detailed history of the war in which they are presently participating, and which are signed "Henry J. Darger, author." The girls become the first readers, and the first critics, of the book in which their story is told:

"Every picture seems to look you straight in the face as if you had some secret to tell them, or as if you suspected them of knowing your thoughts." "And probably he had to use them as company, as he was childless." "Maybe that is so, and he wanted them all to look as if they were paying attention to him," said Jennie. "He must have been a very odd man." "I wouldn't mind seeing him," said Violet.[9]

This is fiction's version of creation's primal scene. The invented world appears so undeniably alive, it is only fit that it should acknowledge the creator who made it. Since this is impossible in his own world, he inscribes this desire for recognition within his invention. Parallels abound in religious literature, where the first duty of created beings is to praise their creator,[10] and in the postmodern novel the scene in which the author (impossibly) confronts his own creations has become something of a cliché.[11] Just like the real world, fully fictional worlds provoke ontological wonder because they cannot be reduced to, or contained within, our own. The more palpable their presence as they stand over against the real world as something not obviously derived from it, the more attention they draw to the threshold that separates the two, and the more their illusory presence and uncanny (in)existence seems like a call for mutual recognition directed at us, their

---

[8] For example, "At Jennie Richie," Bonesteel (2000) 150–51, contains eighty figures, seventy in the foreground, ten in the background, and of these all but two face forward, with about twenty breaking the picture plane with their gaze.

[9] Citation from *In the Realms of the Unreal* in MacGregor (2002) 20–22, with good discussion. This incident seems to have caught John Ashbery's attention. In *Girls on the Run*, his versions of the Vivian Girls speak to him directly, and instruct him to tell their story (p. 3): "Write it now, Tidbit said, before they get back. And, quivering, I took the pen."

[10] The Mayan creation myth is remarkable in this respect in that the gods require several attempts to make beings who are sufficiently intelligent to praise them correctly. See Tedlock (1985) 69–86.

[11] McHale (1987) 213–14. Remarkably, this very scenario is the subject of a flight of fancy on the part of Aristotle in the *Nicomachean Ethics* (9.7.3–4, 1167b34–1168a4): "Every artist loves his own work more than that work would love him if it were to come to life. And this is perhaps especially the case with poets, for they dote upon their own poems and love them as if they were children."

observers. It is with this concern for fictional presence in mind that I want to approach the bucolic world and its place in Hellenistic poetry.

The distinction between truth and deceptive semblance appears early in Greek literature, in the mouth of Hesiod's Muses, who, in the opening lines of the *Theogony*, speak of their ability to tell "many lies resembling the truth," but also to give voice to "true things" when they wish. Pindar gives a polemical edge to this distinction in his seventh *Nemean*, when he blames Homer for creating a version of the Trojan War in which Odysseus is just such a deceptive phantom. An august presence dwells in Homer's words, he claims, so that they have the power to induce men's assent to palpable untruth, leading their minds aside from reality (*Nem.* 7.20–23). Plato, in his own way, echoes Pindar's concerns about the truth status of Homeric narrative, and it is not until Aristotle that we have a discussion of fiction that endeavors to find a value for it that lies beyond the distinction between truth and falsehood.[12] For Aristotle, the value of poetic narrative is unrelated to the question of whether or not it is a true account of past events, and he gives the poet full freedom and full responsibility for the creation of his stories. The poet invents these first, then assigns names to the characters that enact them, which in the case of comedy he invents along with the plot, while in tragedy, by custom, though not by necessity, he uses those of the legendary families of the heroic age, the Homeric heroes and Theban kings. In either case, the bearers of these names are fictions; their function is not to refer to the mythical bearers of their names, but to be the agents of actions that model universal behaviors in the world of the fiction's audience (*Poetics* 9).[13] Because (ideally) chance has been eliminated from the plot of poetic fictions, so that they unfold according

---

[12] The transition from an archaic "poetics of truth" to a post-Aristotelian "poetics of fiction" is traced in Finkelberg (1998). Various positions have been taken on the degree to which Aristotle's account may have been anticipated by sophistic discussions of deception, and its part in literary experience, particularly that of Gorgias (on which see Gill [1993] 74–75, who would minimize it, and, in the same volume, Morgan [1993] 180–81, who would give it a larger role). Cf. Ford (2002) 231, who notes the use of *plassein* in reference to poetry by Xenophanes and Gorgias but concludes that "in neither case do the emotionally powerful and persuasive 'made-up things' belong to a special realm of literary discourse that is distinct from ordinary lying." What I would emphasize here is that Gorgias' account of deception is closely tied to the notion of imaginary presence created through speech, and that this emphasis on speech as the most immediate form of imaginary presence is retained in Aristotle's discussion.

[13] See the account of mimesis as fiction in Halliwell (2002) 166–68, a thorough exposition of the brief notes on this topic in Halliwell (1987) 72–78, 172. Cf. Ford (2002) 231: "The Greek word that can be said to express a concept of fiction is Aristotle's *mimesis*." As the excellent discussion of Aristotle *Poetics* 9 and Antiphanes *Poesis* fr. 189 in Lowe (2000) 260–61 makes clear, Old Comedy's contribution to the poetics of fiction (and here we see its continuity with the fictive speakers of archaic iambic poetry) was made-up characters, not made-up worlds. Even the most fantastic comic fiction takes place in a world that is recognizably a version of Athenian reality.

Introduction: In the realms of the unreal

to strict rules of possibility and necessity, they allow us to recognize general patterns of human life and behavior in them, and so provide a valuable cognitive tool for understanding the world in which we actually live and act. Aristotle, by contrast, would have had little time for the ancient novel, in which contingent detail, chance events, and perfect heroes and heroines who make no mistakes we could learn from are the primary sources of interest,[14] and still less for fictional worlds peopled by beings who are not recognizably moral agents like ourselves, for such worlds would have no efficacy in orienting our behavior in our own world. It follows from this argument, then, that the more fictional the fictional world is, the more its interest is intrinsic to it, and does not consist in its relation to our own world, with regard to which it can only appear as an alternative, and not as a model.

The question of degrees of fictionality is not broached in the *Poetics*, where differences between mimetic genres are explained by reference to the ethical character of the agents they portray – tragedy and epic depict superior people, comedy inferior, and so on; all are equally fictional (*Poetics* 2–5). Distinctions appear later, however, in literary scholarship derived from the *Poetics*. A well-known example is the (bT) scholion to *Iliad* 14.342–51, in which the commentator remarks upon the scene in which Zeus wraps Hera in a cloud of gold and makes love to her within it while golden raindrops fall to the ground, and grass, lotus flowers, crocuses, and hyacinths spring up beneath them:

τρεῖς δέ εἰσι τρόποι, καθ' οὓς πᾶσα ποίησις θεωρεῖται· ὁ μιμητικὸς τοῦ ἀληθοῦς, φιλοπάτωρ, μισογύνης, ἄπιστος, παρρησιαστής· ὁ κατὰ φαντασίαν τῆς ἀληθείας, ὃν δεῖ μὴ κατὰ μέρος ἐξετάζειν, οἷον, ὅτι ψυχαὶ γεύονται καὶ λαλοῦσι, πάντως ἐρεῖ τις καὶ γλῶσσαν ἔχουσι καὶ βρόγχον· τρίτος δὲ ὁ καθ' ὑπέρθεσιν ἀληθείας καὶ φαντασίαν, Κύκλωπες, Λαιστρυγόνες καὶ ταῦτα τὰ περὶ θεῶν.

There are three rubrics under which all poetry may be considered. The first represents reality directly, for example when it portrays "the man who loves his father," "the misogynist," "the untrustworthy man," or "the loudmouth." The second proceeds by way of fantasy upon reality, and one should not probe the details of this type too closely, as when, for example, someone claims that because souls eat and talk they must surely have a tongue and throat. The third exaggerates and goes beyond reality, as is the case with the Cyclopes, the Lastrygonians, and these things [Zeus and Hera's lovemaking] that have to do with the gods.[15]

---

[14] Argued with humor by Morgan (1993) 182–83 and with a wealth of detail in what follows.

[15] My interpretation follows Meijering (1987) 68–69. The threefold division resembles the Latin forensic distinction between the true, the fictive that resembles the true, and the fictive that does not resemble the true; see Morgan (1993) 188–91, who notes how well these categories map onto literary genres – history, New Comedy, tragedy – and suggests an origin in Peripatetic literary theory.

Since *The Misogynist* and *The Untrustworthy Man* are known to be the titles of plays by Menander (the latter is also the title of one of Theophrastus' *Characters*), it is evident that the scholiast has in mind New Comedy, with its representation of universality through omnipresent human types, as his example of poetry that represents reality directly. On this understanding, the human characters and actions of the *Iliad* would constitute a mimetic bedrock that epic poetry shares with more truthful kinds of poetic representation, to which various kinds of additions have been made by the fantasy of the poet. Thus, his second kind of poetry is designed to accommodate those moments in epic where beings from another world (such as the world of the dead) are presented as a kind of fantastic double of actual human beings; while anthropomorphic in general outline, their component parts should not be examined too closely. His final category would explain the monsters of epic, and the marvels that surround the gods, as pure products of the poet's invention that are not modeled on reality at all, but are conceived by a free fantasy that departs from them.

Myth is decaying before our very eyes here, as its once unitary world is parceled out among the mutually exclusive categories of realism, fantastic realism, and fantasy. The ontological status of literary representations is essentially labile, and subject to revision as a result of pragmatic, non-literary developments. If readers no longer believe in actual gods who make love in golden clouds, then gods that do so in literature can only be understood as fictions.[16] From the perspective of the *Poetics*, the *Iliad* scholion is a face-saving strategy. By relegating certain aspects of the text to the category of poetic invention, it allows the remainder to retain the cognitive value that mimetic theory claims for literature as a tool for interpreting real-world experience. Conversely, while the banishment of the gods is not a necessary outcome of the adoption of a mimetic theory of literary value, it is a likely one. Because the gods are not subject to the same laws of probability and necessity that govern human beings, stories in which they are significant agents in their own right are unlikely to offer much in the way of a model of human life. While Aristotle focuses his discussion of poetic fiction on Homer and tragedy, for the scholiast it is evidently New Comedy that functions best as mimetic art, both because its agents are character types who are easily recognizable as universals of real-world human behavior and because these types are presented within a fictional world that has minimal deviation from the real world. As Aristophanes of Byzantium so famously put it, "O Menander and Life, which of you imitated the other?" Realistic

---

[16] Pavel (1986) 39–42; cf. Schmidt (1976) 161–78 on how pragmatic considerations constrain readers' understanding of fictionality.

literature simply works better as mimetic fiction, because there is so much less in it that is extraneous to this function and which has to be bracketed out in its reception.[17]

Hellenistic poetry has been particularly well served by formalist criticism. From the early interest in its mixture of genres[18] to more recent attention to allusion and intertextuality,[19] classical scholarship has constructed a minutely detailed picture of the Alexandrian poets' response to their own literary history. What is needed now is an equally detailed account of the kinds of world-making that are the outcome of this activity – how formal innovations are related to fictionality and the mimetic function. Manifest differences in content with regard to archaic and classical poetry may not be indications of the author's agonistic relationship to his predecessors, but extensions and developments of the repertory of fictional worlds available to him. Bucolic poetry, for example, may be less about demonstrating an oppositional response to epic by portraying low-class or marginal figures in the meter (hexameter) that had been the preserve of their betters,[20] and

---

[17] Aristotelian critical terminology in the prologue to one of Menander's plays explicitly invites the audience to acknowledge the validity of its theoretical concepts in the action of the drama itself. The prologue to the *Perikeiromene* is spoken by Agnoia (Ignorance) who talks about her role in the story; cf. *Poetics* 11, where Aristotle discusses recognition as a change from ignorance to knowledge that contributes to a satisfying plot. For the metatheatrical effect, see Gutzwiller (2000) 116–17.

[18] For "la confusion des genres" in the *Idylls*, see Legrand (1898) 413–36; for "die Kreuzung der Gattungen" exemplified by bucolic, see Kroll (1924) 203–207. For Rossi (1971a) 84, Theocritus is "an illustrious, perhaps the most illustrious, example of this new approach to poetry," and "what is most striking in his poetry is its mixture of genres." For Fantuzzi (1993a) 59, the *Idylls* remain "the most approved and most cited example of the contamination of genres." In a refinement of his earlier position that uses a model of the "literary system" derived from the linguistics of Saussure, Rossi (2000) 149–54 claims that generic mixing is a "functional expedient" by which this system renews itself under altered conditions of literary production. Much of the appearance of hybridization that is supposed to prove generic mixing in fact comes from the hybrid vocabulary of the commentators. Kroll (1924) 203–207 mixes metrical, thematic, and formal observations with terms derived from rhetorical handbooks, dramatic criticism, and ordinary language. Rossi (1971a), likewise, gives the impression that Theocritus is deliberately experimenting with established genres. Wilamowitz (1924) II.141 warned against the misperceptions that result when terminology from late imperial rhetorical handbooks is used to describe poetry, but his warning has largely gone unheeded. For a recent overview of this question that emphasizes both the pragmatic and literary historical constraints upon a purely ludic conception of the Hellenistic poet's relationship to tradition, see Fantuzzi and Hunter (2004) 37–40.

[19] For the demonstration of intertextual mastery as the organizing force of Hellenistic poetry, see Seiler (1997). Hubbard (1998) is a history of pastoral poetry as revisionary intertextuality. Callimachus' acme as scholar poet is perhaps reached in Bing (1988). Notably dissenting voices are Fraser (1972) I. 618–74 and Cameron (1995), to which Bing (2000) acerbically responds.

[20] So Halperin (1983) and Effe (1977, 1978), in their development of the work of Van Sickle (1976). As other scholars have pointed out, this not only makes the category of bucolic so large as to be devoid of descriptive value, but also ignores the reference to a particular represented world (the world of herdsmen) that is inscribed in the category name. Cf. Alpers (1996) 145–47, Gutzwiller (1991) 7 and (1996) 121.

more, as the name suggests, about creating a new fictional genre whose characters are herdsmen (*boukoloi*).[21]

Along with fictionality itself, the investigation of fictional presence – the mediation of the world of the poem by the formal structures that reveal it – will figure largely in the readings in this book. Formal structures are most productively analyzed in close relationship to the fictional worlds they transmit rather than as items in a catalogue of generic innovations. In particular, while formalist criticism approaches the poem as an object of study, I try here to give due attention to the ways in which our relation to it seems, as we read it, to be intersubjective. I look at how its world and the fictional beings who inhabit it present themselves to us, how the poems create the illusion of a living presence.[22] My aim is not therefore to construct an empathetic reader who can (all too easily) be contrasted with his formalist counterpart. For the presence of the bucolic characters is not like our access to the interiority of characters in the modern novel. Just as much as the Homeric characters, the characters of Hellenistic "literary drama" present themselves rhetorically,[23] through speeches, and we can only guess at the inner life that lies behind these speeches, just as we can only guess at the inner life of the writer that is exteriorized through the invention of characters. It is not empathy, or identification with characters, that I will be concerned with – putting ourselves into them – but rather with how they come to presence before us, with the ways in which they appear to us and seem to be before us as fictional beings. In this regard, as I hope to show, Theocritus' bucolic poetry differs in important ways from other Hellenistic literary drama, and from the performed drama that it took for its model.

---

[21] Fantuzzi (2004) 141–67 is a very thorough analysis of the stylization that creates the internal coherence of the bucolic world. As a "selective mixture of idealization and reality" (148), bucolic poetry, like other literary genres, has a particular synecdochic relationship to the real world by virtue of which its fiction is recognizable as a possible version of the extraliterary reality it models. In particular, the abundant reality effects in the fictional modeling of bucolic poetry allow its miniature dramas to stand alongside the well-established image of the real in contemporary mime. Cf. the discussion of genres as possible worlds in Edmunds (2001) 95–107. See Chapter 4 of the present book for a detailed discussion of the role of reality effects in the bucolic fiction of *Idyll* 7, where I argue that here, as elsewhere, these effects help to manifest the blatant fictionality of a world that, like its characters, is deliberately inconsistent from one poem to the next.

[22] My approach is thus very much in keeping with Philip Hardie's remarkable study of Ovid's "poetics of illusion," in which, Hardie (2002) 6, "the emphasis ... is on presence and illusion rather than on fictionality and authority, but these two areas are inextricably connected."

[23] I borrow the term from Bulloch (1985) 6, where it denotes poems in dramatic form that were not, it seems, intended for dramatic performance. Comparing the hymns of Callimachus that are spoken by a dramatic character with the dramatic poems of Theocritus and Herodas, he calls them "a distinct class of Alexandrian experimental poetry."

Direct speech is central to the production of fictional presence in ancient literary theory. In the *Poetics* there is considerable impetus in fact towards equating the dramatic mode with fictionality. Dialogue between characters, as opposed to narration by the poet, is the preferred method of advancing the story, because a fictional narrative presented in this form is more clearly understood as the poet's invention, and not a true history.[24] While there is no necessary relationship between mode of presentation and fictionality (one can transcribe non-fictional dialogue, and tell a made-up story without direct speech), there is, as Aristotle understands it, a felt one. The additional presence that accrues to characters when given speech of their own goes a long way towards giving them ontological independence of their creator.

It will be useful, then, at this point to map the varieties of Hellenistic literary drama against the formal mediation of subject matter in Hellenistic poetry as a whole, which I will consider under the headings of myth, mime, and non-fiction. As many writers have observed, myth provides a fertile breeding ground for fiction; its open structure as a body of narratives allows for embellishments, additions, and retellings that can serve many ends other than supplying explanations of the way the world is.[25] So it is, then, that Hellenistic poets continue to produce mythical narratives alongside scientific ones even as myth itself becomes an object of systematic research and study, and is codified in the body of knowledge we call mythology.[26] Of particular interest in this regard is the use of mythical narrative as a tool for royal self-fashioning in the court poetry of the period.[27] Theocritus' *Idyll* 24, which describes the infant Heracles' throttling of two gigantic snakes sent to kill him by Hera, or Callimachus' *Hymn to Delos*, in which the unborn Apollo remarks upon Ptolemy II's recent war against the Gauls, draw attention to the lurid and fantastic elements in their stories by surrounding them with the kind of circumstantial detail that is not found in archaic versions of the story. This embedding of the fabulous in the mundane has provoked various explanations of Callimachus' attitude towards the myths he treats, ranging from the aggressively ludic to the pious and

---

[24] As Halliwell (1987) 172 argues, Aristotle's wish "to exclude the voice of the poet from his poetry, and to turn the poetry into a 'stage' onto which the poet brings his characters," goes hand in hand with his desire "to clear a distinctive 'space' for poetry outside the sphere of directly affirmative and truth-seeking discourses such as history, philosophy and science."

[25] Pavel (1986) 80–81, Hunter (2003) 231–32.

[26] On the transition from myth to mythology, see Detienne (1986).

[27] Henrichs (1999) 226, 247–48; cf. Stephens (2003), a systematic treatment of the court poetry of Callimachus, Theocritus, and Apollonius, and Cameron (1995) 63–103 on the occasions of Hellenistic poetry as a whole.

reverential.[28] However, in court poetry that makes use of mythical material and in which a panegyrical function has been detected the exemplary character of the plot (the defeat of monsters by an Olympian god, or the emergence of order from chaos) allows for some hilarity in the details, without detracting from the overall seriousness of purpose. For in such poems the allegorical quality of the tale is readily apparent (the audience knows it is really hearing about Ptolemy, not Heracles), and the poet may in fact be ironizing the signified (the myth) as a way of making its referent (the eulogized patron) more apparent. Here, then, we have a propagandistic, ideological use of myth that does not use its gods and heroes for the sake of revealing human universals, as in the Aristotelian account of tragedy (a democratic fiction), but rather treats historical particulars (kings and tyrants) as if they were instantiations of mythical universals.[29]

While Hellenistic mythological narrative revels in the fantastic and the monstrous, it often sets these opportunities for poetic invention within frames that are humble, domestic, and ordinary. In Callimachus' *Hecale* Theseus stays with a poor old woman before fighting the Bull of Marathon, in the *Aetia* Heracles has to hear about the invention of the mousetrap from the pauper Molorchus before proceeding against more dangerous foes, in Theocritus' *Idyll* 24 Hera's terrible serpents find their way into an ordinary family house, where babies are asleep in their cribs. It would be wrong to suppose that these poems entirely domesticate their mythical protagonists. For while the fantastic episodes of the story may lie beyond the narrative itself, the presence of ordinary mortals, with their ordinary claims for recognition and respect, lends additional glamour to the mythical beings whose eyes are set on higher things, and whose breasts contain no ordinary spirit. In their settings, however, these mythological poems do have affinities with another major concern of the period, the representation of daily life, in all its humdrum detail. The model for this poetry is widely

---

[28] For the ludic, see McKay (1962); for the reverential, see Fraser (1972) 662–63, 760–61; for the archaic gods as frankly "demonic" from a civilized Hellenistic perspective, see Bulloch (1984) 228. Hunter (1992b) is a characteristically judicious overview of the question.

[29] This use of myth resembles the assimilation of the victorious athlete to heroic prototypes in epinician poetry, although the Hellenistic poets' more or less overt jesting with the fictionality of their encomiastic constructs points to the wide gulf that separates them from their archaic and classical counterparts. More work needs to be done in this area, as it is not easy to see how poems like Callimachus' *Hymn to Demeter*, or Theocritus' *Idyll* 26 (on the dismemberment of Pentheus), which share many of the lurid features of the overtly panegyrical poems, would fit within the ambit of court poetry. Likewise, the account of the *Argonautica* in Stephens (2003) 171–238 as a calque of Egyptian myth that figures as an allegory of Ptolemaic multicultural and colonialist ambitions needs to be supplemented by a reading that would show how this allegory was legible to contemporary audiences without a detailed knowledge of Egypt.

held to be the mimes of Theocritus' fellow Syracusan Sophron, and ancient commentators saw the reuse of characters from them in the *Idylls* that have contemporary urban settings.[30] In *Idyll* 2 a disappointed teenager tells of her love affair with a local athlete; in *Idyll* 14 a disabused lover discusses his prospects for employment as a mercenary in Egypt; in *Idyll* 15 Alexandrian housewives visit the palace of the royal family. Sophron's *Mimes*, Herodas' *Mimiambi*, and Theocritus' urban *Idylls* all make use of real-world locations and allude to contemporary history. The intention seems to have been to offer an imitation of everyday life without the full-scale dramatic plots and character types of New Comedy. Gorgo and Praxinoa in *Idyll* 15, or Kynno and Phile in *Mimiambus* 4, can hardly be identified, or distinguished from one another, as types; as fictional particulars, they do not embody real-world universals, and the poems in which they appear offer genre scenes rich in circumstantial detail rather than a representative range of characters in the manner of Theophrastus' *Characters*, or New Comedy.

These poems, then, that have affinities with the popular genre of mime give their fictional characters the vivid presence imparted by the exclusive use of direct speech, but the fictional world they inhabit has no features that would disbar it from being understood as an image of contemporary reality. The mythical, the divine, and the fantastic are all scrupulously excluded, setting its representation of low-life characters apart from that of Old Comedy, where lucky slaves may ascend to heaven on gigantic dung beetles to present their claims to Zeus, or journey to the Land of the Birds. By contrast, poems that have recourse to mythical stories – the *Aetia*, the *Hecale*, *Idylls* 16, 18, 24, and 26, the *Argonautica* – use a frame narrator as the means of access to this world. Rather than a guarantor of the truth of the story, the narrator of these poems has become a kind of warning sign about the world they represent, a persona that explicitly separates the poet from the storyteller in the poem. Likewise, for Callimachus' *Hymns*, it has been shown that, in those poems that feature a speaker clearly fixed in a fictional time and place (the "mimetic" *Hymns*), this potentially unreliable narrator makes use of apparently omniscient sources to recount the sacred narrative that is the centerpiece of all the *Hymns*, while, in the other poems, the uncharacterized and seemingly transparent narrator tends to interfere with the story he is telling.[31] In both cases, formal mediation of the sacred narrative signals a kind of ontological caution in the presentation of the

---

[30] In the Introduction to his new edition of the fragments, Hordern (2004) 26–29 gives a brief account of their influence.
[31] By Harder (1992).

fabulous world of myth, even as particularly fabulous episodes from that world are selected for retelling.

A similar caution is apparent in the didactic poetry of the Hellenistic period. Here we can see a radical restriction of the sphere within which a poet may hope to make legitimate truth claims in his own voice. While Hesiod may claim knowledge about the birth of the gods, or Pindar offer prescriptive maxims for moral behavior, the Hellenistic poet instead offers a poetry of fact, presented with the elegance proper to scientific knowledge itself, but manifestly a poetry of non-fiction. The points of departure for Aratus' poetry on the movements of the stars, or Nicander's on the bites of venomous animals, are prose treatises by scientific authorities (Eudoxus, Apollodorus), with which their poems could easily have been compared.[32] Their work is understudied by comparison with other Hellenistic poetry, but it is to be hoped that future research will relocate its concern for the relationship between truth, fiction, and the poet's voice within the mainstream of Hellenistic poetics.[33]

Against this background it is easy to appreciate the singularity of the bucolic poems, and how their distinctive character would have made them immediately identifiable and imitable as a new kind of poetry. They have the form of literary drama, but their characters are manifestly not representations of contemporary life. It is not simply that the sole occupation of the herdsmen within the poems is singing (rather than herding). These are herdsmen that take part in musical competitions with Pan and the Muses. They pretend to be Daphnis and Polyphemus in their songs, they elaborate on the pleasure they have taken in contemplating works of art, or offer their thoughts on Hellenistic literary theory. Their world is also characterized negatively in reference to actuality in that its time and place cannot usually be determined. Clearly these are not the rustic counterparts of the urban slaves of ancient comedy and mime, whose stories unfold in the real cities of the ancient world. Nor, on the other hand, do they belong to myth. The nameless goatherd of *Idyll* 1 cannot, by his very anonymity, be found in the mythical record. Anonymity is a marker of fiction where it is found in earlier literature,[34] and the presence of unnamed characters in the bucolic poems seems to be programmatic: while fictional beings elsewhere people

---

[32] As Gow and Scholfield (1953) 18 point out, "the difference between the two poets is that whereas the uninstructed reader may learn a good deal of astronomy from Aratus, the victim of snake-bite or poison who turned to Nicander for first-aid would be in sorry plight."

[33] Cf. Hunter (1995) 12: "The versifying of prose treatises is not inherently an idle game, but is at base a serious response to a crucial question of poetics."

[34] Finkelberg (1998) 130.

the interstices of mythical narratives – the shield of Achilles in the *Iliad*, whose invented cities are filled with anonymous inhabitants, or the messengers and minor characters of tragedy – here they alone occupy the stage. Likewise, while the goatherd's companion in *Idyll* 1, Thyrsis, impersonates the mythical herdsman Daphnis, he is unknown to myth himself, and this story is kept at one remove – it is a matter for dramatic reenactment by the poem's characters, but is not retold by the poet himself. While much Hellenistic poetry, through its exploration of *aetia* (the mythical causes of present-day practices), seeks to connect the world of the myth with the world of the present by constructing solid chronological links between them, the bucolic poems are not anchored to either, and their world floats free of both. The poems flaunt the absence of a single origin for their world, which can be derived neither from myth alone nor from actuality alone. While elements derived from each are present – Daphnis and Polyphemus on the one hand, ordinary rural workers on the other – their copresence prevents the reader from understanding any single bucolic poem as belonging to one or the other. The irreducibility of the bucolic world's origins once again enhances its ontological mystique; what is sourced from myth and actuality has undergone a thorough fictionalization in its transduction to its new home, and the bucolic characters belong to no world that we can identify outside the poems in which they appear. The poet, however, does not hedge this world within embedded narration but lets it manifest itself directly to the reader through the speeches of its inhabitants; the illusory presence of its fictional beings is made immediately palpable to us.

The poems thus identify literary pleasure with the discovery of a fictional world, and, in the four chapters of my book, I investigate some of the consequences of this move. In the first, "The pleasures of the imaginary," I focus on *Idyll* 1, which according to the ancient commentators is the most delightful and well-constructed poem in the collection, and is, for this reason, suitably placed at the beginning as its "gleaming front."[35] The poem opens with a dialogue between two herdsmen who compare the landscape they inhabit to the music they are accustomed to make for one another. One of them then goes on to describe the pleasure he has found in contemplating the carvings on a wooden bowl, and he offers this bowl to his companion if he will sing for him a song called "The Sorrows of Daphnis," which he does. All three elements of the poem – landscape, ecphrasis, and song – exhibit a harmonious adjustment to one another and may be seen as equivalents. As trees and streams repeat the herdsmen's music, so a work of

[35] *Id.* 1 arg., Wendel (1914) 23.

visual art is offered in exchange for song. All three offer the same stimulus to the imagination, and the world in which the poem is set is a source of the same pleasure as the nameless goatherd discovers in contemplating his decorated bowl and listening to his companion's song. His enthusiasm for them dramatizes the appeal of imaginary experience and so guides our response to the fictional world of the poem.

Here, then, I embrace the suggestion of Ross Chambers in his *Story and Situation* that certain kinds of fiction thematize their own powers of seduction through representations of the act of storytelling, and control their impact on their audience by dramatizing the reactions of a listener within the story.[36] I also consider how the fictionality of this exemplary bucolic poem is related to the question of its performance. Scholars since Wilamowitz have noted that the herdsmen's songs are not metrically distinguished from the surrounding dialogue, given that both are written in hexameters. Fictionality is thus inscribed in their very texture: Thyrsis' supremely enchanting vocal performance, which receives so much acclaim from his audience within the poem, cannot be produced outside the poem by a performer of *Idyll* 1, it can only be imagined by a reader. Moreover, even as we are asked to hear "The Sorrows of Daphnis" as the acme of oral song, it reveals itself to the eye of a reader as a collage of textual sources. The poem undoes the fiction of oral performance it so persuasively presents, unmaking its own illusion as imaginary experience.

In the second chapter, "The presence of the fictional world," I investigate the relationship between fictional presence and mode of presentation. I argue, with reference to the discussions of literary form in Plato's *Republic* and Aristotle's *Poetics*, that differences in the mode of storytelling (in particular, the dramatic versus the narrative mode) are not merely a useful tool for categorizing genres, but, for the Hellenistic poets who embraced the possibilities of "literary drama," continue to represent an important difference in the degree of vividness and felt presence imparted to the story world. I begin with a brief discussion of how fictional space is mapped onto the real-world space of the audience in archaic and classical dramatic poetry, then compare the construction of fictional space by the poem's dramatic speaker in Callimachus' *Hymn to Apollo* and Theocritus' *Idyll* 3. In both poems an unapproachable location within the fictional world functions as a focalizing device for our desire to enter the world of the poem in which it is contained (the temple of Apollo in the *Hymn*, the cave of Amaryllis in *Idyll* 3). This motif reappears in *Idyll* 11 and *Idyll* 13, where a lover

---

[36] Chambers (1984) 211, cf. 23.

Introduction: In the realms of the unreal 17

(Polyphemus, Heracles) longs for a sight of his absent love, concealed within an underwater world to which he cannot gain access. Readerly interest is once again mapped onto the character's gaze into a secondary space within the world of the poem that is off limits to its protagonist. The mediation of this world by the poet is more complex than in *Hymn* 2 and *Idyll* 3, however. The poems begin with a framing device in which the poet addresses the poem to a person who is apparently a real-world addressee, and presents his story as the illustration of gnomic reflection on the nature of love. However, this structural similarity only draws out the difference in the felt presence of the fictional world that is created by having the writerly frame enclose in one case a literary drama (the monologue of Polyphemus in *Idyll* 11), in the other a poem narrated entirely by the poet and containing only a single line of direct speech, and that, very unusually, within a simile.

While the bucolic characters, as I have suggested, cannot easily be understood as imitations of anything outside the bucolic poems themselves, they are frequently imitations of one another. In my third chapter, "Becoming bucolic," I suggest that a defining characteristic of the herdsmen is that they take other imagined herdsmen as models for their own self-invention. The nameless goatherd of *Idyll* 3 matches his own situation against a list of pastoral figures from epic myth, and Thyrsis in *Idyll* 1 plays the role of Daphnis in the song he performs. Likewise, in *Idyll* 7 Lycidas, the goatherd who is, for the poem's narrator, the archetypal herdsman singer, looks forward to hearing of his mythical predecessors from another singer, Tityrus, and wishes that he could have been the audience of Comatas. The most revealing poem in this regard, however, is *Idyll* 6: here Daphnis adopts the role of a friend of Polyphemus to advise his friend Damoetas, and Damoetas replies in the persona of the Cyclops. To hear bucolic song is to be filled with a desire to enter the world it presents, and dramatic impersonation is one way in which this desire manifests itself. By imagining themselves as Daphnis or Polyphemus, the herdsmen strive to become equivalents of one another, minimizing their differences and staging their imaginative involvement with the fictional world of which (from the reader's perspective) they are already a part. Being bucolic means becoming bucolic: merging the self with an imagined counterpart is one of the attractions of this world. Mostly the two selves blend easily, so that, by singing of their counterparts, the herdsmen come to resemble them: Thyrsis in *Idyll* 1 becomes like Daphnis by impersonating him, Comatas in *Idyll* 5 resembles Daphnis in his mastery of the song contest in which he competes, Lycidas in *Idyll* 7 embodies the archetypal herdsman singer for Simichidas, Daphnis and

Damoetas become Polyphemus and his advisor. The selves that are fully fictional when viewed from outside the bucolic world are mimetic within it: they model themselves on others and are in turn used as models by others. Exploring this aspect of the bucolic fiction, I draw on the early work of René Girard, which theorized mimetic desire as the attempt to replicate in one's own life a self discovered in a work of the imagination.[37]

The progress of the pastoral self is thus a kind of replacement therapy. In the face of intense erotic desire, the herdsmen sing to alleviate its pain, but they do not seek its causes in themselves, nor do they attempt to mitigate its pain by discovering that physical relations with the object of their desire are unworthy of the highest aspiration. Lycidas, who longs for the boy Ageanax in *Idyll* 7, Polyphemus, who would sacrifice his single eye for Galateia, the herdsman of *Idyll* 3, who craves an inaccessible nymph, try to gain relief from their love by replacing their desire for erotic satisfaction with the desire for the world of pastoral song. In each case it is by contemplating a version of the pastoral world that they themselves inhabit that they are able to gain some measure of respite. Self-knowledge has no role in the process; rather the self temporarily conceals its longings from itself. Substituting one desire for another through song, the singer is able to stand outside himself for a time, and, because the wound of desire is no longer aggravated by repeated contemplation of the love object, some kind of healing is able to occur. As an illustration of the therapeutic value of imaginary experience for a self conceived along these lines, I will conclude this chapter with a reading of the understudied *Idyll* 12, an erotic monologue by a male speaker who resembles the herdsmen of the pastoral poems in a number of ways, but especially insofar as he frees himself from his erotic yearning by projecting a series of imagined worlds to himself. In this case the objects of his imagination are the historical worlds of the distant past and the distant future, which here appear, like the pastoral world, as saving realms of imaginary experience.

The staging of mimetic desire in the bucolic poems reveals the power of fictional worlds to transform lives in their own image. As we saw with Henry Darger, and as Girard showed with Proust, the desire to belong to the world of a literary work may be felt by its creator as well as by its inhabitants.[38] It is the poet's own play with a fictional identity, then,

---

[37] I refer therefore to Girard (1966) and the refinement of the idea in Girard (1978) rather than to the generalized model of all human desire as in some sense mimetic that Girard developed from it.
[38] Girard (1966) 38: "Novelistic genius begins with the collapse of the 'autonomous' self... when what is true about Others becomes true of the hero, in fact true about the novelist himself."

and the possibility of encountering his own fictional creation, that are the subjects of my fourth chapter, "From fiction to metafiction." In *Idyll* 7 the poem's narrator, Simichidas, tells how he made a journey from the city of Cos to a harvest festival at the country estate of some friends. On the way he met a goatherd named Lycidas, and they exchanged songs and poetic theory before going their separate ways. When he eventually arrives at his friends' estate, Simichidas describes how he is enraptured by the rustic setting, and ends the poem wishing that he might be allowed to repeat the experience in the future. While the narrator does not have the same name as the poet, the poem is full of "reality effects" that set it apart from the other bucolic poems; it is localized in a real-world geographical location, and, rather than the present tense of dramatic fiction, it gives a retrospective, past-tense account of the speaker's experience. Theocritus, in other words, seems to have done his best to give the poem the feel of a poet's autobiography, and ancient commentators read it as his own. However, while the character of Simichidas points in the direction of actuality, the character of Lycidas points towards fiction. Lycidas appears suddenly to Simichidas like the epiphany of a Homeric god. He is dressed in rags and smells foul, yet theorizes eloquently about poetic technique, and he sings a song that, in its wistful evocation of past bucolic singers, is perhaps the supreme example of its kind. If Simichidas looks like Theocritus, Lycidas looks very much like one of his fictional herdsmen. Likewise, Simichidas' rapturous pastoral experience at the festival resembles the rustic symposium that Lycidas predicts for himself in the song he sings to Simichidas earlier in the poem, and the longing to repeat the experience with which Simichidas ends the poem echoes the wish expressed by Lycidas that he could have belonged to the pastoral world of his predecessor Comatas. What we seem to see here is fiction imitating life imitating fiction, an interpretation that the poem encourages by having Lycidas describe Simichidas as "fabricated for the sake of truth."

In my effort to make sense of this puzzling, beguiling poem, which has drawn more scholarly attention in the modern period than the rest of the bucolic poems together, I will once again turn to a modern parallel for illumination. The poets of the early twentieth century offer numerous examples of the creation of semi-fictional alter egos through which to explore questions of poetics in narrative rather than theoretical form. Pound's Hugh Selwyn Mauberley, Rilke's Malte Laurids Brigge, Valéry's Monsieur Teste all allowed their inventors to reflect upon critical moments in their own poetic development with the intellectual distance of maturity figured as the author's critical distance from a fictional double.[39] One poet, however, stands out for his elaboration of the project of fictionalized autobiography, and that is Fernando Pessoa. Pessoa's achievement was to divide his own poetic work among a number of invented poets – Alberto Caeiro, Ricardo Reis, and Alvaro de Campos – whom he called "heteronyms." These heteronyms not only comment upon each other's work, they are even credited with inspiring poems signed "Fernando Pessoa." Thus Pessoa has Campos record a meeting between himself and Caeiro in which Caeiro appears as the master of his inventor: "Pessoa, completely shaken upon hearing Caeiro read poems from his *The Keeper of Sheep*, immediately went home to write verses of a kind he never could have produced otherwise."[40] The heteronym is a richer concept than the pseudonym. While the latter functions merely as a disguise of the author's identity, the heteronym confers independent life upon aspects of his creative personality. The heteronym, I will argue, is a useful way of thinking about the interaction between Simichidas and Lycidas in *Idyll* 7 because it allows us to understand the poem as an encounter between a version of the poet and one of his own fictional creations. Reading the poem in this way preserves the gesture towards autobiographical authenticity in the retrospective first-person narration and non-fictional geographical setting, and accounts for the fact that, within the poem, Lycidas appears as the poetic master of Simichidas. The poem dramatizes the invention of pastoral as the encounter between a version of its creator and a fictional character from that world who inspires it, much as Pessoa's encounter with Caeiro imagines the poet inspired by his own creation. By having a fictional character who embodies a poetic world of their own invention appear in a narrative that looks like autobiography as the inspiration for that world, the poets not only assert that what came into being through their own creative fiat is now independent of them, they even suggest that it precedes its creator. It is as if they were the discoverers of that world rather than its inventors. It is because, not in spite, of the fact that *Idyll* 7 contains manifestly fictional elements

---

[39] The work of J. M. Coetzee, whose *Foe* (1986) will be discussed in Chapter 2, offers interesting parallels. His *Youth* (2003), like Rilke's *The Notebooks of Malte Laurids Brigge: A Novel*, explores the coming of age of a youthful writer in exile, while *Elizabeth Costello* (2003) addresses (among other things) issues of moral responsibility in fictional representation in the person of an aging author on the literary prize circuit, who, in spite of her gender, bears more than a passing resemblance to Coetzee himself. Elizabeth Costello reappears in Coetzee's most recent novel, *Slow Man* (2005), where she arrives inexplicably at the house of the protagonist, recites the book's opening paragraph to him, and berates him for his failure to be an interesting fictional character.
[40] See Pessoa (1998) 6, 41 and Guillén (1971) 242.

alongside its reality effects that it is true creative autobiography (Pessoa's term is "autopsychography"),[41] and I will endeavor to find a place for it as such within the categories of writing about the self that have been elaborated by autobiographical theory.[42]

I adopt the term metafiction to refer to the triangulation of the relationship between author, narrator, and fictional character that is staged in this poem. The term has been used to describe a range of contemporary fiction that asks its readers to participate imaginatively in the creation of a world even as they are simultaneously made aware that this world is an invention.[43] The scene in which the author enters his own writing and appears there alongside his characters figures largely in such fiction, where it bridges (in the fiction) the ontological difference that ought to keep them safely grounded in the worlds to which each of them rightfully belongs.[44] Mimetic desire is a similar attempt to bridge this gap; by endeavoring to become a fictional subject, the impersonator attempts to make present in his own life what is properly located in a fictional world. The songs of the herdsmen manifest this desire clearly, and *Idyll* 7 can therefore usefully be thought of as metafiction because in it the youthful version of the poem's narrator (who is also, within the poem, a bucolic poet) acts just like the fictional herdsmen. In this way we can distinguish pastoral fiction from comic fantasy. There is no possibility that the fantasies of the comic poets – underworld rivers of soup, preroasted birds that fall into the mouths of the hungry, dung beetles that fly to the throne of Zeus – will ever become a reality. Pastoral, however, lies just across the border from reality. When we aspire to it, we seem to inhabit its world for a while, and, when we have done so, we will, like Simichidas, long to return there.

My conclusion, "The future of a fiction," looks at the responses to this possibility in the ancient scholia on Theocritus and in the poem in which the author's presence in his own fiction becomes an established feature of the genre, the anonymous *Lament for Bion*. The approach favored by the scholia is to try to fit the poems to the account of mimesis in the *Poetics*. However, they report one strand of interpretation that is more insightful in its view of how the bucolic characters unsettle the boundary between fiction and reality. This voice belongs to the critic Munatius, who sees Theocritus himself in the nameless goatherd of *Idyll* 3, as well as in Simichidas of *Idyll* 7 (this view is shared by all the scholiasts). While Munatius is roundly

---

[41] Pessoa (1998) 2. [42] In particular, Lejeune (1989) and the essays collected in Olney (1980).
[43] Hutcheon (1980) 1–7. [44] McHale (1987) 213, cf. 71–72.

abused by the scholiasts, his ideas are in keeping with the later Greek bucolic of the *Lament for Bion* and the Latin pastoral of Virgil's *Eclogues*, which embrace the possibility that the poet can appear in his own fiction. The *Lament for Bion* expresses a bucolic poet's grief for his own master, who has predeceased him. It presents a series of lamentation scenes in which a variety of beings mourn the dead poet, the last of whom are his own bucolic characters (verses 58–63): "Galateia too weeps for your song, whom you used to delight as she sat beside you on the shore. For you did not play like the Cyclops. The lovely Galateia shunned him, but you she looked upon with more delight than the sea, and now, having forgotten about its waves, she sits upon the lonely sands, and tends your flocks till this hour." This poem, for the first time, calls a historical poet a herdsman,[45] but this assertion follows, and depends upon, the far more remarkable fact that it posits a world in which the historical poet is known to, and lamented by, his own fiction. He can be called a herdsman because he inhabits the same world the herdsmen do. Likewise, the *Eclogues* at moments collapse the fictional world of the shepherds into the world of the poet and his readers,[46] a possibility that will be decisive for the later history of pastoral.

Not all of the *Idylls* that feature herdsmen are discussed in detail in this book; *Idylls* 4 and 5 are mentioned only in passing. Conversely, *Idylls* 12 and 13, which do not feature herdsmen, are read closely. My interest here is in those poems of Theocritus that do feature herdsmen that stand out from other kinds of literary drama because they foreground the question of fictionality and fictional presence in particularly interesting ways. While one strand of imitation leads towards pastoral mannerism and a weak form of literary drama in the spurious *Idyll* 8 and *Idyll* 9,[47] another leads to the continuing exploration of mimetic desire, and the relationship between absolute fictions and the reality of the reader in the *Eclogues*. Some of the bucolic *Idylls* are clearly more important for this line of development, and these will be the center of attention here. Likewise, some poems that do not feature herdsmen are discussed as a way of bringing into sharper focus the issues that concern me in those that do. While the *Eclogues* consist of both specific acts of emulation and an organized, book-length imagination that is not reducible to such emulation, there are a cluster of elements in the bucolic *Idylls* – shepherds, the dramatic mode and its framing, song, full fictionality, the presence of the poet in the poem – that allow us to recognize the Virgilian development in the Theocritean model. Some of

[45] Van Sickle (1976) 27, Alpers (1996) 153.   [46] Hardie (2002) 21.   [47] See Rossi (1971b).

these elements are thematic, some formal, some ontological, and in no one *Idyll* are they configured in quite the same way. My goal is not to impose a spurious closure on a group of poems that clearly have many points of contact with the collection as a whole but to consider what it was in them that allowed a distinctive genre to emerge that took them as its origin.

CHAPTER I

The pleasures of the imaginary

The ancient scholia on Theocritus consider *Idyll* 1 the poem most worthy of standing at the head of the collection. It is, they claim, composed with greater skill and charm than the others, and they cite Pindar on the appropriateness of its coming first as a consequence: "At the beginning of a work one ought to place a gleaming front."[1] They note next that the poem has the form of a dramatic exchange by its characters in which the poet himself does not feature.[2] It is a dialogue between Thyrsis, a shepherd and singer, and an unnamed goatherd who is also a syrinx player. An introductory conversation between the two (1–14) sets the scene of their encounter and is followed by a long speech by the goatherd (15–63), in which he describes a decorated bowl or *kissubion* (27–60) that he promises to give to Thyrsis if the latter will sing "The Sorrows of Daphnis" for him. Thyrsis responds by performing the song (64–145), and the goatherd greets his performance with enthusiastic admiration when it is over (146–52).[3] For the scholia, then, part of the poem's appeal, its charm, or *charis*, is the skill with which these diverse components are interwoven; they speak of the poem as being particularly well put together, even though the poet's own voice does not appear in it as a unifying force. This chapter hopes to demonstrate some ways in which the scholiast's claim is justified, especially insofar as the poem's component parts – dialogue, ecphrasis, and song – work together as a unified exploration of fictionality.

---

[1] *Id.* 1 arg. b, Wendel (1914) 23.
[2] In the Platonic schema employed by the scholia it is δραματικόν, "dramatic," rather than διηγηματικόν, "narrative," or μικτόν, "mixed." See Prolegomena D, Wendel (1914) 4–5.
[3] While Thyrsis' performance is the major event in the poem (81 of its 152 lines), the ecphrasis is a secondary focal point that balances it (thirty-three lines); cf. Legrand (1898) 407, Friedländer (1912) 13, Lawall (1967) 30, Nicosia (1968) 36, Ott (1969) 132–33.

THE DIALOGUE

The poem begins with Thyrsis' praise of the goatherd's piping (1.1–6):

ἁδύ τι τὸ ψιθύρισμα καὶ ἁ πίτυς, αἰπόλε, τήνα,
ἁ ποτὶ ταῖς παγαῖσι, μελίσδεται, ἁδὺ δὲ καὶ τύ
συρίσδες· μετὰ Πᾶνα τὸ δεύτερον ἆθλον ἀποισῇ.
αἴ κα τῆνος ἕλῃ κεραὸν τράγον, αἶγα τὺ λαψῇ·
αἴ κα δ' αἶγα λάβῃ τῆνος γέρας, ἐς τὲ καταρρεῖ
ἁ χίμαρος· χιμάρῳ δὲ καλὸν κρέας, ἔστε κ' ἀμέλξῃς.

Sweetly somehow that pine tree by the springs sings its whispering song, goatherd, and sweetly too you pipe. After Pan you will carry off the second prize. If he chooses the horned goat, you will take the female. And if he takes the female, the kid will come to you. And kids' meat is good until you milk them.

The repetition of ἁδύ, "sweet," gives a clear structure to Thyrsis' thought: the sound of the pine tree is sweet, and so is Thyrsis' syrinx playing. Yet the first clause already contains an identification of human and natural music: the pine tree is the subject of a verb of human song, μελίσδεται, "sings," and the noise it produces, "whispering," is reminiscent of the human voice. The effect is emphasized by the subsequent echo of the sound it makes, ψιθύρισμα, in the word for human music, συρίσδες, "you pipe."[4] Yet the pine tree does not simply sing its whispering song sweetly, it sings it "sweetly somehow."[5] The modified adverb in the first phrase contrasts with its unaccompanied use to describe the goatherd's piping, "sweetly too you pipe." Rather than a simple description of the sound, "sweetly somehow," fronted not just in its own clause but as the first words of the poem, dramatizes Thyrsis' hesitation as he attempts to translate what he hears into words. The object that he points to – "that pine tree, the one by the springs" – invites a simple pictorial response from the reader, but the verb and adverb that accompany it ask us already, at the very outset of the poem, to think about the transformation of landscape into imaginary object that takes place in Thyrsis' attentive listening.

---

[4] Donnet (1988) 160.
[5] For adverbial ἁδύ τι (here parallel to ἁδὺ δὲ καὶ τύ | συρίσδες), cf. 5.88–89, ἁ Κλεαρίστα | ... ἁδύ τι ποππυλιάσδει; [Theocr.] *Epigr.* 5.1–2, ἀεῖσαι | ἁδύ τί μοι; Call. *Hymn* 2.4, ἐπένευσεν ὁ Δήλιος ἡδύ τι φοῖνιξ. Gow (1952) *ad loc.* 1.1ff. compares Terentianus Maurus 2129, *dulce tibi pinus summurmurat*. Dover (1971) *ad loc.* 1.1f. understands ἁδύ τι as an appositional phrase: "Lit., 'something pleasant the whispering that pine-tree ... makes music', i.e. 'sweet is the whispered music which that pine-tree makes'." Similarly Hunter (1999) *ad loc.* 1.1–3: "'Something sweet, goatherd, the whispering [which] that pine-tree by the springs sings.'"

Pan's potential participation in the herdsmen's musical exchanges marks off the world of the poem from the world of ordinary human experience. In contrast to the references to the landscape, by which the herdsmen point to objects they can see, there is no actual deixis here; the goats are introduced without articles (3), and the demonstrative pronouns that refer to the god (4, 5) are anaphoric rather than deictic: they refer back to his earlier mention in the speech, rather than pointing out his actual presence. Pan is made an element of the poem's imaginary world, which tells us what kind of world we are dealing with (one in which divinities may take an active part in the musical contests of herdsmen), without his having to appear in it. This is a world in which gods have face-to-face relationships with mortals, though for now they remain somewhere just out of sight, which distinguishes this world at once from the secular reality of mime, even though we are not dealing with figures from myth; Thyrsis, just as much as the anonymous goatherd, is unknown in that domain.[6] Moreover, by rendering the two possible outcomes to the song contests with the gods in syntactically matching if-clauses (αἴ κα... αἴ κα), Thyrsis suggests that there is little to choose between the music of the goatherd and Pan. While the herdsman is second to his god, their music is nonetheless complementary, like the natural and human music of the opening verses.

The goatherd's reply is an equally elaborate praise of Thyrsis' singing (1.7–11):

> ἅδιον, ὦ ποιμήν, τὸ τεὸν μέλος ἢ τὸ καταχές
> τῆν' ἀπὸ τᾶς πέτρας καταλείβεται ὑψόθεν ὕδωρ.
> αἴ κα ταὶ Μοῖσαι τὰν οἴιδα δῶρον ἄγωνται,
> ἄρνα τὺ σακίταν λαψῇ γέρας· αἰ δέ κ' ἀρέσκῃ
> τήναις ἄρνα λαβεῖν, τὺ δὲ τὰν ὄιν ὕστερον ἀξῇ.

Your song falls more sweetly, o shepherd, than that echoing water falls from the rock above. If the Muses lead away the sheep as a gift, you will take the penned lamb as prize. But if they are content to take the lamb, you will lead away the sheep afterwards.

Thyrsis assimilated the sounds of the pine to human speech in his praise of the goatherd's music. The goatherd turns the compliment around: Thyrsis' song is like the sound of falling water, but sweeter still. His speech also begins by pointing to features of the landscape – "that echoing water . . . the rock

---

[6] Cf. Martinez-Bonati (1981) 106–107: "All singular judgments carry universal implications. The thetic projection of a mimetic sentence establishes not only a singular fact of the imagined world . . . but, at the same time, inevitably, a general axiom for that world . . . If a fictional character were to tell us that the King's daughter kept a unicorn in her garden, one of the general implications would be that such creatures are materially possible in that world."

The pleasures of the imaginary

above" – then matches Thyrsis' vision of harmonious musical rivalry with the gods. Of the poem's first eleven verses, seven are taken up with imagining the outcome of this hypothetical song contest. Moreover, Thyrsis' "you pipe" (1.3), and the goatherd's "your song falls" (1.7–8), do not denote what they are doing at that moment. They are generalizing present tenses, as the speaker recollects his previous impressions of the other's music. The first two speeches are entirely occupied with imaginary experience; the reader listens to the herdsmen as they describe a remembered music to one another, and in doing so locate themselves in a landscape with its familiar gods.

In reply, Thyrsis points to the place where he would like the goatherd to play for him (1.12–14):

> λῆς ποτὶ τᾶν Νυμφᾶν, λῆς, αἰπόλε, τεῖδε καθίξας,
> ὡς τὸ κάταντες τοῦτο γεώλοφον αἵ τε μυρῖκαι,
> συρίσδεν; τὰς δ' αἶγας ἐγὼν ἐν τῷδε νομευσῶ.

Will you, for the sake of the Nymphs, will you, goatherd, sit over there, where there is that sloping mound and the tamarisks, and play? I myself will look after your goats in the meantime.

As in the first two speeches, deixis locates the speaker and his interlocutor in the center of a landscape the elements of which lie neither immediately at hand nor very far away. As Thyrsis points to "that pine tree by the springs" (1.2), and the goatherd compares his song with "that echoing water," so Thyrsis here invites him to sit "over there," where there is "that sloping mound and the tamarisks." The herdsmen create a mood of calm by pointing to the objects that lie around them, as immobile and restful as they are. After the goatherd has alerted Thyrsis to the danger of irritating Pan with noonday piping, he extends his own invitation (1.21–23):

> δεῦρ' ὑπὸ τὰν πτελέαν ἑσδώμεθα τῷ τε Πριήπῳ
> καὶ ταῖν κρανίδων κατεναντίον, ἅπερ ὁ θῶκος
> τῆνος ὁ ποιμενικὸς καὶ ταὶ δρύες.

Let us sit over here under the elm opposite Priapus and the springs, where there is that shepherd's seat and the oaks.

Thyrsis has given one half of the scene, now the goatherd supplies the other: his "over here" matches Thyrsis' "over there," so that the landscape appears as the expression of their complementary desires.[7]

The herdsmen do not indicate how each element in the landscape is related to the others. They simply point to "that sloping mound and the

---

[7] Cf. *Id.* 5.45–52, 101–103, where Comatas and Lacon create a similar picture through antagonistic comparison.

tamarisks," and "that shepherd's seat and the oaks," and let the reader imagine how they are situated in relation to one another: are the tamarisks on the mound? Is the seat under the oaks?[8] Perhaps the strangely inexact way in which the herdsmen point out their surroundings can be explained as a reality effect. Because they have the landscape before their eyes, they need only gesture towards it in order to make themselves understood; they do not dwell on the scene more than people in their situation would in fact need to, and what they say about it fits their occupation as herdsmen. For them it is a workplace in which they also take their leisure, but they do not set it before themselves as an object of contemplation.[9] It is simply at hand for them as a place in which to conduct their business and to rest. Yet, for the reader, their cursory references to their surroundings have a different function. The lack of descriptive precision on the part of the characters invites us to go further with the game of world-building that they initiate. If the poem does not tell us how to arrange the shepherd's seat and the oaks in relation to the elm, Priapus, and the springs, we may nonetheless work out these details for ourselves.[10] While the deictic gestures never amount to a sustained description and, considered individually, do not introduce any large vistas,[11] the accumulation of individual details soon has the reader putting together the pieces of the picture, constructing a scene that extends beyond the immediate foreground. While the herdsmen may not know they are in a landscape, the audience surely does.

THE ECPHRASIS

After his invitation to Thyrsis to sit beneath the trees the goatherd reminds him again of his preeminence as a singer and offers him a two-part reward for his song (1.25–28):

> αἶγά τέ τοι δωσῶ διδυματόκον ἐς τρὶς ἀμέλξαι,
> ἃ δύ' ἔχοισ' ἐρίφως ποταμέλγεται ἐς δύο πέλλας,
> καὶ βαθὺ κισσύβιον κεκλυσμένον ἁδέι κηρῷ,
> ἀμφῶες, νεοτευχές, ἔτι γλυφάνοιο ποτόσδον.

I will give you a goat that has borne twins to milk three times, which, despite having two kids, fills two pails with milk, and a deep bowl sealed with sweet wax, two-handled, newly made, still smelling of the knife.

---

[8] As Elliger (1975) 326 n. 27 notes, "die Landschaft wird durch punktuelle Angaben, nicht durch Bezüge und Abhangigkeiten der einzelnen Teile evoziert."
[9] Arland (1937) 13, cf. Schmidt (1987) 125 n. 38.
[10] Gow (1952) *ad loc.* 1.22: "Since the remoter demonstrative τῆνος is opposed to δεῦρο, and δρύες to πτελέαν, it seems that the rustic seat and the oaks are by the springs and the figure of Priapus, and opposite to the elm under which Thyrsis is invited to sing." Cf. Elliger (1975) 326.
[11] Legrand (1898) 197.

However, while the goatherd offers to give Thyrsis the bowl, he does not invite him to look at it right away, or at any point during his description of it.[12] It is only when the song is over that he produces the object itself and with a flourish invites Thyrsis to see if it matches up to his earlier description (1.149): "Behold the bowl; see, my friend, how sweetly it smells."[13]

If the bowl only makes its entrance at the end of the poem, this should remind us that the ecphrasis is more a response to a work of art than a description of one.[14] It is the goatherd's impressions that we hear as he encourages Thyrsis to imagine the object for himself. He describes its shape and plant motifs briefly (1.27–31); the figures portrayed on it form the bulk of his description (1.32–54). The first figure that he describes is a woman (1.32–33):

> ἔντοσθεν δὲ γυνά, τι θεῶν δαίδαλμα, τέτυκται,
> ἀσκητὰ πέπλῳ τε καὶ ἄμπυκι·

Within a woman, some ornamental work of the gods, is fashioned, adorned with a robe and headband.

Since this is the first extant occurrence of the word δαίδαλμα, we may wonder what he means by it. The stem might lead one to suppose that the word is simply a metrical alternative to δαίδαλον, a piece of ornamental work. However, when the scholia comment upon these lines they suggest that the men portrayed "are laboring in vain," because, they ask, "how could anyone persuade a statue?"[15] The scholia, in other words, look to the suffix -μα and deduce that δαίδαλμα means not merely a piece of ornamental work but, like ἄγαλμα, a statue. In context, the word presents us with a choice: is the woman carved on the bowl something made by the gods, or is she, more concretely, a statue of one of them?

The scholia appear to have been influenced by the following line: ἀσκητά, "adorned with," belongs to the language of the decorative arts, and in the sense "curiously wrought" is used elsewhere of manufactured objects (*LSJ* s.v. ἀσκητός 1.1). Yet there are several levels at which the epithet might function. A statue on which robe and headband are "curiously wrought" may be portrayed on the bowl. A flesh-and-blood woman may

---

[12] In the "mimetic–dramatic" type of ecphrasis to which Gutzwiller (1991) 90 refers, joint inspection of an object is always accompanied by invitations to look: ἄθρησον, Theocritus *Id.* 15.78; οὐκ ὁρῇς, ὄρη, Herodas 4.23, 27, 35; ἰδού, ἄθρησον, σκέψαι, λεύσσεις, Euripides *Ion* 190, 201, 206, 209.
[13] Cf. Dover (1971) *ad loc.* 1.144f.: "Thyrsis does not get the bowl until 149." ἠνίδε and θᾶσαι are just the kinds of invitation that are missing from the ecphrasis.
[14] Cf. Miles (1977) 147: "We are not actually shown the bowl. We are presented a version of it as seen through the eyes of an inhabitant of the bucolic world."
[15] Σ 1.38e, Wendel (1914) 42.

be depicted "adorned with" robe and headband.[16] The image of a woman may be "curiously wrought" with robe and headband on the surface of the bowl. Not only is there a choice to be made about who the woman is, the epithet that accompanies her may describe how she looks within the scene in which she is portrayed, or the skill with which she has been rendered by the artist who portrayed her.

The scholiast's question seems to reflect a rather crude attempt to get a definite picture from the goatherd's indefinite words. In later usage δαίδαλμα, like its parent δαίδαλον, does not designate a particular object but conveys the wonder that objects of surpassing craftsmanship inspire.[17] Yet perhaps we should ask what impelled this leap on the commentator's part. If other scholia on poetic texts explain δαίδαλον as δαίδαλμα, why do they gloss δαίδαλμα with ἄγαλμα here? Does it point to something unusual in the goatherd's use of the word? Richard Hunter compares δαίδαλα at *Iliad* 18.482 (the images on the Shield of Achilles), *Argonautica* 1.729 (on the Cloak of Jason), and *Europa* 43 (on the Basket of Europa), and suggests that "δαίδαλμα belongs to the standard language of *ekphrasis*."[18] In these passages, however, there are always δαίδαλα πολλά, "many images." The phrase occurs at the beginning of the ecphrasis and summarizes the pictures that will then be described individually. In *Idyll* 1, by contrast, δαίδαλμα is used without an adjective to mark out a single figure on the bowl. It separates the woman from her companions and suggests that she is somehow more artificial than the other images around her.

Moreover, the woman is not simply a δαίδαλμα, she is a θεῶν δαίδαλμα, an ornamental work "of the gods." Does this mean that she was made by the gods, that she looks like the gods, or that her representation

---

[16] Gow (1952) *ad loc.* 1.33: "ἀσκητά is used elsewhere of the garment (e.g. 24.140) or the wool (18.32 n.) rather than the wearer except in what seems a reminiscence of this passage by Antipater at *A.P.* 6.219, but T.'s use arises naturally from that of the verb at, e.g., Aesch. *Pers.* 182 πέπλοισι Περσικοῖς ἠσκημένη."

[17] The *TLG* gives twenty-six occurrences in addition to our present passage and its scholia. The only one earlier than *Idyll* 1, Pindar *Paian* 8 fr. 52i.81, proves insecure; see Morris (1992) 46: "The crucial word is incomplete beyond the restored fourth letter and its syntactical function is unclear." The remainder are considerably later than Theocritus. The word is used for statues (Lucian *Amores* 13; Eusebius *De laudibus Constantini* 11.8; Himerius *Oration* 28.41) and objects of divine manufacture like the walls of Troy (Colluthus *Rape of Helen* 310), ornamentation on a shield made by Hephaestus (Nonnus *Dionysiaca* 37.127), and the "visible adornments of the entire universe" (Eusebius *De laudibus Constantini* 11.11). The scholia to Pindar *Pythian* 5.46 write δαιδάλματα τῶν τεκτόνων, where Pindar's text has τεκτόνων δαίδαλ(α), and Eustathius has δαιδάλματα where *Iliad* 18.483 (the Shield of Achilles) has δαίδαλα; cf. his commentary on Odysseus' brooch at *Od.* 19.226: δαίδαλον δὲ τὸ δαίδαλμα, τὸ ποίκιλμα, συγκοπὲν ἐκ τοῦ δαιδάλεον. Cf. Morris (1992) 4: "a survey of epic δαίδαλα in terms of metrical, syntactical, and thematic distribution reveals far greater powers of connotation than specific denotation."

[18] Hunter (1999) *ad loc.* 1.32.

on the bowl resembles the gods' handiwork? The scholia are tempted by the first explanation, and report that "some say she is Pandora."[19] The -μα suffix suggests manufacture, manufacture implies a maker, and so she is a woman made by the gods. Hence, Pandora.[20] If the scholia hesitate, it may be because this solution overlooks the goatherd's τι, "some," which, they note, belongs with δαίδαλμα, and makes the statement less definite. But how exactly? Some editors understand τι θεῶν δαίδαλμα as simply in apposition to γυνά: "Within a woman, some ornamental work of the gods, is fashioned." The texts of Ahrens, Gow, and Hunter accordingly all have a comma after γυνά, "woman." Not punctuating after γυνά does not of course preclude understanding the phrase as appositional, and some editors who print the line without punctuation (Meineke, Wilamowitz, Gallavotti) may intend it to be read in that way. Dover, however, rejects this interpretation and understands the phrase as predicate: "Lit., 'a woman is depicted <as> a-sort-of . . .'."[21] Both constructions point to reflective or interpretive activity on the part of the goatherd. If we accept the majority view, the goatherd is emphasizing the quality of the bowl's craftsmanship. The image of the woman is the kind of thing the gods might make. If we accept Dover's view, the emphasis is on the woman's appearance. She is a human woman, who has nonetheless been depicted in such a way that she looks god-like, as the other figures around her do not (and this difference from her companions is the point of departure for the scholiast's interpretation). Perhaps the τι also reflects the fact that the goatherd does not have the bowl in front of him, and dramatizes a momentary engagement with the figure in his imagination, much as Thyrsis' ἁδύ τι, "sweetly somehow," in the poem's opening line dramatizes his effort to express the sounds of nature in language.[22] However we interpret the phrase, imaginative effort is required to translate the goatherd's description back into image.

---

[19] Σ 1.32, Wendel (1914) 40.
[20] A more obvious choice than the deceitful image of Helen fashioned by the gods, a "statue of cloud," νεφέλης ἄγαλμα, in Euripides' *Helen* 1219 (cf. 262–63). The scholia may also have in mind Hesiod's description of the creation of Pandora at *Theogony* 578–81, where there is also a conjunction of ἀσκήσας and δαίδαλα: "And about her head she [Athena] set a golden band, which the glorious Lame One made himself, fashioning it (ἀσκήσας) with his hands, gratifying Zeus his father. And on it were fashioned many devices (δαίδαλα πολλά), a wonder to behold." Pandora herself, however, is not described as a *daidalon*, or as the object of daidalic manufacture. The *daidal-* words are used of her crown, as above, and of the πολυδαίδαλον ἱστόν, the "weaving with many images", which Athena is to teach her how to make at *Works and Days* 64.
[21] Dover (1971) *ad loc.* 1.32: "Punctuation before the postpositive τι, making τι θεῶν δαίδαλμα a phrase in apposition, is to be avoided."
[22] Cf. Gorgo at *Idyll* 15.79, who, when describing the tapestries at the palace of Ptolemy Philadelphus in Alexandria that are right before her eyes, shows no such hesitation: "you would say they were garments of the gods."

After describing the woman the goatherd fills in the scene around her (1.33–38):

> πὰρ δέ οἱ ἄνδρες
> καλὸν ἐθειράζοντες ἀμοιβαδὶς ἄλλοθεν ἄλλος
> νεικείουσ' ἐπέεσσι· τὰ δ' οὐ φρενὸς ἅπτεται αὐτᾶς·
> ἀλλ' ὅκα μὲν τῆνον ποτιδέρκεται ἄνδρα γέλαισα,
> ἄλλοκα δ' αὖ ποτὶ τὸν ῥιπτεῖ νόον· οἱ δ' ὑπ' ἔρωτος
> δηθὰ κυλοιδιόωντες ἐτώσια μοχθίζοντι.

And beside her men with beautiful hair alternately from either side contend with words; yet these do not touch her mind. But at one time she looks at one man smiling and at another she turns her mind to the other. And they, for a long time hollow-eyed from love, labor in vain.

He describes appearances – the men have "beautiful hair," they "contend with words" – but also the inner experience he imagines these appearances reflect: "these things do not touch her mind." Like the men, he is drawn to the god-like woman, and translates her indifference into action: "at one time she looks at one man smiling and at another she turns her mind to the other." The goatherd is making a story out of a picture;[23] he introduces time into the visual representation and constructs a "back story" to explain what he has seen: the men are hollow-eyed "from love," and have been so "for a long time." Finally, his description also hints at the likely outcome of the scene: "they labor in vain."

While the goatherd's narrative integrates the images of the carved figures by attaching the feelings and motivations that have suggested themselves to his imagination, this very reconstruction bequeaths further reconstruction to the imagination of the reader. His use of pronouns is sparing in the extreme. While the two men are "long hollow-eyed from love," he does not spell out that they are in love with the woman.[24] Similarly, "these things do not touch her mind" suggests a more than human unconcern; her laughter combines the unfathomable mirth of Aphrodite, who will later visit Daphnis smiling (γέλαισα, 95–96), with the unresponsiveness of an artwork.[25] Perhaps it is not so surprising that the scholia see Pandora, or a statue, here.[26] The men's behavior is also hard to read. Hunter notes that the scene

---

[23] A "narrative response to pictorial stasis," as Heffernan (1993) 4–5 calls ecphrastic storytelling.
[24] Cf. Homeric desire at *Iliad* 3.438–46 (Paris and Helen) and 14.313–28 (Zeus and Hera). The abundance of pronouns leaves no doubt about who is feeling what for whom.
[25] Hunter (1999) *ad loc.* 1.36–37.
[26] On erotic infatuation with statuary, see Steiner (2001) 185–207 and Hardie (2002) 193, for whom the Pygmalion story thematizes "the close connection between erotic desire and the response to works of

rewrites the legal dispute on the Shield of Achilles (*Il.* 18.497–508)."[27] But as what exactly? When the men "contend with words," νεικείουσ' ἐπέεσσι, this sounds like a formulaic Homeric phrase, but in the Homeric formula verb and noun are accompanied by an adjective that makes clear exactly how the speaker is addressing his interlocutor: his words are "reproachful," "shameful," "angry," "gentle," "harsh," or "shocking," as the case may be.[28] Without qualification it is unclear whether the men are chiding, quarreling, or competing, just as the absence of pronouns means that we cannot tell whether their words are directed at each other or the woman. It has been suggested that "contend in words" might refer to "rivalry in hexameter verses as well as in simple speech," and that the use of ἀμοιβαδίς, "from either side," "looks forward to the convention of 'amoebean song' which was destined to become a hallmark of the bucolic poetry of Theocritus and his imitators."[29] On the other hand, while at *Id.* 7.48 "labor in vain" is used of unsuccessful poets, in other poems "lovers do not . . . 'contest' before their rivals."[30] Once again the goatherd is more certain than we can be about what he is describing.

The goatherd's description of the scene supplies "more 'than is actually there' (the thoughts and emotions of the figures for example)."[31] Yet this excess is puzzling; it is an interpretive response that we cannot compare with the object itself. The goatherd's interpretations invite interpretations of our own. The scholia disambiguate at the level of individual words: by deciding that the woman is a statue, or Pandora, they see something specific on the bowl. Their approach seems crude, a violation of the poem's suggestive vagueness. Yet the desire for clarity can hardly be separated from the act of reading; even Hunter's inconspicuous summary is quite a bit clearer than the goatherd himself: "The woman laughs while the men suffer from the *eros* for which she is responsible."[32]

---

art," insofar as both map the viewing subject's desire for an imagined presence onto an irremediably unresponsive object. Cf. Ott (1969) 105 n. 296: "Außerdem soll der Vergleich einem Standbild die Ungerührtheit der Frau bezeichnen."

[27] Hunter (1999) *ad loc.* 1.34–35.

[28] ὀνειδείοις, *Il.* 2.277, 21.480; αἰσχροῖς, *Il.* 3.38, 6.325; χολωτοῖσιν, *Il.* 4.241, 15.210, *Od.* 22.26, 225; μειλιχίοις, στερεοῖς, *Il.* 12.267; ἐκπάγλοις, *Od.* 8.77, where the verb δηρίσαντο is preceded by νεῖκος (75).

[29] Halperin (1983) 178, cf. 242–43.

[30] Hunter (1999) *ad loc.* 1.34–35 also compares Longus *Daphnis and Chloe* 1.15.4–17.1; yet surely this is more interpretation than imitation of *Idyll* 1?

[31] Hunter (1999) p. 63.

[32] Hunter (1999) *ad loc.* 1.36–37 Cf. Friedländer (1912) 14 on the bowl's layout. He notes that it has undergone a twofold reduction compared with the Shield of Achilles. Firstly, far fewer scenes are

The next scene is easier to picture (1.39–44):

τοῖς δὲ μετὰ γριπεύς τε γέρων πέτρα τε τέτυκται
λεπράς, ἐφ' ᾇ σπεύδων μέγα δίκτυον ἐς βόλον ἕλκει
ὁ πρέσβυς, κάμνοντι τὸ καρτερὸν ἀνδρὶ ἐοικώς.
φαίης κεν γυίων νιν ὅσον σθένος ἐλλοπιεύειν,
ὧδέ οἱ ᾠδήκαντι κατ' αὐχένα πάντοθεν ἶνες
καὶ πολιῷ περ ἐόντι· τὸ δὲ σθένος ἄξιον ἅβας.

Next to them is fashioned an old fisherman and a steep rock, on which the old man eagerly drags a large net for a cast, looking like a man who is laboring hard. You would say that he is fishing with all the strength of his limbs, the tendons bulge so all over his neck, even though he is grey-haired. But his strength is worthy of youth.

Here there is no conflict between visual representation and narration; the present tense of "drags" is not combined with temporal markers like "at one time and another," or "for a long time," as in the previous scene. Similarly, the goatherd's inferences are more obviously derived from the visual information: if the fisherman resembles "a man who is laboring hard," and "you would say that he is fishing with all the strength of his limbs," this is because "the tendons bulge so all over his neck." Only in the final verse does he add something to the image: "his strength is worthy of youth." Here, as in the conclusion to the previous scene, he seems to anticipate how events will turn out.

He also anticipates his audience's response: "you would say that he is fishing with all the strength of his limbs." But who is he talking to with his "you would say"? Kathryn Gutzwiller thinks that the words are intended for Thyrsis alone: "To remove any doubt that φαίης in 42 is addressed to Thyrsis rather than an anonymous 'you,' we need only compare Gorgo's remarks on the tapestries in *Idyll* 15.79, 'you would say (φασεῖς) they are garments fit for the gods.' Even Gorgo's θεῶν περονάματα recalls the goatherd's τι θεῶν δαίδαλμα (32), both conveying the speaker's subjective impression of an art object."[33] Yet the scene does not unfold dramatically like *Idyll* 15, or Herodas 4, to which Gutzwiller also refers. In these poems, when one character invites another to respond to an image, we are given the companion's response. In *Idyll* 15, after Gorgo's initial reaction

portrayed, and, secondly, there are far fewer figures within those scenes. This facilitates synoptic perception and induces a sense of symmetry in the insets: "Denn liegt es freilich nicht allzu fern, den Fischer in ein emblemartiges Mittelfeld zu setzen und die beiden Dreifigurenszenen antithetisch an den Rand. *Aber gesagt wird davon nichts, und der Dichter hat wohl ein ganz scharfes Bild weder gehabt noch geben wollen.*" (My emphasis.)

[33] Gutzwiller (1991) 92.

The pleasures of the imaginary

(78–79) – "Praxinoa, look at the tapestries first, how fine and delightful they are, you would say they were garments of the gods" – we hear Praxinoa's reply (80–83): "Lady Athena, what sort of weavers worked on them. What sort of artists drew their precise shapes. How true they stand and how true they move, living, not woven. People are so clever!" Similarly, in Herodas 4, after Phile's first reaction (20–22) – "What beautiful statues, dear Kynno: what craftsman fashioned this stone and who set it up?" – we hear, after the names of the artist and dedicator, further commentary by Kynno: "Look at that girl looking up at the apple; wouldn't you say she will faint soon if she can't get the apple?" (28–29).[34] Moreover, their responses are brief; in *Idyll* 15 the description of the tapestries lasts nine verses (78–86), and in Herodas 4 the women respond succinctly to a succession of objects. Both poems ask us to focus on the characters, as by question and answer they formulate a shared response to what they are viewing; the object itself is less important than their reaction to it.[35]

The dramatic interaction between object, first viewer, and respondent in these poems is quite different from *Idyll* 1. The goatherd describes a single object in great detail, yet that detail creates a conflict between his description and the object it represents. After the first scene there are two bowls in the audience's mind: the one the goatherd describes, and the one we picture on the basis of his description. The two are bound to be different, since the second cannot incorporate all the information included in the first. Yet in the second scene the goatherd's interpretation is less intrusive; the image seems to offer itself to us more directly. Similarly, while "you would say" is apparently addressed to Thyrsis, it is not intended to elicit a response from his companion like Gorgo's question to Praxinoa, for he goes on with his description without a pause. The assertion looks beyond the poem's dramatic illusion, and finesses the *kissubion* in the audience's mind. The first scene gives us the goatherd's interpretive narration of whatever clues he has picked up from the images on the bowl. The second gives us just the images, and so lets us find clues of our own.[36]

---

[34] The ecphrastic scene at the temple in Euripides' *Ion* (184–218) is also a series of questions and answers between the chorus members.

[35] Gutzwiller (1991) 90. How we should react to their reaction is another question. Recent work on *Idyll* 15 has distanced itself from ironic treatment of Gorgo and Praxinoa. Goldhill (1994) 217–22 and Burton (1995) 103–104 analyze the women's use of Hellenistic art theory. For a judicious overview of the issues, see Hunter (1996b) 149–69. On Hellenistic ecphrasis and its relationship to contemporary art and its audiences, see Zanker (2004).

[36] Cf. Ott (1969) 103 n. 290: "Die 'Momentaufnahme' des Fischers zeigt nur seine Anstrengung, die Frage, ob ihm Erfolg oder Mißerfolg beschieden ist, muß der Leser für sich selbst beantworten. M. E.

The final scene is the longest of the three (1.45–54):

> τυτθὸν δ' ὅσσον ἄπωθεν ἁλιτρύτοιο γέροντος
> περκναῖσι σταφυλαῖσι καλὸν βέβριθεν ἀλωά,
> τὰν ὀλίγος τις κῶρος ἐφ' αἱμασιαῖσι φυλάσσει
> ἥμενος· ἀμφὶ δέ νιν δύ' ἀλώπεκες, ἁ μὲν ἀν' ὄρχως
> φοιτῇ σινομένα τὰν τρώξιμον, ἁ δ' ἐπὶ πήρᾳ
> πάντα δόλον τεύχοισα τὸ παιδίον οὐ πρὶν ἀνησεῖν
> φατὶ πρὶν ἢ ἀκράτιστον ἐπὶ ξηροῖσι καθίξῃ.
> αὐτὰρ ὅγ' ἀνθερίκοισι καλὰν πλέκει ἀκριδοθήραν
> σχοίνῳ ἐφαρμόσδων· μέλεται δέ οἱ οὔτε τι πήρας
> οὔτε φυτῶν τοσσῆνον ὅσον περὶ πλέγματι γαθεῖ.

And a little way off from the sea-worn old man a vineyard is nicely laden with dark clusters which a little boy is guarding as he sits on a dry-stone wall. And about him are two foxes; one roams among the vine rows, damaging what is ready to be eaten, the other, fashioning every possible scheme against his wallet, thinks that she <will not let the boy go until she has sat down having feasted upon dry food>.[37] But he is weaving a lovely cage for crickets, fitting together asphodels and reeds. And he has no concern at all for his wallet or the plants, his pleasure in the weaving is so great.

The description begins with a still image (45–48). The two foxes are more animated: one "roams among the vine rows," the other makes plans on the boy's wallet. The figures come to life because the goatherd imagines their inner life on the basis of their appearance: σινομένα, "damaging," suggests deliberate mischief,[38] "fashioning every possible scheme," and φατί, "thinks," (if this is correct) are overtly humanizing. There is no conflict between visual representation and narration as there is in the first scene; the grapes and the wallet are easily pictured as objectives of the foxes' actions. Similarly, the description of the cricket cage gives the materials of its construction and a clear sense of how they are being used, and it is from this picture that the goatherd projects the boy's inner experience (53–54): "And he has no concern at all for his wallet or the plants, his pleasure in the weaving is so great." In contrast to the second scene, we are aware that the goatherd is imagining more than what he sees, yet his imagination seems to harmonize with the visual information; it does not create the puzzles of the first scene.

---

gibt jedoch die in beiden andern Szenen thematisierte Erfolglosigkeit den entscheidenen Hinweis: auch der Fischer müht sich vergebens, das volle Netz ist zu schwer. Aber diese Meinung ist subjectiv." My own subjective opinion would be that "his strength is worthy of youth" points to success.

[37] Verse 51 is almost certainly corrupt. I have supplied the stop-gap translation of Hunter (1999) *ad loc.* 1.50–51, based on the "minimum necessary change" of ἀκράτιστον to ἀκράτιστος.

[38] *LSJ* s.v. σίνομαι I gives pirates, Cyclopes, Scylla, and marauding armies as subjects of this verb.

The pleasures of the imaginary

Having considered the content of the individual scenes, let us now consider how they relate to one another. The bowl, we are told, has ivy decoration around its lip (29–31), and "within" (ἔντοσθεν, 32) is the first of the figures the goatherd describes, that of the woman. Beside this woman (πάρ, 33) stand the two men, and "contend in words from either side" (ἄλλοθεν ἄλλος, 34). "By (or with) these" (τοῖς δὲ μετά, 19) is the fisherman. "A little way off" from him (τυτθὸν δ' ὅσσον ἄπωθεν, 45) is the vineyard and the boy, and "about him" (ἀμφὶ δέ νιν, 48) are the foxes. Finally, acanthus spreads "in every way around" the bowl (55).

The ivy and acanthus belong exclusively to the bowl's visual surface, and do not participate in the scenes that they surround. While ἔντοσθεν, "within," may indicate either that the two men and the woman are inside the bowl, or that they are inside an ivy frame, it clearly separates the decorative plant motif from the human figures. But how are we to understand the bowl's other spatial markers? Do "by (or with) these" (τοῖς δὲ μετά, 19) and "a little way off" (τυτθὸν δ' ὅσσον ἄπωθεν, 45) mark divisions within a single scene, or is each scene a world of its own? And how should we understand "beside" (πάρ, 33) and "from either side" (ἄλλοθεν ἄλλος, 34)? Do we picture the two men standing beside the woman within a pictorial space that they share, or does she, "the ornamental work of the gods," occupy a different visual field? Does the goatherd see the men as in love with an image that lies between them, but in another plane of representation, and is this why their words can never touch her mind? Is this what the scholia mean by their question, "Who could persuade a statue?" Any attempt to reconstruct the bowl as a physical object must decide questions which the goatherd's language leaves open, just as all attempts to do so necessarily share one fundamental assumption: that the goatherd has told us everything there is to see.[39]

Rather than guides to turning an imaginary object into an actual one, it would perhaps be better to understand the frequent spatial markers as a reminder that what we are listening to is a fiction; "within," "beside," "from either side," "a little way off," and "about him" never let us forget that the characters we are hearing about are figures on the surface of a bowl. This is what J. A. Heffernan calls "representational friction" in the

---

[39] See Gow (1952) *ad loc.* 1.27–56, Gallavotti (1966) 421–36, Nicosia (1968) 36, Ott (1969) 132–33, and Manakidou (1993) 15–47. The difficulties that lie in wait for the attempt were already well appreciated by Friedländer (1912) 14: "Betrachten wir nun die Einlage selbst genauer, so zeigt sich, daß der Dichter eine Vorstellung vom Ganzen besitzt und dem Leser übermittelt. Allein diese Vorstellung ist alles andere als exakt. Das Gefäß heißt 'zweihenklig,' aber es wird mit einem homerischen Kunstwort (κισσύβιον) benannt, das keine bestimmte Form vor das Auge stellt."

Shield of Achilles: "By explicitly noting the difference between the medium of visual representation (gold) and its referent (cattle), Homer implicitly draws our attention to the *friction* between the fixed forms of visual art and the narrative thrust of his words."[40] Yet Heffernan also suggests that, because of the length of the narrative sequences in the description of the Shield, the conversion of image to narrative is at times so thorough that "we can hardly see a picture through Homer's words."[41] The scenes on the bowl, by contrast, are of much smaller scope: seven, six, and ten lines apiece. Concentration emphasizes the power of the fiction; we assent to the narrative illusion even as we are reminded that what we are hearing about is a two-dimensional surface.

One might also approach the question of voice in the passage as a deliberate, even ostentatious, fiction. A goatherd describes an object that belongs to his rustic world, and yet what Theocritus has placed in his mouth is epic ecphrasis that has its place beside Apollonius' description of Jason's cloak, and Moschus' description of Europa's basket. Gorgo and Praxinoa describe the palace tapestries briefly and in character, but what the goatherd speaks is an emulation of Homer's Shield of Achilles and Hesiod's Shield of Heracles. While *Idyll* 1 is in the dramatic mode, the ecphrasis can hardly be construed as a reality effect; it rather strongly marks the poem as fiction. Even the word *kissubion* belongs to literature, not life.[42]

The ecphrasis, then, is a manifest fiction, and what it offers the reader is a concentrated experience of fictional involvement and a paradigm of the way in which this involvement can further fictionalize fictional facts by providing them with all kind of imaginary motivations and contexts. In twenty-three verses we enter and leave three microcosmic scenes in succession, with new settings, new characters, and new stories to imagine each time. Moreover, the goatherd's narration leaves us in no doubt that what we are listening to is in part invention. The ecphrasis is a fictional character's imaginative engagement with a work of visual fiction. To participate in it fully, he creates a world from the hints its still images offer. In this sense the goatherd's response to the bowl can be seen as a *mise en abyme* of the reader's

---

[40] Heffernan (1993) 4.
[41] Heffernan (1993) 13. Cf. *Iliad* 18.491–515, 523–49, 579–606, which, as Heffernan (20) observes, close with, or are followed by, reminders that the Shield is a physical object.
[42] Friedländer (1912) 14, Halperin (1983) 167–77. Hunter (1999) *ad loc.* 1.41 compares ἐοικώς with Hesiod *Aspis* 215, Aratus *Phaenomena* 63–67, and *Argonautica* 1.739, and notes, *ad loc.* 1.42, that this verse is Theocritus' only use of the Homerism φαίης κεν: "Here the form plays against the precious poeticisms γυίων and ἐλλοπιεύειν: would *anyone* 'say' such a thing?"

The pleasures of the imaginary 39

response to the poem itself.[43] The quick succession of scenes, and our effort to correct the goatherd's interpretive decisions regarding them, surely make us aware that our own willingness to participate in these fictional worlds rivals his own.[44] We may feel that a desire for meaning differentiates our response from his.[45] The goatherd interprets the bowl insofar as he endows its two-dimensional figures, human and animal, with thoughts and feelings appropriate to the stories in which he thinks they are participating. He does not, however, reflect on their significance, either individually or as a whole, whereas a sense that the *kissubion* is in some way symbolic has been a staple of modern critical reception.[46] Yet if our hermeneutics are enabled or even invited by the limitations in his, then our response to the ecphrasis looks very much like his response to the *kissubion*. As he reads narrative and psychology into the figures on the bowl, so we read symbolism into his narration. By seeking to go beyond his response we in fact resemble it most. For it is in the nature of verbal accounts of visual art to imagine the explanations the image does not supply. As Alain Robbe-Grillet has observed, writing rarely imitates the picture's refusal to explain, where "everything is given as

---

[43] Dällenbach (1989) 94–106 and *passim* is the most complete treatment of ecphrasis as a *mise en abyme* of the text in which it occurs. Thomas (1983) and Fowler (1991) are good introductions to the extensive literature on this figure in *Aeneid* 1, where it points to the limits of fiction as a tool for self-understanding.

[44] Cf. Iser (1978) 133–34, an analysis of readers' self-conscious involvement in a text as they correct false impressions formed earlier in their reading: "It is at this point that the discrepancies produced by the reader during the gestalt-forming process take on their true significance. They have the effect of enabling the reader actually to become aware of the inadequacy of the gestalten he has produced, so that he may detach himself from his own participation in the text and see himself being guided from without. The ability to perceive oneself during the process of participation is an essential quality of the aesthetic experience; the observer finds himself in a strange, halfway position: he is involved, and he watches himself being involved. However, this position is not entirely nonpragmatic, for it can only come about when existing codes are transcended or invalidated. The resultant restructuring of stored experiences makes the reader aware not only of the experience but also of the means whereby it develops."

[45] Miles (1977) 156: "Thyrsis and his friend fail to appreciate the significance of the content of their art . . . The effect of *Idyll* 1 is . . . to reveal how alien the herdsmen's way of looking at things is from ours and how unbridgeable is the gulf that separates them from us." Fowler (1991) 33 and Boyd (1995) 74 discuss the relationship between characters' and readers' points of view in the ecphrastic scene of *Aeneid* 1.

[46] I can only give a selection here. For Lawall (1967) 30, the three scenes represent not merely the three ages of man but their "essential psychological condition;" for Edquist (1975) 106, they show "the totality of significant human experience from childhood to old age." For Miles (1977) 146–49, the bowl depicts grim scenes of Hesiodic realism that are systematically misread by the goatherd; for Halperin (1983) 186, these scenes "represent the themes of bucolic poetry itself." For Cairns (1984) 102–104, the final scene is a climactic symbol of poetic composition within an object that has (101) "literary programmatic significance." Cf. Gutzwiller (1991) 92: "analogical readings, which seek to find meanings insinuated by the author and unintended by the character, have predominated over mimetic ones."

in movement, but frozen in the middle of that movement, immobilized by the representation which leaves in suspense all gestures, falls, conclusions, etc., eternalizing them in the imminence of their end and severing them from their meaning."[47]

THE SONG

The goatherd's offer of the bowl is intended to elicit a song from his companion. Frequent references to Thyrsis' skilful singing (7–8, 19–20, 61–62), including a previous victory in a song contest against Chromis from Libya (23–24), anticipate his performance. The *sphragis*, or seal of ownership, with which he begins his song (65) – "I am Thyrsis of Etna, and the voice of Thyrsis is sweet" – praises his own singing, and, as he sings, the refrain is a constant reminder that we are listening to a song. After its first appearance at verse 63, variations on "bucolic . . . song" recur at verses 70, 73, 76, 79, 84, 89, 94, 99, 104, 108, 111, 114, 122, 127, 131, 137, and 142: eighteen times in eighty-one lines. When Thyrsis has finished singing, the goatherd greets his performance with lavish praise and the promised gift of the *kissubion* (146–50); the song has evidently lived up to his expectations. "The Sorrows of Daphnis," then, is a supreme display of pastoral singing, and the poem strongly marks the fiction that its hexameters – a spoken meter – are here to be heard as if they were a song.[48] So how are we to imagine the performance that the goatherd so admires?

After the *sphragis* Thyrsis continues with questions addressed to the Nymphs (1.66–69):

πᾷ ποκ' ἄρ' ἦσθ', ὅκα Δάφνις ἐτάκετο, πᾷ ποκα, Νύμφαι;
ἦ κατὰ Πηνειῶ καλὰ τέμπεα, ἢ κατὰ Πίνδω;
οὐ γὰρ δὴ ποταμοῖο μέγαν ῥόον εἴχετ' Ἀνάπω,
οὐδ' Αἴτνας σκοπιάν, οὐδ' Ἄκιδος ἱερὸν ὕδωρ.

Where were you then, when Daphnis was dying, where were you, Nymphs? In the lovely valleys of Peneius or Pindus? For surely you did not keep to the great stream of the river Anapus, or the peak of Etna, or the holy water of Acis.

---

[47] Robbe-Grillet (1989) 86. His own interest in the ecphrastic *mise en abyme* is well known. The novel *In the Labyrinth*, for example, contains a detailed description of a print, "The Defeat of Reichenfels," which portrays scenes from the story in which it is found. As they are described, these representations merge insensibly with the world of the primary narrative.

[48] Wilamowitz (1906) 137: "ein Reflex des Liedes in einer anderen poetischen Gattung;" Gow (1952) *ad loc.* 1.64–142: "the 'songs' which T. puts in the mouth of his characters can do no more than suggest in another medium the verses which they actually sang;" Rosenmeyer (1969) 147: "Theocritus suggests the music instead of putting it on the boards." This suggestion is, however, insistent.

The pleasures of the imaginary

His tone is passionate; the interjection ἄρ', as Hunter observes, "marks an urgent question,"[49] and the effect is heightened by the repeated "Where were you?" Similarly οὐ γάρ, "for surely," with which Thyrsis responds to his own question, is not so much an answer as a show of indignation, surprise, or even contempt.[50] At the same time the sonorous geography – Peneius, Pindus, Anapus, Etna, Acis – is a counterpoint to the emotional display; each name invites us to imagine a pleasant haunt of the divinities far away from the scene of Daphnis' death.

In the verses that follow Thyrsis shifts from direct address to narrative, evoking the animals' response to Daphnis' death through their various cries: jackals and wolves "howled" (71), the lion "lamented" (72), cattle "wept" (75). Having suggested these inhuman voices, Thyrsis introduces a series of articulate visitors. Hermes, the first to arrive, does not grieve like the animals but speaks (εἶπε, 77) to Daphnis as one sensible fellow remonstrating with another (77–78): "'Daphnis, who is wearing you out? Who are you so enamored of, my good friend?'" The words of the cowherds, shepherds, and goatherds who arrive next are reported indirectly – "everyone asked him what was the matter" (81) – and are followed by the appearance of Priapus. Priapus speaks directly, like Hermes, but appears more sympathetic (82): "'Poor Daphnis, why are you wasting away?'" The scholia call his words a speech of consolation,[51] but his rhetoric appears to miss its mark. Daphnis is not reconciled to his fate, and does not reply (92).

His silence is theatrical.[52] Yet, if Daphnis' unwillingness to respond is a kind of acting, will this not be reflected in Thyrsis' performance? Should we not imagine some kind of pause for effect here, to communicate this silence to the goatherd? For there are other signs of communication between the performer and his audience. Hunter notes that the goatherd's approval of the song is not impaired by Priapus' satirical portrait of his profession in verses 86–88:[53]

'βούτας μὲν ἐλέγευ, νῦν δ' αἰπόλῳ ἀνδρὶ ἔοικας.
ᾡπόλος, ὅκκ' ἐσορῇ τὰς μηκάδας οἷα βατεῦνται,
τάκεται ὀφθαλμῶς ὅτι οὐ τράγος αὐτὸς ἔγεντο.'

---

[49] Hunter (1999) ad loc. 1.66.   [50] Denniston (1950) 77–79.
[51] Σ 1.82–85f., Wendel (1914) 60: παρηγορητικὸς ὁ λόγος, cf. 1.82–85k: παρηγορῆσαι θέλων τοῦτό φησι πρὸς αὐτόν.
[52] Lawall (1967) 20–21 compares Daphnis to Aeschylus' Prometheus. Walsh (1985) 9 cites Aristophanes *Frogs* 832–34, 912–20: "Even [Daphnis'] silence seems theatrical, a way of miming significance, the trick for which Aeschylus was famous." For Gutzwiller (1991) 241 n. 61, Daphnis resembles Phaedra in Euripides' *Hippolytus*, "because it is *love* that compels both of them to their fate."
[53] Hunter (1999) ad loc. 1.86–91.

'You used to be called a cowherd, but now you resemble a goatherd. For the goatherd, when he sees how the females are mounted, cries because he himself was not born a goat.'

Hunter concludes that "the framing context never completely disappears;" the world portrayed in "The Sorrows of Daphnis" reflects the world of *Idyll* 1, in which the song is performed. But Thyrsis' repetition of αἰπόλος, "goatherd," is emphatic; it appears to be a deliberate jest incorporating his audience into the song.[54] The verses are a fiction of oral composition and dramatize the singer's adaptation of his song to fit its performance context.[55]

Thyrsis' portrayal of Aphrodite is also conditioned by his audience. Unlike the previous visitors, whose attitude towards Daphnis is expressed through their speech alone, Aphrodite's feelings are narrated by Thyrsis (1.95–96):

ἦνθέ γε μὰν ἁδεῖα καὶ ἁ Κύπρις γελάοισα,
λάθρη μὲν γελάοισα, βαρὺν δ' ἀνὰ θυμὸν ἔχοισα.

And yes, Cypris came too, smiling sweetly, smiling secretly, but bearing heavy anger in her heart.

These verses, and their relationship to verses 138–39, are famously difficult to interpret, for we do not know why Aphrodite is smiling, or if she played a part in Daphnis' death in a now unknown myth that preceded the poem's composition. Yet, if we examine the lines in light of the interaction between Thyrsis and the goatherd, perhaps their difficulty will seem less oppressive. As Hunter observes, "γε μάν marks the climactic point of an enumeration;"[56] Aphrodite is the last of Daphnis' visitors, and the effect is heightened by καί: "Cypris came too." Thyrsis is increasing the tension as the most important arrival approaches. Yet his creation of suspense surely plays upon the goatherd's knowledge that Aphrodite has a crucial role in Daphnis' death. As we might guess from his request to hear "The Sorrows of Daphnis" specifically (19), he already knows the story; verse

---

[54] Gow (1952) *ad loc.* 1.86 draws the opposite conclusion: "T. has probably forgotten that the sole audience of Thyrsis' song is himself a goatherd."

[55] Cf. Pretagostini (1992) 71: "La *performance* di Tirsi sulla morte di Dafni ... mostra come un componimento ... poteva essere adattato dall'autore-esecutore alle mutate necessità e circostanze della nuova esecuzione: il riferimento finale alla libagione in onore delle Muse con il latte appena munto è un esempio molto interessante di un'aggiunta estemporanea, dettata dal contesto situazionale relativo al momento dell'esecuzione." While the end of the song is the clearest indication of Thyrsis' adaptation of "The Sorrows of Daphnis" to its performance context, it is not the only one. Incorporation of the audience into the song is most fully dramatized in the song contest of *Idyll* 5, where mockery of the other singer is an essential ingredient of the performance. Cf. Finnegan (1977), especially Chapter 3, "Composition," 52–87, for this feature of oral poetry in a range of cultures.

[56] Hunter (1999) *ad loc.* 1.95–96.

The pleasures of the imaginary

95 is addressed to a listener who (unlike us) understands what lies behind Aphrodite's behavior.

The words that Thyrsis has Aphrodite address to Daphnis also presuppose his audience's knowledge of this "back story" (1.97–98):[57]

κεῖπε 'τύ θην τὸν Ἔρωτα κατεύχεο, Δάφνι, λυγιξεῖν·
ἦ ῥ' οὐκ αὐτὸς Ἔρωτος ὑπ' ἀργαλέω ἐλυγίχθης;'

And she said, 'Daphnis, did you not indeed assert that you would bind Love, and have you not now been bound by fierce Love yourself?'

This speech finally provokes a response. Daphnis reproaches Aphrodite for her cruelty and, promising that, even in the underworld, he will remain hostile to desire (100–103), hints at her illicit sexual relations with Anchises by aposiopesis, breaking off suddenly in the middle of speaking (105): "'Don't they say about Cypris that the cowherd . . . ?'" The figure is theatrical, and we should no doubt imagine another pause here. Daphnis then orders Aphrodite to "'begone to Ida, begone to Anchises'" and ironically sketches the pastoral scene she can expect to find upon arrival (106–107). He reminds her that Adonis too is "in season" (109) and tells her, in language reminiscent of comedy (112),[58] 'αὖτις ὅπως στασῇ Διομήδεος ἆσσον ἰοῖσα,' "'go and stand next to Diomedes again.'" He even puts into her mouth the words with which she is to greet him (113).

From here on Daphnis addresses his mute companions. He bids farewell to the wild animals (115–16), then to the spring Arethusa and the rivers of Thybris (116–17). After his colloquial abuse of Aphrodite he now sounds like a tragic hero saying goodbye to his world.[59] Envisioning his death, he composes an epitaph for himself (1.120–21):

'Δάφνις ἐγὼν ὅδε τῆνος ὁ τὰς βόας ὧδε νομεύων,
Δάφνις ὁ τὼς ταύρως καὶ πόρτιας ὧδε ποτίσδων.'

'I am that Daphnis who herded his cows here, Daphnis who watered his bulls and calves here.'

---

[57] Ogilvie (1962) 106: "[the song] is throughout allusive, seeming to assume from the listener familiarity with the story." (Although Ogilvie means the poem's audience rather than the goatherd, on which see below.) Cf. Ott (1969) 112: "Die Vorgeschichte bleibt außerhalb des erzählten Geschehens."

[58] Aristophanes *Clouds* 824, 1177, *Frogs* 378, 627, *Birds* 131, *Peace* 77, etc. Cf. Gow (1952) *ad loc.* 1.112: "The proposal to regard ὅπως στασῇ as a final clause dependent on ἕρπε in 106, and to treat what intervenes as parenthesis, gives unsatisfactory sense, and its gross clumsiness is accentuated by the imperative in 113."

[59] Ott (1969) 126 n. 365 compares Sophocles *Ajax* 856–65, *Philoctetes* 936–40. Cf. Walsh (1985) 9: "What Thyrsis uncovers as he tries to reach the hidden parts of Daphnis' 'tragic' consciousness is a public performance, a substitute for the inner man."

Its form recalls the *sphragis*, and so associates Daphnis with Thyrsis himself.[60] The resemblance becomes closer in the invocation of Pan that follows (1.123–26):

> 'ὦ Πὰν Πάν, εἴτ' ἐσσὶ κατ' ὤρεα μακρὰ Λυκαίω,
> εἴτε τύγ' ἀμφιπολεῖς μέγα Μαίνολον, ἔνθ' ἐπὶ νᾶσον
> τὰν Σικελάν, Ἑλίκας δὲ λίπε ῥίον αἰπύ τε σᾶμα
> τῆνο Λυκαονίδαο, τὸ καὶ μακάρεσσιν ἀγητόν.'

'O Pan, Pan, whether you are on the high mountains of Lycaeus, or whether you wander great Mainolus, come to the island of Sicily, and leave the peak of Helice, and that steep tomb of the son of Lycaeon, which is a wonder even to immortals.'

The list of locations in which a god might be found is a standard feature of kletic hymns, which call on them to appear, but here the blend of heightened emotion and geography recalls the address to the Nymphs with which the song began: the Daphnis created by Thyrsis' performance resembles the performer who created him.

The prayer continues with Daphnis offering his syrinx to the god (1.128–30):

> 'ἔνθ', ὦναξ, καὶ τάνδε φέρευ πακτοῖο μελίπνουν
> ἐκ κηρῶ σύριγγα καλὸν περὶ χεῖλος ἑλικτάν·
> ἦ γὰρ ἐγὼν ὑπ' Ἔρωτος ἐς Ἄιδαν ἕλκομαι ἤδη.'

'Come, lord, and carry off this pipe, honey-scented from the pressed wax, well bound around its lip. For I myself am now being dragged off to Hades by love.'[61]

The pathos of the appeal to the absent pastoral divinity is emphasized by the repeated ἔνθ', "come" (124, 128), the verb which marks the arrival of Daphnis' unsolicited visitors (77, 80, 81, 95). Moreover, the demonstrative in τάνδε ... σύριγγα, "this pipe," suggests that a gesture from Daphnis accompanies the offer. We know from the opening of the poem that the syrinx is the goatherd's instrument (1–3); Thyrsis asked him to play it for him (12–14), and the goatherd refused because it might anger Pan (15–16). Thyrsis, then, has Daphnis point to the goatherd's pipe as he offers his own to Pan. By indicating that they are both syrinx players, Thyrsis suggests that Daphnis resembles the goatherd as well as himself. It is an adaptation of his song in performance that celebrates his listener's skill even as it acknowledges his refusal to play.

---

[60] Hunter (1999) *ad loc.* 1.120–21.
[61] My translation follows Hunter (1999) *ad loc.* 1.129: "καλόν is adverbial, περὶ ... ἑλικτάν in tmesis, and χεῖλος accusative of respect."

The pleasures of the imaginary 45

Yet why does Thyrsis spend two verses describing the pipe's look and smell as he approaches the song's emotional climax? Does this not risk spoiling the impact of its most sublime moment?[62] The verses seem to be a miniature ecphrasis echoing the goatherd's description of the bowl: the syrinx is πακτοῖο μελίπνουν | ἐκ κηρῶ, "honey-scented from the pressed wax," just as the *kissubion* is κεκλυσμένον ἁδέι κηρῶ, "sealed with sweet wax," and ἔτι γλυφάνοιο ποτόσδον, "still fragrant from the carving" (27–28); it is καλὸν περὶ χεῖλος ἑλικτάν, "well bound around its lip," just as on the bowl χείλη μαρύεται ὑψόθι κισσός, "ivy curls above the lip" (29).[63] While it is natural for the goatherd to dwell on the *kissubion*'s decoration rather than its function, since this is what makes it remarkable, Thyrsis' emphasis upon the pipe's appearance rather than its music seems best explained as a response to the goatherd's description. By referring to it in this way, he makes a point about the superiority of his own art. While visual representations may be able to elicit fascination, drawing the viewer into their world, the verbal arts can reach out to their audience, actively intervening in their lives as they attend to the performance. The point is similar to Pindar's in the opening of *Nemean* 5, where he contrasts the immobility of statues doomed to remain where they stand with the mobility of the poem that speeds in all directions bringing news of the athlete's victory. The point of the contrast here, however, is not the capacity of a text for unlimited dissemination, but rather the fiction of a live performance in which the singer can respond directly to the living presence of his audience. Face to face with his listener, he confronts him with the illusion of a fictional world that maps itself actively onto his own real space and time, just as (as we shall see in the next chapter) the deixis of performed drama maps the fictional space of the play onto the real space of its audience.

Daphnis ends his speech by inviting the world to change because he is dying (132–36). The last disorder he invokes is an unprecedented song contest (136): "let owls sing against nightingales from the mountains."[64] The image reminds us that the herdsmen look to nature for paradigms of their music (cf. 1–3, 7–8).[65] As the nightingale is more melodious than the owl, so the quality of the singing is all important when they judge their

---

[62] Demetrius *On Style* 119: the use of an elevated style on small matters is a source of frigidity.
[63] The resemblance is noted by Cairns (1984) 101–102, who sees both objects as symbols of bucolic poetry.
[64] Hunter (1999) *ad loc.* 1.136: "'cry in competition with . . .', i.e. 'rival.'"
[65] For Miles (1977) 154, the herdsmen's delight in "inarticulate sound" here and in the opening of the poem emphasizes "the superficiality of their response to the very art which they value so highly."

own songs.[66] Thyrsis begins by celebrating his "sweet voice" (65), and in conclusion promises the Muses not that he will remember another song, but that he will sing to them more sweetly on another occasion (145). The singing is also what the goatherd admires in his performance (1.146–48):

> πλῆρές τοι μέλιτος τὸ καλὸν στόμα, Θύρσι, γένοιτο,
> πλῆρες δὲ σχαδόνων, καὶ ἀπ' Αἰγίλω ἰσχάδα τρώγοις
> ἁδεῖαν, τέττιγος ἐπεὶ τύγα φέρτερον ᾄδεις.

May your lovely mouth be filled with honey, Thyrsis, and filled with honeycomb, and may you eat the sweet figs of Aegilus, since you sing better than a cicada.

We might guess as much from the form of the song. Thyrsis' declamatory opening gives his own voice center stage as one half of a supposed dialogue with the Nymphs. After this there are several kinds of vocal representation: narrative for animals, indirect speech for human beings, dramatic impersonation for the gods and Daphnis. Each new speaker's entrance is marked, though no exits are reported.[67] Unlike drama, the characters are only present as long as Thyrsis is singing their part, and the most important part is Daphnis. This is the centerpiece of the performance, the means by which the celebrated pastoral singer stages his resemblance to his legendary predecessor: of the eighty-one verses of the song, eighteen are refrain, twenty-nine impersonation of Daphnis.[68]

This song, however, is a stylistic medley. It incorporates tragedy, comedy, epitaph, and hymn in a rhetorical *bricolage* held together by the performance itself. The poem deconstructs its own illusion of primitive, oral song even as it produces it. The verbal spell that (within the poem) makes Daphnis and Aphrodite present to the goatherd with the immediacy of a quasi-magical enactment is, to the reader, a collage of textual sources.[69] The more the goatherd insists upon his pleasure, the greater the cognitive dissonance grows. For to understand his enthusiasm, we have to imagine an experience of the song that is quite different from our own. His grasp of the story is clearly superior to our own, since the identity of the anonymous maiden at verse 82, the role of Aphrodite (95–98, 138–39), and the nature of Daphnis' death (139–41) are not obstacles to his enjoyment as they are to ours. Even

---

[66] Cf. *Id.* 5.136–37, where Comatas appears to win the song contest because he is a better singer than Lacon: "it is not right for jays to compete with a nightingale, Lacon, nor hoopoes with swans." Note also how he taunts Lacon at 5.29 as "a wasp buzzing against a cicada."
[67] ἦνθ' Ἑρμᾶς, 77; ἦνθον τοὶ βοῦται, τοὶ ποιμένες, ᾠπόλοι ἦνθον, 80; ἦνθ' ὁ Πρίηπος, 81; ἦνθε ... ἁ Κύπρις, 95.
[68] Cf. Lycidas in *Idyll* 7, where the archetypal goatherd sings of Daphnis and Comatas. Here too the voice is emphasized (7.82, 88).
[69] Cf. Hardie (2002) 13–23 on the creation and unmasking of such presence effects in Ovid.

The pleasures of the imaginary 47

if we accept that the poem's original audience would have enjoyed piecing the myth together from allusions in the song,[70] this pleasure is hardly that of the goatherd himself.[71] Finally, since the entire poem, and not just "The Sorrows of Daphnis," is in hexameters, the pleasure the goatherd finds in the latter can only be guessed at; it requires imagining for ourselves a difference between the sound of the poem's various parts that we do not experience in reading them and which would not fully manifest itself in performance either. The representation of the human voice within the poem could only ever contrast with the reproduction of that voice in a staging of the poem. In its representation of oral performance, the poem playfully stages its own distance from orality.[72] Its impossibly melodious shepherd is the product of a poet who knows that he can depend on the imagination of readers to bring his world to life.[73]

Homer, by contrast, avoids drawing attention to the difference between speech and song within his poems by reporting the content of the songs that occur within them indirectly. Thus, in Book 8 of the *Odyssey*, when Odysseus reaches the land of the Phaeaecians, and he and the court are entertained by the songs of their resident bard, Demodocus, we are told what Demodocus sang about, but his actual singing is not staged for us in the poem. Moreover, there is no mention of the quality of Demodocus' voice, so that the rhapsode who performs the *Odyssey* is not obliged to emulate a superb display of singing in his performance of the poem. The text of the poem, in other words, anticipates a performance that is dramatic (in Demodocus' longer song, the story of Ares and Aphrodite, there is a good deal of dialogue between the characters once the frame of indirect reporting has been established), but which does not feature vocal display as a primary attraction. Conversely, the alternation of meters in tragedy allows the choruses to be performed as the songs they claim to be, and differentiates them from the dialogue between characters. These texts, then, ensure that the difference between speech and song does not become problematic

---

[70] For Ogilvie (1962) 110, the song contains "clues – no doubt intentionally difficult clues – to lead [Theocritus'] well-read and educated readers to fill in the gaps for themselves and to admire his ingenuity of allusion." Cf., however, Gow (1952) II.1: "T.'s story was no more intelligible to his scholiasts than to us." For modern responses, see Arnott (1996) 63, "mysterious and elusive;" Fantuzzi (2000) 146, "obscure presentation."
[71] Cf. Miles (1977) 56.
[72] Cf. Zumthor (1987) 37, for whom everything within a text that "nous renseigne sur l'intervention de la voix humaine dans sa *publication*" is an index of orality.
[73] I would therefore disagree with the suggestion of Henderson (1999) 145 that pastoral poetry is in fact not "past-oral" but merely "post-oral," still haunted, in other words, by its distance from its origins in "the improvisational singing that must contain its true, real essence."

in performance; if this difference cannot be materially instantiated, the representation of it circumvents the need for its production.[74]

In *Idyll* 1 the "non-performativity" of the text thus becomes another marker of its fully fictional character. While face-to-face storytelling (as the poem portrays it) responds directly to its audience's desires, the text must seduce its readers with the promise of an experience they cannot have outside it.[75] In the gap that opens up between representation and performance Theocritus places the reader, whose representative within the poem is the nameless goatherd. It is he who shows us the work of the imagination in his description of the bowl, so that we see how we are to bridge this gap in our reading of the song, when he, in direct contact with its immediacy, can no longer be our guide.

---

[74] Likewise, when traditional operas wish to mark certain moments within them as song, not speech (as is often the case when the fictional characters are singers, as in Monteverdi's *Orfeo* and Wagner's *Die Meistersinger von Nürnberg*), the shift from recitative to aria allows this difference to manifest itself.

[75] Chambers (1984) 11–12. Finkelberg (1998) 91–93 makes a similar claim.

CHAPTER 2

The presence of the fictional world

This chapter looks at the fictionality of the bucolic world from the perspective of narrative mode; that is to say, whether that world is brought into being through the dramatic speech of its fictional characters, through narration by the poet, or through some combination of the two. By way of introduction to the discussion of this question in Theocritus, I consider the relationship between fictional presence and dramatic enactment in pre-Hellenistic poetry, in Hellenistic poetry other than the *Idylls*, and in ancient literary theory.

In an important discussion of "the mimetic poetic of Greek hymns," Jan Maarten Bremer and William Furley have emphasized that the function of dramatic imitation in early cult hymns was to foster a sense of identity between the participants in the cult and the mythical beings their performance instantiated. Thus, for example, in the Cretan Palaikastro Hymn to Zeus armed warriors known as Kouretes reenact the rescue of the infant Zeus from his infanticidal father. Amid the clashing of cymbals (to drown out the cries of the baby), they address him as "the greatest Kouros," describe the performance of their own hymn around his altar, and invite him to leap into (or for) their homes and fields.[1] For the young Cretan men who perform the hymn, the reenactment of their ancestors through dramatic performance is a way to identify themselves with them, and so replicate in themselves the ideal of young manhood these ancestors represent. For the audience who observes them, their performance is both a demonstration of their success in this regard and a way to make these absent ancestors present as a reminder of their continuing value as role models.

One can likewise speak of the rhapsode's performance of Homer as a "presentification" to his audience of the model heroes of epic. Socrates calls Ion "rhapsode and actor," just as he calls his audience "spectators" (*Ion* 535a–b), and he emphasizes the audience's complete absorption as it

[1] Bremer and Furley (2001) II.6–18.

50   *Theocritus and the Invention of Fiction*

contemplates the heroes staged by his performance.² While the rhapsode is simultaneously aware of the imaginary world produced by his performance and the real world of his audience, whom he eyes with the care of a professional performer, the latter lose all self-possession in the presence of the characters he stages. For the duration of the performance, the world it manifests usurps the reality of the world in which it appears, and, as in the Hymn, the performer's body and voice are the medium by which the absent world of the past becomes visible and tangible in the present world of the audience.³

The classical and Hellenistic stage work similarly in their production of the worlds of tragedy and New Comedy. David Wiles has described how the fictional space enacted on the stage projects beyond the dramatic space itself, and imposes itself on the space occupied by the audience.⁴ Euripides' *Ion* offers a striking example. In this play the protagonist is, unknown to himself, the offspring of his mother's rape by the god Apollo. Having been abandoned by her at birth, he was brought to his father's temple at Delphi by Hermes, where he now serves as an attendant. One of his custodial duties is to drive away from the temple's roof the flocks of birds that threaten to land there (153–63):

> ἔα ἔα·
> φοιτῶσ' ἤδη λείπουσίν τε
> πτανοὶ Παρνασοῦ κοίτας.
> αὐδῶ μὴ χρίμπτειν θριγκοῖς
> μηδ' ἐς χρυσήρεις οἴκους.
> μάρψωσ' αὖ τόξοις, ὦ Ζηνὸς
> κῆρυξ, ὀρνίθων γαμφηλαῖς
> ἰσχὺν νικῶν.
> ὅδε πρὸς θυμέλας ἄλλος ἐρέσσει
> κύκνος. οὐκ ἄλλᾳ φοινικοφαῆ
> πόδα κινήσεις;

Ah! Ah! The winged ones are coming now and leaving their nests on Parnassus. Don't you dare land on the roof or in the golden house. I'll get you too with my bow, herald of Zeus, who surpass the strength of birds with your beak. Here comes another one winging its way towards the precincts, a swan! Will you not take your purple foot elsewhere?⁵

---

[2] On the rhapsode as actor, see Herington (1985) 51.
[3] See Vernant (1991) 151–63 for a discussion of the power of the archaic cult image "to make the invisible visible, to assign a place in our world to entities from the other world." Gumbrecht (2004) 30–31 likewise discusses the manifestation of the divine in medieval drama as a "production of presence" mediated through the materiality of the actors' bodies.
[4] Wiles (1991) 37.   [5] My translation of the text of Diggle (1994).

Just as in the opening of the play Hermes announces that the stage on which he stands is "this land of Delphi," so here Ion points to what the audience can see – the stage building and the slopes behind the theater – as a way to get it to imagine what it cannot see: nests on the cliffs of Parnassus, an eagle, a swan with purple feet. The poet exploits a wide range of deictic expressions – vocatives, imperatives, demonstratives, and verbs of motion – so that his audience will reimagine the here and now of its actual physical location through his character's eyes.[6] The impossibility of staging everything that Ion points to is, as Demetrius *On Style* 195 observes, a chance for the performer to show his skill: "The rush for the bow provides many movements for the actor, as does looking up into the air as he speaks to the swan, and all the rest of the stage business which is fashioned for the actor." As Demetrius' observations make clear, imaginary deixis is a risky business, and its effectiveness depends upon the charisma of the performer. It is, however, anchored in the transformation of the dramatic space that has already taken place in the audience's mind, and in the body of the performer, by whose gestures it continues to be realized. Its function is not metatheatrical; it rather extends the fictional world of the drama so that it embraces the space that surrounds the theater.

It is interesting to compare the Euripidean stage with the stage of New Comedy in this respect. In the prologue to Menander's *Dyskolos* a character (who in due course will reveal himself to be the god Pan) appears from the central door of the stage and speaks to the audience (1–7):

> τῆς Ἀττικῆς νομίζετ' εἶναι τὸν τόπον,
> Φυλήν, τὸ νυμφαῖον δ' ὅθεν προέρχομαι
> Φυλασίων καὶ τῶν δυναμένων τὰς πέτρας
> ἐνθάδε γεωργεῖν, ἱερὸν ἐπιφανὲς πάνυ.
> τὸν ἀγρὸν δὲ τὸν [ἐ]πὶ δεξί' οἰκεῖ τουτονὶ
> Κνήμων, ἀπάνθρωπός τις ἄνθρωπος σφόδρα
> καὶ δύσκολος πρὸς ἅπαντας οὐ χαίρων τ' ὄχλῳ.

Imagine that this place is Phyle in Attica, and that the shrine from which I appear belongs to those who live here and are capable of cultivating these rocks. It's a famous holy place. The farm here on the right is the home of Knemon, your typical recluse, a bad-tempered man who shuns the crowd.[7]

As many scholars have suggested, the informative prologue of New Comedy has its origins in the prologues of Euripides, where a god who knows the full story gives the prehistory to the dramatic action that is about to unfold.

---

[6] Cf. Wiles (1997), especially Chapter 5, "The chorus: Its transformation of space," 114–32.
[7] My translation of the text of Handley (1965).

So in the *Ion*, for example, it is Hermes who appears on stage first, and informs the audience that the character we are about to see is, unknown to himself, the love child of Creusa and Apollo. He does not, however, address them directly, or in any way acknowledge that he is in the presence of observers, and it is here that a distinctive difference of New Comedy can be noted.[8] While the prologue speech of Euripides contains an implied imperative to the audience to imagine the world of the fiction ("I have come to this land of Delphi," says Hermes), in Menander this has become an explicit compact between playwright and audience expressed through the prologue speaker who is in a liminal position with regard to the play as such, neither quite inside, nor entirely outside it.[9] The presence of the god on stage as an agent or explicator of the plot occurs before, or at least apart from, the main dramatic business transacted by its human agents, so that he figures as a stand-in for the poet himself.[10] Menander's mediation of fictional space by means of this stand-in is bold yet subtle. He does not ask his audience to map an unfamiliar location onto the visible geography, as Euripides asks his audience to see the site of the theater as Delphi. Rather, he asks for something that may in fact be more difficult to accomplish, namely that they conform their knowledge of a real, local shrine – the temple of the Nymphs at Phyle – to the needs of stage presentation. The distinctive cliffside cave that is the real-world site of the sanctuary becomes, in the play, a typical wayside shrine, with houses and farms around it.[11] The spatial transformation of real particular into fictional universal is immediately echoed in the definition of the play's leading character. After identifying the stage's central door as that of the shrine Pan points to "the farm here on the right" as that of Knemon, "your typical recluse" (the subtle universalizing force of ἀπάνθρωπός τις ἄνθρωπος is hard to capture in translation), and "a bad-tempered man," the generalizing adjective that gives the play its title. Having given the back story of the plot that is about to unfold, Pan reminds the audience that it is set amid familiar local places. The bad-tempered man, he tells us, hates everyone, from "his wife and neighbors here" all the way to "Cholargos way down there." From his location in

---

[8] Bain (1975) 22. For the ongoing debate as to whether or not Old Comedy presents a consistent dramatic illusion comparable to those of tragedy and New Comedy, which it occasionally breaks through parabases and other such metatheatrical moments, or should rather be considered essentially non-illusionistic, see Slater (1995) 29–30, who takes the view that the presentation of a consistent dramatic illusion is in fact one of the characteristic developments of New Comedy.

[9] Bain (1977) 186; Gutzwiller (2000) 115.

[10] In the *Aspis* Menander delays the prologue some one hundred lines, offering a beginning *in medias res*, which is then supplemented by the overview of the goddess Tyche (Chance).

[11] See Handley (1965) 20–25.

Phyle, Pan looks down the road to Athens, extending Knemon's loathing as far as the village of Cholargos, and so stopping just short of the city itself in which the audience is now watching the play. As in Euripides, imaginary deixis extends the play's fictional geography from the stage out into the world of the audience, superimposing itself upon it. Menander, however, uses this technique as a way to have his audience reimagine this world as the site of universal stories, like the one he is about to tell them.

Callimachus' use of the dramatic mode to create fictional space is best exemplified by the *Hymns*. These are usually divided into mimetic (*Hymns* 2, 4, 5) and non-mimetic poems (*Hymns* 1, 3, 6), with the former being spoken by a dramatic character who is localized in a fictional time and space and responds dramatically to people and events within it, and the latter being spoken by a narrator, who, like the speaker of the *Homeric Hymns*, shows relatively little sign of individualization.[12] The mimetic *Hymns* make use of the present tense of drama, and an abundance of deictic words, to dramatize their speaker's response to events occurring within the world of the poem. So *Hymn* 2 begins:

> Οἷον ὁ τὠπόλλωνος ἐσείσατο δάφνινος ὅρπηξ,
> οἷα δ' ὅλον τὸ μέλαθρον· ἑκὰς, ἑκὰς ὅστις ἀλιτρός.
> καὶ δή που τὰ θύρετρα καλῷ ποδὶ Φοῖβος ἀράσσει·
> οὐχ ὁράᾳς; ἐπένευσεν ὁ Δήλιος ἡδύ τι φοῖνιξ
> ἐξαπίνης, ὁ δὲ κύκνος ἐν ἠέρι καλὸν ἀείδει.
> αὐτοὶ νῦν κατοχῆες ἀνακλίνασθε πυλάων,
> αὐταὶ δὲ κληῖδες· ὁ γὰρ θεὸς οὐκέτι μακράν·
> οἱ δὲ νέοι μολπήν τε καὶ ἐς χορὸν ἐντύνασθε.
> ὡπόλλον οὐ παντὶ φαείνεται . . .

How the shoot of Apollo's laurel shakes! How the whole temple shakes! Stand back, stand back, whoever is polluted. It must be that Apollo is now striking the doors with his lovely foot. Do you not see? The Delian palm suddenly nods sweetly, and the swan in the air is singing beautifully. You, bars, now draw back from the gates yourselves, and you bolts too! For the god is no longer far away. And the youths there, get ready for song and dance. Apollo does not appear to everyone . . .[13]

---

[12] Cf. Harder (1992), who argues that Callimachus is playing with mimetic and diegetic modes of storytelling in these poems, just as he does in his other works. In the *Homeric Hymn to Apollo* the rhapsode apparently performs the poem as a dramatic character, in the persona of Homer, the "blind man [who] lives in rocky Chios" (172); see Zanetto (1996) 37, Nagy (1996) 62. This is in keeping with the poem's praise of mimesis, the lines addressed to the Delian women, who, in their own song, "know how to imitate the voices . . . of all men" (162–63). Even here, however, very little attention to this impersonation is apparent in the text of the *Hymn*; if it was Callimachus' model for the dramatic speakers of his mimetic *Hymns*, he has expanded this aspect of the poem to the point that his imitation constitutes, for all practical purposes, a new kind of poem.

[13] My translation of the text of Williams (1978). I follow his interpretation of ὅρπηξ (16), and the structure of the doors (18, 21).

The speaker begins with an expression of amazement at an event unfolding before his eyes. As the urgency of Ion's speech before the temple at Delphi encourages the audience to imagine the invisible birds that threaten its roof, so here the speaker's dramatic reaction asks the reader or listener to imagine a presence that lies just outside the fictional space in which he himself is located, the god who is just about to burst into it. However, to communicate these effects, Callimachus uses the fiction of questions addressed to a κωφὸν πρόσωπον, or mute companion, a feature of both choral lyric and mime.[14] Callimachus exploits a silent presence in the speaker's foreground in order to point to – rather than simply describe – events taking place somewhat further away: "Do you not see? The Delian palm suddenly nods sweetly, and the swan in the air is singing beautifully." Rather than the assumed compact between dramatist and audience in Euripides, or the explicit one in Menander, Callimachus uses an "I/thou" structure to mediate the poem's fictional world to a reader or listener who will adopt the "thou" position relative to the poem's speaker. In the case of choral lyric or mime, the speakers address a figure who, though silent, is physically present to them in the performance space, a chorus member or fellow actor, who is therefore also present to them within the imaginary world their performance enacts. By adopting this device for the *Hymns*, Callimachus creates an addressee for the poem's speaker who is fictionally present within the world of the poem, yet not instantiated as the poem is enacted, whether this enactment takes the form of reading, or solo recitation.[15] For if no one shares the stage with

---

[14] Fantuzzi (1993b) 934, 945. Depew (1993) likewise derives the mimesis of the *Hymns* from the resources of choral lyric. As Danielewicz (1990) and Felson (1999) have shown, fictional deixis (*Deixis am Phantasma*) is a feature of choral lyric, where it contrasts with a real deixis (*demonstratio ad oculos*) that refers to the here and now of the audience and choral celebrant. From this perspective, the innovation of the *Hymns* is to fictionalize the primary deixis directed at the real world the chorus shares with its audience. For the silent addressee in mime, see Wiemken (1972) 22, Albert (1988) 80–83.

[15] For the continuing debates about the performance of the *Hymns*, see Falivene (1990) and the response to Cameron (1995) in Bing (2000). Various arguments have been advanced about the performance of other Hellenistic literary drama. Legrand (1898) 414–18 argued that the multiple parts and changes of place in *Idyll* 15 made performance inconceivable. Mastromarco (1984) 21–63 claimed that ambiguities of space, persons, exits, and entrances in the poems of Herodas could only be clarified through a full staging with more than one actor. Puchner (1993) 19, 30, by contrast, argued that clarification of textual ambiguity through performance reverses the known procedures of ancient dramaturgy, in which stage directions are written into the text. The poems contain no objective "playable" space, and their world is experienced as a narrative that unfolds through the eyes of the principal speaker. Hunter (1993) 39–40, on the other hand, notes that every poem (except 8) contains more than one speaking character, and that in every poem one character predominates, a form that seems well suited to performance by a small troupe dominated by the leading mime. Noting, however, that other scholars have charged Mastromarco with underestimating a solo performer's ability to project more than one role, he concludes: "General agreement on these questions may be hardly possible, because they depend upon subjective assessments of what is and is not possible in performance."

the performer as the poem is recited, his speech positions the live audience as a fictional addressee just as it would a reader.

It is possible, then, to see the role of deixis in the poem along the lines laid out by theorists of deixis in modern fiction, that is, as effecting a "vicarious transport" from the reader's real time and place to the fictional "here and now" in which the imagined action takes place, a process usually referred to as "deictic shift."[16] While the *Hymns* surely achieve this, however, an account of the dramatic mode in the Hellenistic poets that saw its function solely in effecting the same kind of transport to a fictional location that could be effected by a non-dramatic narrator would miss an important aspect of its handling by them. For these poems begin with the speaking voice of the character, without preamble or introductory setting by the poet. The reader is not transported gradually to a fictional world located within the pages of a book but confronted by a voice that accosts him face to face, from the written page. The mimetic *Hymns*, in particular, preserve the frontality of actual drama; by using the device of the fictional addressee, they project their world outward, into the world of the reader, just as the world of the dramatists pushes out into the world of the audience. It is in this that their uncanny effect resides, and it makes reading them quite unlike reading a work of narrative fiction.[17]

This unsettling quality is the difference between entering a fictional world as its unseen observer and having that world present itself to you. It is in these terms, then, that I want to briefly reconsider the difference between showing and telling, mimesis and diegesis, as it appears in the theoretical discussions of narrative form in Plato, Aristotle, and Longinus. In Book 3 of the *Republic* Socrates, having settled what kinds of things poets ought and ought not to tell in their stories, moves on to the question of how they ought to tell them. He explains that "everything that is said by storytellers or poets is a narrative (διήγησις) of past, present, or future things." Poets accomplish this *diegesis* either by narrative alone (ἁπλῇ διηγήσει), or by a *diegesis* that comes about through imitation (διὰ μιμήσεως γιγνομένη), or by a *diegesis* that comes about through both narrative and imitation (δι' ἀμφοτέρων) (392c–d). Thus, in the opening of the *Iliad*, when Homer tells the story speaking in his own voice, this is narrative alone, whereas, when he tells the story through the direct speech of Chryses, this is narrative that

---

[16] For "deictic shift" in modern fiction, see Galbraith (1995) 19–59. "Vicarious transport" is the title of Felson (1999), where it refers to the imaginary journey undertaken by the audience of Pindar's *Pythian* 4.

[17] Hunter (1992b) 13 captures this aspect of the poems well: "'Do you (sing.) not see?' asks the poetic voice (*H.* 2.4), and we are compelled to answer 'Well, no.'"

comes about through imitation. Because the *Iliad* and the *Odyssey* consist of the poet speaking in his own voice and in the voice of his characters, they belong to the third kind of *diegesis*, that which comes about through both narrative and imitation. Drama, on the other hand, because the poet's own voice is excluded, belongs to the second kind of *diegesis*, that which comes about through imitation, whereas the first kind, that which consists of narrative alone, without direct speech, is best exemplified by the dithyramb (392e–394c). The importance of these distinctions becomes apparent in the ensuing discussion. For Plato, the agency of poetic speech is not confined to the poetic world in which it is spoken. Expressions of feeling on the part of poetic characters not only affect their interlocutors in the poem, but compel an involuntary accommodation of the listener's soul to the world the poem enacts. The effects of exposure to such speech are long-lasting; the powerful emotions voiced in epic and drama leave traces in the soul of the listener that may induce him to replicate the behavior of the poetic character if suitable real-world triggers are present (Book 3, 395c–d, 401b–c; cf. Book 10, 605c–606b).

For Plato, the border between poetic worlds and the real world is an open one; the illusory presence that emanates from poetic speech and insinuates itself into the soul of the listener accords well with what we have seen of dramatic enactment in archaic and classical performance – the presentification of an absent world in the Palaikastro Hymn, and the usurpation of real-world geography by fictional geography in Euripides and Menander. In Aristotle, by contrast, there is a strict separation of these domains. Narrative poetry offers a model of the real world that is more useful in understanding that world than historical narrative because contingent details that obscure the perception of universal behaviors have (ideally) been eliminated from it (*Poetics* 9). The value of poetry is in its plots, a point on which Aristotle is abundantly clear, and the kind of cognitive processing of them that he envisages allows for little direct influence of fiction upon reality – what is evidently a model will hardly have the same ontological conviction as the thing it models. Likewise, while tragedy is usefully affective, it is so because the catharsis that occurs in response to it gets something inessential out of the soul, rather than introducing some alien element into it.

As Stephen Halliwell has pointed out, it is a little difficult to grasp why, on this understanding of the function of narrative literature, Aristotle should attach so much importance to the dramatic mode of presentation.[18]

[18] Halliwell (2002) 168.

He retains Plato's distinction between three modes of literary *diegesis* – narrative, dramatic, and mixed – though in the *Poetics* (Chapter 3) they are called modes of mimesis.[19] However, while Plato rejects narrative that makes abundant use of direct speech because of the threat it poses to the soul of the listener, Aristotle praises Homer's poems because, in their extensive use of it, they approach so nearly to the condition of drama (Chapter 24). How, then, to explain Aristotle's "pro-mimetic prejudice,"[20] which seems unrelated to the larger cognitive goals that he proposes for literary representation? For plot can surely be grasped as well, if not better, in narrative as in dramatic form. The teleological progress he envisages towards "the ideally dramatic status of poetic fictions"[21] is not simply a reflection of the literary historical developments of his own time. While dithyramb (Plato's example of poetic narrative without direct speech) may no longer have been available as an example, since it was no longer purely narrative in form,[22] epic poetry in catalogue form continued to enjoy great success throughout the fourth and third centuries: the *Lyde* of Antimachus is a collection of unhappy love stories in the tradition of Hesiod's *Catalogue of Women*, a catalogue of heterosexual loves appears in the *Leontion* of Hermesianax, and of homosexual loves in the *Erotes* of Phanocles.[23] From such fragments as remain, it would appear that these poems contained as little direct speech as the works of Hesiod that they imitate. Indeed, rather than being a thing of the past, poetry in the form of pure narrative seems, like its opposite, literary drama, to have been rather in vogue in the early Hellenistic period, perhaps as a result of the regard for Hesiod over Homer on the part of some Hellenistic poets. Aristotle's preference for direct speech as the form in which exemplary plots should be enacted is neither an accommodation to historical developments nor a necessary outcome of his own account of poetic value. It can only be explained by supposing that, for Aristotle, the dramatic mode made the fictional events of which such plots consist more immediately present, and so made these plots more concrete and graspable.[24]

While Aristotle's ideas about the value of narrative fiction for life require firm boundaries between the two domains in order to maintain the useful, but subordinate, position of the former as model, his valuation of the

---

[19] See Lucas (1968) *ad loc.* 1448a20–24 on the close resemblance to the *Republic*.
[20] Genette (1992) 22.   [21] Halliwell (1989) 66.
[22] Lucas (1968) *ad loc.* 1447a13; cf. Hordern (2002) 18.
[23] The fragments are collected in Powell (1925). Cameron (1995) 380–86 considers the importance of catalogue poetry in the Hellenistic period. Cf. Fantuzzi (1995) 29, with n. 86.
[24] Halliwell (2002) 168.

58   *Theocritus and the Invention of Fiction*

dramatic over the narrative mode can be seen to be continuous with the experiments on the part of fourth- and third-century poets with the kinds of presence effects that can be achieved by one mode or another. While the *Poetics* privileges the dramatic over the narrative and mixed modes, the poets continue to be interested in the varied possibilities offered by all three. In addition to these macrostructural possibilities available at the outset, the Hellenistic poets also show a keen awareness of the effects that can be produced by different kinds of transition from narrative to speech within a poem. Callimachus, for example, in the *Hymn to Zeus*, ends almost one third of the passages of direct speech without any formula to indicate that the speech has come to an end and narrative by the poet has been resumed.[25] The occasional difficulty in ascertaining whether the voice that is present to us in reading is that of the poet or one of his characters is in keeping with the tendency in the non-mimetic *Hymns* for the narrator to become a palpable presence in the telling of the sacred narrative.[26] Apollonius' practice is more conservative in this regard; he carefully varies the formulas with which direct speech is introduced and concluded, but not so noticeably as for his narrator to intrude as a factor in the shaping of the story in this way.[27] Here Theocritus offers the most striking innovation. His *Idyll* 22, a hymn to Castor and Pollux, begins, like a Homeric Hymn, with the voice of the poet stating his intention to praise his subjects, and then going on to tell their story in the manner of an epic narrator. However, as he recounts the scene in which Pollux, in the course of his voyage as one of the Argonauts, encounters the monstrous Amycus and engages him in a boxing match, he eschews the "he said/she said" tags with which speech is conventionally framed in epic narration, and presents the dialogue as an exchange of single lines of direct speech that resembles such exchanges in tragedy.[28]

The discussion of this device that is most revealing for an understanding of its effect upon a contemporary reader is in Longinus. In Chapter 27 of *On the Sublime* he considers unexpected transitions to direct speech as a source of sublimity. He calls such shifts an "outburst of feeling," in which "the writer, exchanging places, suddenly turns himself into his character," and cites *Iliad* 15.346–49 as an example: "Hector shouted aloud, calling on

---

[25] McLennan (1977) 147.   [26] Harder (1992) 394.
[27] For a detailed study of such formulas in Book 1 of the *Argonautica*, see Fantuzzi (1988) 65–81.
[28] Thomas (1996) 236 sees the passage as "internal intertextuality," recalling the agonistic passages of *Idylls* 4 and 5. This, however, misses the surprise in the unexpected change in the mode of presentation: the Idylls to which he refers employ the dramatic mode from the outset. *Idyll* 25, most likely not by Theocritus but a gifted imitator, apparently goes even further in this regard; in the form in which it has been transmitted, it opens with a character replying to a question that has been put to him before the poem begins. For a sympathetic account of the poem, see Hunter (1998).

the Trojans to return to the ships and to leave the bloody spoils. 'Whomever I see apart from the ships of his own free will, for him I will there plan death.'"[29] In this passage, he imagines, the poet "took up the narrative as belonging to himself, then suddenly, without any kind of advanced notice, transferred the abrupt threat to the angry prince." It would be anticlimactic, he adds, if the poet were to add a verb of speaking, and, as it stands, the change of construction (ἡ τοῦ λόγου μετάβασις) has suddenly overtaken him as he is changing into his character (τὸν μεταβαίνοντα). Longinus cites a similar use of the figure in Hecataeus, and compares its emotional effect to the sudden change of addressee within a speech, examples of which he provides from pseudo-Demosthenes *Oration* 25, and *Odyssey* 4.681–89, where Penelope shifts suddenly from criticizing the herald who has led the suitors to her hall to censuring the suitors themselves. For Longinus, then, the omission of a verb of speaking, and the unexpected shift in the mode of presentation this enacts, have an effect far more powerful than we readers of modern fiction, long accustomed to this narrative shorthand, can easily imagine. For in this moment of transition the presence of the poet as the shaping force behind his own poem is suddenly revealed, as he morphs before our eyes into the characters that are the externalizations of his own imaginative energies. Critical attention to this matter can likewise be found in the scholia to Homer and the dramatic poets.[30] Moreover, the Prolegomena to the scholia to Theocritus note as remarkable the fact that, in his bucolic poetry, he made use of all three of the modes of presentation outlined in the narrative theory of Plato and Aristotle, and they follow up this observation in the introductions to the individual *Idylls* by noting how each poem exemplifies this theory by either including or omitting the voice of the poet.[31] "Modistics," as Gérard Genette christened this branch

---

[29] As Russell (1964) *ad loc.* 27.1 notes, Longinus punctuates the passage differently from modern editors, who understand ἐπισσεύεσθαι and ἐᾶν as imperatival and part of the direct speech rather than dependent on ἐκέκλετο in 347.

[30] Fantuzzi (1988) 52–54.

[31] Prolegomena D, Wendel (1914) 4–5: "All poetry has three characters, narrative, dramatic and mixed. Bucolic poetry is a mixture of every kind, simply mingled together. For which reason it is in fact more appealing because of the diversity of the mixture, consisting at one time of the narrative kind, at another of the dramatic, at another of the mixed, that is to say, the narrative and the dramatic." Cf. Prolegomena E [d.], Wendel (1914) 5. For the introductions to the individual *Idylls*, see, for example, *Id.* 1 arg., Wendel (1914) 23, *Id.* 5 arg., Wendel (1914) 154. Contra Van Sickle (1976) 31, then, the use of these Hypotheses to introduce dramatic and non-dramatic poems does not indicate that the dramatic *Idylls* dominated the generic conception of the collection formed by the person who composed them, and who then extended this conception illegitimately to other poems. For the Hypotheses are in fact used to note variations in the mode of presentation. For Plato's tripartite scheme as standard throughout antiquity, see Halliwell (2002) 168 n. 44. The scholia to Theocritus originate in the work of Theon, who was active in Alexandria between 50 BCE and 20 CE, though his work was likely a synthesis of numerous predecessors. See Guhl (1969) fr. 1, cf. p. 3, Cameron (1995) 191.

of literary theory,[32] is clearly more than a means of categorization for both Hellenistic poets and critics, and retained its vitality as an area for creative experiment and critical analysis long after the particular conditions of textual production and performance in which the Platonic theory originated had passed. Generally speaking, the choice of the dramatic over the narrative mode privileges the presence of the characters over the presence of the poet. However, particular uses of this mode allow for subtle mediations of their presence. As we shall see in *Idyll* 3, the use of a quasi-dramatic prologue encourages a quite specific, corporeal imagining of the poem's main character, while the use of writerly framing devices in *Idyll* 11 and *Idyll* 13 underscores the particular kinds of imaginative presence that belong to beings of pure narrative (in *Idyll* 13) and beings who have the more intimate presence of fictional speakers (in *Idyll* 11).

IDYLL 3: THE HERDSMAN AS ACTOR

The speaker of Callimachus' *Hymn* 2 is the leader of a public rite; his monologue has a function within the events to which he responds. Conversely, his address to fellow participants identifies him for the poem's audience; we know who he is because of the instructions he gives to others, and these have their place within an event that is underway as the poem begins. The speaker has a reason to speak, and the poem's narrative premise allows its fictional world to be revealed naturalistically. Likewise, while the nature of the dialogue in *Idyll* 1 emphasizes the fictionality of the world in which it is produced, there is narrative motivation for the dialogue itself. Thyrsis and the goatherd have occasion to refer to the particulars of the world in which they are located, though that world may not resemble any that we know. The situation in *Idyll* 3 is quite different, for the speaker reveals, by his opening words, that he is alone. He is not speaking to anyone, and so, by the standards of the real world, has no reason to be talking in the first place (3.1–5):

> Κωμάσδω ποτὶ τὰν Ἀμαρυλλίδα, ταὶ δέ μοι αἶγες
> βόσκονται κατ' ὄρος, καὶ ὁ Τίτυρος αὐτὰς ἐλαύνει.
> Τίτυρ', ἐμὶν τὸ καλὸν πεφιλημένε, βόσκε τὰς αἶγας,
> καὶ ποτὶ τὰν κράναν ἄγε, Τίτυρε· καὶ τὸν ἐνόρχαν,
> τὸν Λιβυκὸν κνάκωνα, φυλάσσεο μή τυ κορύψῃ.

I go to serenade Amaryllis, my goats graze on the hill, and Tityrus herds them. Tityrus, my dearly beloved, graze the goats, and lead them to the spring, Tityrus. And watch out for the male, the yellowish one, in case he butts you.

---

[32] Genette (1992) 83.

The goatherd has, it seems, already left his goats behind, and his reference to the hill where he has left them is not deictic (there is no article or demonstrative adjective); he is rather recalling to himself what has just happened. If the poem had begun with the imperatives addressed to Tityrus in verses 3–5, it would have resembled other literary drama, where the first words are addressed in a natural way to characters within the dramatic setting, and so invite the reader to imagine the fictional location in which the poem's action is taking place. Instead, because the goatherd begins by referring to Tityrus in the third person, as if he were not present, when he does refer to him in the second person in what follows, the effect is to suggest not his presence within a fictional space he shares with the speaker but an imaginary address in which the speaker continues to talk aloud, but to himself.

The effect is disorienting. At the outset, the goatherd appears to address the reader directly. We will not, it seems, have to imagine the world of the poem by positioning ourselves as the speaker's addressee within it, as in the Callimachus hymn. Rather, that world will be revealed to us without mediation, as the divine speakers of dramatic prologues tell the audience what they need to imagine without the presence of a second party as stage addressee.[33] The goatherd, however, breaks off this communication as soon as it is begun, and turns instead to apostrophizing his absent friend. Because we have first accepted the fiction that we are being addressed directly by the character from within his world, it is disconcerting to then have to trade places, and imagine the world of the poem through the eyes of someone within it. In addition, the goatherd is not in the same place as Tityrus, and so we cannot imagine his surroundings through deictic references to a place shared by the two of them. Instead, he occupies a transitional space that is no longer the hillside where he has left his flocks, nor yet the cave to which he has announced his intention of proceeding. The theatrical illusion is empty; it is as if the speaker emerged from an entrance marked "Hill," pointed to an exit marked "Cave," and now lingered on a stage devoid of all fictional characteristics. Theocritus employs a recognizably theatrical technique, but suspends its illusionary purpose; the voice speaks from the page in a place we are not given to imagine.

It is possible to read the goatherd's emergence ironically. The theatricality that surrounds it points ahead to the deliberately staged performance that he will give before the cave of Amaryllis. Caves, after all, are not only the home of real Nymphs and their shrines, but also a standard stage set in

---

[33] Thus Hunter (1985) 25 argues that Euripides' prologues, while not explicitly audience addresses, are functionally identical with those of Menander in this respect.

Athenian drama.[34] Tityrus, moreover, plays no further part in the poem.[35] In *Idyll* 2 Simaetha's unspeaking servant Thestylis, who is introduced in the poem's opening lines, remains on hand for further instructions until she is dispatched to the house of her mistress's ex-lover, and, even after her departure, Simaetha refers to her in the story that she tells. Her presence situates her mistress, and her mistress's speech, within a network of social relationships to which they both belong. Here, by contrast, the goatherd will perform his song outside the social setting created by his opening words; he hands off his animals to a friend, and approaches Amaryllis in the role of singer. No sooner does he introduce himself as a herdsman than he sets this part aside for that of lover. His character is less an identity than a role, and what we are being asked to imagine is not so much a fictional character within a fictional world, but rather the enactment of a fictional character by a gifted performer.[36] On this reading, then, the poem's opening would ironize the song that follows; we cannot take it entirely seriously because we cannot help but see it as a performance (3.6–14):

> ὦ χαρίεσσ' Ἀμαρυλλί, τί μ' οὐκέτι τοῦτο κατ' ἄντρον
> παρκύπτοισα καλεῖς, τὸν ἐρωτύλον; ἦ ῥά με μισεῖς;
> ἦ ῥά γέ τοι σιμὸς καταφαίνομαι ἐγγύθεν ἦμεν,
> νύμφα, καὶ προγένειος; ἀπάγξασθαί με ποησεῖς.
> ἠνίδε τοι δέκα μᾶλα φέρω· τηνῶθε καθεῖλον
> ὦ μ' ἐκέλευ καθελεῖν τύ· καὶ αὔριον ἄλλα τοι οἰσῶ.
> θᾶσαι μάν. θυμαλγὲς ἐμὶν ἄχος. αἴθε γενοίμαν
> ἁ βομβεῦσα μέλισσα καὶ ἐς τεὸν ἄντρον ἱκοίμαν,
> τὸν κισσὸν διαδὺς καὶ τὰν πτέριν ἅ τυ πυκάσδει.

Lovely Amaryllis, why do you no longer peep out from this cave and call me, your sweetheart? Do you hate me? Do I look snub-nosed to you up close, my nymph, with a chin that sticks out? You will make me hang myself. See, I bring you ten apples. I picked them from the place you told me. And tomorrow I'll bring others. Look then. I'm in terrible pain. If only I could become that buzzing bee and go into your cave, flying through the ivy and ferns that conceal you.

What is striking about this performance, however, is that it deliberately, and surprisingly, reconnects its scene with the time and place of the opening verses. While we had seemed to leave the world of Tityrus and rural labor

---

[34] As in Sophocles' *Philoctetes* and Menander's *Dyskolos*. See Handley (1965) 21–22.
[35] Gow (1952) *ad loc.* 3.2: "the elaborate address here to a κωφὸν πρόσωπον inessential to the subject of the Idyll is somewhat odd."
[36] Hunter (1999) 109.

behind, it is clear that the scene we are witnessing is a repeated one: today the goatherd brings apples, as he has been told to on a previous visit, and tomorrow he will bring more. Similarly, as the song continues, and he begins to despair at Amaryllis' absence, he threatens to leap from "the rock where Olpis the fisherman watches for tuna" (3.26), recalls the sieve divination of Agroeo, "who was recently my companion while cutting grass" (3.31–32), and promises to give the goat and kids intended for Amaryllis to "the dark-skinned day-laborer of Mermnon" instead (3.34–36). Olpis, Agroeo, and dark-skinned day-laborers belong to the same world as the cave-dwelling Nymph who torments her goatherd admirer with demands for apples, and the goatherd's behavior is evidently unexceptional within the fictional world of this poem. Just as in *Idyll* 1 the fact that Pan and the Muses compete in singing competitions with the herdsman establishes that world as neither mythical nor an imitation of life, so here the copresence of theatrical performance and unromantic agricultural labor establishes the world of the poem as manifestly fictional.

The goatherd disarms the irony with which we had been prepared to approach his song by showing that it is a repeated element in an internally consistent fictional world; this is a performance he gives on a daily basis. So too, the role play that is apparent in it encourages us to imagine his textual existence with the solidity and corporeal presence of an actor's body. Drama makes imaginary beings present by instantiating them in the body of a performer. *Idyll* 3 reverses this procedure; by inviting us to conceive not just the possibility of its being acted, but also the possibility that it is being acted, the poem invites us to imagine its protagonist and his world with the physical presence of a dramatic enactment. While *Idyll* 1 asks us to contemplate the impossibility of instantiating its song in actual performance, *Idyll* 3 asks us to imagine that its song already is one, and it is in this peculiar act of the imagination that much of this slight poem's unsettling effect resides.

A similar tension between irony and imaginative involvement complicates our response to the poem's fictional space. The goatherd's seeming inability to enter the cave where the Nymph lives, though no physical barrier prevents him from doing so, appears to ironize his use of the song of an excluded lover. This type of song is meant to be performed in front of a city house, where real doors keep the lover out. By using it here, the goatherd apparently demonstrates his ignorance of its conventions, not to mention a lack of awareness of his real situation.[37] Yet it is clear that he has

---

[37] On the form, see Copley (1956), Hunter (1999) 108.

been to this place before, and believes he has received instructions from the Nymph to return, with apples. The apples, fictionally real, from a place whose existence can be asserted by an emphatic deictic gesture (τηνῶθε), grounds the reality of the Nymph in the fictional world he himself inhabits, in his own mind at least. Rather than proving his naivety, his song identifies a space within the poem that he cannot enter with the promise of a divine female body that the reader is not permitted to see. As in *Idyll* 11, where this space is the ocean that withholds the body of Galateia from Polyphemus' view, the poem creates a double of its own fictional world that is off limits for its protagonist and for us. The cave is a canceled *mise en abyme* of the poem itself; it figures the allure of fictional experience as the desire to enter a world available only through that experience.[38]

Excluded from the cave itself, then, the goatherd takes new heart from a twitching in his eye that seems to presage the Nymph's appearance. He steps beneath a pine tree and begins his song again, in a new vein (3.40–51):

> Ἱππομένης, ὅκα δὴ τὰν παρθένον ἤθελε γᾶμαι,
> μᾶλ' ἐν χερσὶν ἑλὼν δρόμον ἄνυεν· ἁ δ' Ἀταλάντα
> ὡς ἴδεν, ὡς ἐμάνη, ὡς ἐς βαθὺν ἅλατ' ἔρωτα.
> 　τὰν ἀγέλαν χὠ μάντις ἀπ' Ὄθρυος ἆγε Μελάμπους
> ἐς Πύλον· ἁ δὲ Βίαντος ἐν ἀγκοίναισιν ἐκλίνθη
> μάτηρ ἁ χαρίεσσα περίφρονος Ἀλφεσιβοίας.
> 　τὰν δὲ καλὰν Κυθέρειαν ἐν ὤρεσι μῆλα νομεύων
> οὐχ οὕτως Ὤδωνις ἐπὶ πλέον ἄγαγε λύσσας,
> ὥστ' οὐδὲ φθίμενόν νιν ἄτερ μαζοῖο τίθητι;
> 　ζαλωτὸς μὲν ἐμὶν ὁ τὸν ἄτροπον ὕπνον ἰαύων
> Ἐνδυμίων· ζαλῶ δέ, φίλα γύναι, Ἰασίωνα,
> ὃς τόσσων ἐκύρησεν, ὅσ' οὐ πευσεῖσθε, βέβαλοι.

Hippomenes, when he wanted to marry the maiden, took apples in his hand and completed the race; and Atalanta, as soon as she saw them, was immediately infatuated, and plunged into deep desire. And Melampus the seer led the herd from Othrys to Pylus, and in the arms of Bias the lovely mother of wise Alphesiboea reclined. And did not Adonis as he tended his sheep in the mountains bring the lovely Cytherian to such a degree of madness that even when he is wasting away she never puts him out of her breast? Envied by me is Endymion, sleeping the unturning sleep; I envy, dear lady, Iasion, who is allotted such things as you profane ones will not learn.

---

[38] For the *limen*, or threshold, in Latin erotic elegy as the barrier that both forbids and invites the reader's access to the body of the beloved, see Pucci (1978). Hardie (2002) 3 develops the image of the locked door as a screen that separates the reader from the world of the text; cf. his observations at 145–48 on Ovid's Narcissus, whose ardent wish to enter the pool in which he beholds his own reflection figures the desire of the viewer of illusionist art to believe in the reality of the images he encounters in it.

The goatherd's choice of mythological examples has caused much debate among the poem's commentators. Gow notes that, in alluding to the story of Hippomenes, "the dropping of the apples in the race is . . . inapposite to the goatherd's purpose," and that the reference to Endymion "is not altogether happy," since "Endymion profited little from the infatuation of the goddess."[39] Dover similarly proposes that "the goatherd's citation of mortals whose enjoyment of the love of goddesses was so brief and tragic . . . suggests . . . a comically insensitive and ignorant choice of *exempla*."[40] Whitaker, on the other hand, sees a "smooth transition" from hope to despair in the examples selected,[41] and Stanzel detects a therapeutic function in their progression: the goatherd concludes by recognizing that Amaryllis' love is not worth the risk.[42]

Certainly the examples are compact and well organized. The stories of Hippomenes, Melampus, and Adonis are three-line narratives; the first two offer the simplest possible expression of desire and its fulfilment – striving occupies the first clause, accomplishment the second – while the third reworks this bipartite structure as a result clause expressed as a rhetorical question: "And did not Adonis as he tended his sheep in the mountains bring the lovely Cytherian to such a degree of madness that even when he is wasting away she never puts him out of her breast?" The final triplet is even simpler; by expressing only the fulfilment of desire, it is able to compress an entire story into each half of its three lines: "Envied by me is Endymion, sleeping the unturning sleep; I envy, dear lady, Iasion, who is allotted such things as you profane ones will not learn." While the organization of the material, then, hardly suggests a clumsy or stupid speaker, its use in this particular discursive situation is somewhat puzzling. Aristotle, in the *Rhetoric*, calls example (παράδειγμα) and enthymeme two kinds of proof (πίστις), the function of which is to persuade (2.20.1–3). While he is speaking here of prose oratory, he cites the poet Stesichorus' use of invented, rather than historical, examples, one form of which he calls fables (λόγοι), like those of Aesop. Similar observations have been made by modern scholars about examples in Homer. Mythical examples are introduced "when one character wishes to influence the actions of another," and these persuade because of the "parallelism between the mythological story and the immediate situation."[43] Thus Phoenix in Book 9 of the *Iliad* endeavors to persuade Achilles to fight by demonstrating his supposed resemblance

---

[39] Gow (1952) *ad loc.* 3.40, 3.50.
[40] Dover (1971) *ad loc.* 3.40–51, cf. Lawall (1967) 40, Rosenmeyer (1969) 174. For Fantuzzi (1995) 16–35, the passage is typical of the "collapse of exemplarity" in the bucolic poems as a whole.
[41] Whitaker (1983) 52.   [42] Stanzel (1995) 137, 202.   [43] Willcock (1964) 147.

to Meleager, and Achilles in Book 24 persuades Priam to eat by showing his resemblance to Niobe. In both cases the person attempting to persuade tells a tale in which the person to be persuaded ought to recognize his similarity to the central figure in the story.

The protagonists of the goatherd's tales, however, are Hippomenes, Melampus, Adonis, Endymion, and Iasion, figures from myth who in his mind have some sort of bucolic associations. The person who has to be persuaded, Amaryllis, figures only obliquely, as the object of their quests. If the goatherd is trying to persuade anyone with these examples, it can only be himself. This becomes clear in the story of Iasion, in which he asserts that Amaryllis will never experience what is imagined in his narrative: "I envy, dear lady, Iasion, who is allotted such things as you profane ones will not learn." He excludes her, in other words, from seeing herself as a participant in the kind of love story that he imagines for himself. Rather than attempting to persuade his listener, the series of mythical lovers he imagines in his song diverts his attention, for a time, from his own present suffering. The straightforward syntax of their stories contrasts with the hesitant, self-referential song he sings about himself (3.6–23), even as their protagonists' accomplishments contrast with his own lack of success. The dissociation of these myths from the goatherd's world is shown not only by the "stylistic pretension" with which they imitate epic language,[44] but also by the fact that what he sees in each of them is an identical narrative of desire and its accomplishment that is at odds with his own lack of success. Their similarities to one another only emphasize the different ethos of myth, where, as the goatherd sees it, herdsmen simply go out and get what they want, rather than being paralyzed in the presence of the object of their desire, and consoling themselves for their failure with song. The world of myth and the world of pastoral are quite dissimilar, even though herdsmen inhabit them both.

It is only when his song is over, and he realizes that he has a headache, that the goatherd returns to the here and now (3.52–54):

> ἀλγέω τὰν κεφαλάν, τὶν δ' οὐ μέλει. οὐκέτ' ἀείδω,
> κεισεῦμαι δὲ πεσών, καὶ τοὶ λύκοι ὧδέ μ' ἔδονται.
> ὡς μέλι τοι γλυκὺ τοῦτο κατὰ βρόχθοιο γένοιτο.

My head hurts, but you don't care. I won't sing any longer, but I'll lie where I have fallen, and the wolves will eat me here. May it be sweet as honey in your throat.

---

[44] Hunter (1999) *ad loc.* 3.40–51.

The poem ends with the goatherd encouraging his unseen addressee to picture his body collapsed in front of her cave. The invitation to Amaryllis, offstage, is also an invitation to the reader to once again imagine the poem's fictional space as a stage, on which the goatherd's body continues to rest for a few moments now that the drama is over. By calling attention to the theatrical aspect of his performance at the end of his song, however, the goatherd only makes us aware of the degree to which his performance has fallen short of a genuine dramatic reenactment. Like *Idyll* 1, the poem is a literary drama that contains a performance within it. Thyrsis, however, in *Idyll* 1, is able to make his desired identification with Daphnis present to his audience, the poem's anonymous goatherd, through impersonation; his performance suggests the possibility of reenacting archetypes in lived experience. In *Idyll* 3, the goatherd's ability to imagine and present himself to his listener as the enactment of such an archetype is more limited; he can only narrate the lives of such characters, but not instantiate them in performance. While his performance is theatrical, it does not actually make present in his own world a being from another one; the poem stages a narration, not an act of presentification. We are left with the curious experience of watching a character whose inner life clamors for dramatic performance unable to enact the roles to which he aspires. However, his failure to achieve the kind of persuasive dramatic impersonation that gives Thyrsis his power over his listener gives the goatherd of *Idyll* 3, as a body to be imagined in the performance of theatrical gestures unseen by his audience within the poem, a distinctive imaginary presence to the reader outside it. The literary drama becomes not merely the means to create a fictional world with the added vividness that comes from eliminating authorial narration, but a way to explore the intangible boundary that separates the world of fiction form the world of the reader. The more vividly we imagine the goatherd with the corporeal presence of an actor's body, the more unsettling his imagined presence as a textual being becomes. *Idyll* 3 explores this uncanny presence while remaining (just) within the resources of a fictional world that manifests itself in a way that resembles drama. The remainder of this chapter will explore Theocritus' use of framing devices that are specific to written, non-performative literature, and embed their fictional world within an explicitly written communication.

IDYLL 11: THE CYCLOPS AS SINGER

The experience of reading *Idyll* 3 can rightly be described as an uncanny one; so palpable is the corporeal presence of its speaker that a kind of ontological doubt lingers around him even as we reflect on the conditions of his textual production.[45] In *Idyll* 11, Theocritus experiments even more radically with the boundary that separates fictional character from real-world reader. In this poem we overhear the Cyclops Polyphemus, as he sings a song for the sea Nymph Galateia. As with the goatherd and Amaryllis, here too there is little chance that she is listening to him, since she is somewhere beneath the ocean, and he is sitting on its shore. Moreover, Theocritus makes it clear that the song is really intended for the friend that he addresses in its opening lines, for he tells him that he is presenting the Cyclops' song to him as a demonstration of the idea that poetry is the only cure for love. The presence of a framing address to a real-world reader makes the strangeness of our assent to a textually produced fictional world more evident still. We give our imaginative assent to it even as we are made aware that it has been shaped to produce an effect upon a reader who is outside it. Framing makes explicit what is implicit in the form of *Idyll* 3, and in the ecphrastic scenes of *Idyll* 1, that it is the movement into and out of fictional worlds that makes the reader aware of their powers of seduction.

The poem begins with a gnomic proposition about love (11.1–4):

οὐδὲν ποττὸν ἔρωτα πεφύκει φάρμακον ἄλλο,
Νικία, οὔτ' ἔγχριστον, ἐμὶν δοκεῖ, οὔτ' ἐπίπαστον,
ἢ ταὶ Πιερίδες· κοῦφον δέ τι τοῦτο καὶ ἁδύ
γίνετ' ἐπ' ἀνθρώποις, εὑρεῖν δ' οὐ ῥᾴδιόν ἐστι.

There is no other medicine for love, Nicias, it seems to me, either rubbed or sprinkled, than the Pierides. This one is easy and pleasant for men, and yet not easy to find.

Song is a treatment (*pharmakon*) for love, although we do not know how it works yet; while other medicines are applied to the surface of the body, this one is not like them: it is easy and pleasant, although difficult to discover. The image is that of a rare magical herb, like the one Hermes gives to Odysseus as a remedy against the charms of Circe, or Helen's Egyptian drug that brings forgetfulness of all pain.[46] Like Odysseus and Telemachus, Nicias has apparently not been able to discover it for himself. Yet, since he is a doctor, and also "particularly dear to the Muses," he will recognize that what Theocritus is proposing is the treatment indicated in an

---

[45] While I do not wish to pursue the uncanny as a psychoanalytic concept, Freud's account of it in literary experience as the rational mind's lingering conflict of judgment as to whether or not what it has just read is really possible seems apposite here; see Freud (2003) 156.
[46] *Odyssey* 10.281–320, 4.219–234.

illness of this kind (11.5–6). At this point the poet introduces Polyphemus for comparative study (11.7–9):

οὕτω γοῦν ῥᾶιστα διᾶγ' ὁ Κύκλωψ ὁ παρ' ἁμῖν,
ὡρχαῖος Πολύφαμος, ὅκ' ἤρατο τᾶς Γαλατείας,
ἄρτι γενειάσδων περὶ τὸ στόμα τὼς κροτάφως τε.

So at any rate our Cyclops fared well, the Polyphemus of old, when he loved Galateia, as he was just getting a beard around his mouth and temples.

Theocritus lets Nicias, the doctor, examine the Cyclops he sets before him. For at first we might not recognize this Polyphemus who is "just getting a beard around his mouth and temples." He is "our Cyclops," or, more literally, "the one by us (ὁ παρ' ἁμῖν)," a Cyclops who, like Theocritus and Nicias, lives in Sicily: "my countryman," as Gow's translation puts it.[47] This local hero is also "the Polyphemus of old (ὡρχαῖος Πολύφαμος)," presumably Homer's Cyclops, and the one who loved Galateia. It is at this point that we are likely to recall that there is no such Cyclops. If the "Polyphemus of old" is Homer's Cyclops, this Polyphemus did not love Galateia at all, nor did he live in Sicily.

Ancient storytelling knows very well that the proper name is a "rigid designator," that it refers to an individual whether or not the individual named bears all the characteristics usually associated with him, so that it is possible, for example, to write about a Napoleon who won the Battle of Waterloo, or a Richard Nixon who is not responsible for the events of Watergate but whom we nonetheless still identify with the historical person who bore that name.[48] Without the ability to relocate the bearer of a name within a different possible version of his own history, ancient storytelling would hardly be possible. Yet, if Theocritus' Cyclops is manifestly fictional with respect to his Homeric antecedent, it remains to see how the fictional world he occupies is positioned with respect to that of the *Odyssey*. For redescription of a story world from the perspective of a marginal character within it has the potential to change our understanding of the protoworld by allowing us to see that its construction was not in fact neutral and objective, but conditioned by the needs of the storytelling situation in which this first version was produced.

Redescription of the world of a previous fiction from the perspective of a marginalized character within it is a familiar subgenre of the postmodern novel. Notable examples include J. M. Coetzee's *Foe*, a retelling

---

[47] Gow (1952) *ad loc.* 11.7.
[48] These are the conventional examples in the theoretical literature. See especially Ronen (1994) 132–36. The term "rigid designator" originates with Kripke (1980) 48.

of *Robinson Crusoe*, and Christa Wolf's *Cassandra*, a retelling of the fall of Troy, though the closest parallel to *Idyll* 11 is perhaps John Gardner's *Grendel*, which retells the *Beowulf* story as the encroachment of culture upon nature from the perspective of its vanquished monsters. Typical of the postmodern novel has been an interrogative or even antagonistic stance towards the version of events in the predecessor, so that the rewrite endeavors to bring to light what was deliberately suppressed in the first fiction. By its disavowal of the version of events given in the model, the rewrite claims the fictional world found in it as ontologically independent of the writing by which it was transmitted. It endeavors to correct or restore our understanding of a world that it imagines to have been subjected to various kinds of distortion in the first fiction. By going behind the words of this fiction to its world, truths about it that were lost in the telling can be reclaimed. While many postmodern fictions undertake quite specific ideological revisions of their protoworlds, one influential account of such rewrites has argued that their effect is to supplement, rather than invalidate, the canonical protoworld, enriching, rather than deleting, the world of the previous fiction by redescribing it.[49] This seems, on the whole, to be closer to the practice of ancient poets. While gestures towards large-scale polemical revision certainly exist (Euripides' *Trojan Women* and Pindar's scathing comments in *Nemean* 7 on Homer's untruthful presentation of Odysseus spring to mind), ancient poetry perpetuates itself by inventing a theoretically endless number of Odysseuses, Heracleses, and Medeas who originate in a preexisting literary world but migrate unproblematically to new ones that accommodate contemporary needs more easily.

How, then, to situate Theocritus' Cyclops with regard to Homer's, and those of comedy and dithyramb that came between them? *Idyll* 11 certainly exploits the possibility of inventing a Polyphemus who is as dissimilar as possible to these predecessors. When ancient comedy and satyr play reinvented Polyphemus, they reinvented him as a bearer of contemporary vices. In Euripides' *Cyclops* he is a fussy eater who talks like a sophist on a variety of fashionable intellectual issues. Similarly, in the comic tradition he seems to have been represented as a gastronome, with ridiculously pretentious tastes.[50] While myth provides material for comic appropriation in these genres, contemporary reality provides the point of view from which it is reused.[51] Likewise, as far as we can tell from the scraps of Philoxenus' dithyramb, the Cylops featured in it as a cipher for the tyrant Dionysius of

---

[49] Dolezel (1998) 220, cf. McHale (1987) 10–13, 90–91.   [50] Seaford (1984) 51–59.
[51] Bakhtin (1981) 23.

Syracuse, on whom the poet was avenging himself by means of this representation, and his portrayal of Polyphemus was likely, as a consequence, to have been as unflattering and unsympathetic as it is in the comic tradition.[52] The Polyphemus of *Idyll* 11, however, is neither the representative of all that is opposed to civilization, as he is in the *Odyssey*, nor the monstrous manifestation of all the excesses of civilization, as he is in the comic tradition. He is instead a young lover, a herdsman, and a singer. While he has shed all the traits of the Homeric Cyclops other than his one eye and his flock, the new ones that he has acquired do not make him a vehicle for contemporary satire, but identify him with the herdsman of the other bucolic poems. His relationship to his predecessors is not one of mere intertextual affiliation, for Theocritus has maximized the dissonance between his Cyclops and his epic (and comic) models. Yet neither is it that of a revisionist rewrite; if his Polyphemus is "non-compossible" with his predecessors, the effect is not to suggest a deletion of these models but rather to emphasize the uniqueness of his own fiction relative to them, and its allegiance with the bucolic fiction of other *Idylls*.[53] A radical, if playful, fictionality is the defining characteristic of Theocritus' Cyclops, a fictionality that extends to the suggestion implied by the poem's status as prequel to the *Odyssey*, that, if we want to get from *Idyll* 11 to Homer's poem, the way to do so is by imagining a fiction of our own, in which the disappointed lover turned to savagery as a consequence of his erotic rejection.

Moreover, if we pay close attention to the way in which Polyphemus uses song in response to his love, fashioning a pastoral vision of his own as an escape from the pain of desire, we will be able to find a new approach to the much discussed question of whether or not he is cured by his singing. For, I shall argue, his invocation of the pastoral world in his own imagination is entirely in keeping with that of other bucolic characters, who imagine a more perfect version of the world they themselves inhabit as a relief from their present affliction. Polyphemus, then, suffered from the internal wound of love, yet he found the *pharmakon* with which to alleviate it. Ring composition reminds us that the *pharmakon* of song that Polyphemus applies to his wound is the very *pharmakon* that Nicias has not been able to discover (11.1). Moreover, this *pharmakon* is the song that Nicias is now

---

[52] See Hordern (1999).
[53] Cf. Gow (1952) I.xxvii: "I do not doubt that the bucolic Idylls (1, 3–7, 10, 11) form a unity and cannot be widely separate in date . . . Two of the poems commonly classed as bucolic are however less conspicuously so than the rest. *Id.* 11 contains no human rustics, though the flouted Cyclops is a shepherd and has much in common with the lovesick peasants of *Idd.* 3 and 10. Wilamowitz regarded *Id.* 11 as the earliest of Theocritus's poems, and I agree that it is early and may well be first."

about to hear (11.17–18): "sitting on a high rock, looking out to the sea, he used to sing thus," καθεζόμενος δ' ἐπὶ πέτρας | ὑψηλᾶς ἐς πόντον ὁρῶν ἄειδε τοιαῦτα. After beginning as a paradigmatic anecdote addressed to someone in the same world as its writer,[54] the poem morphs into dramatic fiction before our very eyes. With the transition to direct speech, the world of the poem, an example kept at arm's length until this point, comes alive, and calls for our attention as a living presence. Now we are right beside the Cyclops, overhearing his song. Theocritus maps his own creative fiat onto the change in narrative mode – the appearance of Polyphemus' voice marks the moment at which the poem's fictional world presents itself before us – so that this transition signals a change in the kind of speech act that the poem is. The discursive handling of Polyphemus as a topic to be discussed between friends cedes to the illocutionary force of the poet's "let it be" that brings a fictional world into full dramatic presence.[55] Homer's "Tell me Muse" grounds the world of his poems in his communication with the unseen goddesses who are his explicit addressees. What we hear is what they know to have been. The world of *Idyll* 11 manifests itself without any such ontological guarantees. Despite the reference to "the Polyphemus of old," this is not an act of represencing, and the mention of the Muses in the opening lines (they are the cure for desire, and all nine of them care for Nicias) only draws attention to the fact that Theocritus does not call upon them for his own poem, and that his invention does not originate with them. Rather, the transition to direct speech points to the act of world creation characteristic of fiction, "an extreme case of world-change, a change from nonexistence into (fictional) existence."[56] Enacting this change with the author manifestly present as his real-world self (the poem begins by addressing someone who is positioned, with regard to its fictional world, as a real-world addressee) is very bold. Pointing to the author's creative fiat reveals the world that is its outcome as mere invention, and so risks becoming an obstacle to the imaginative assent required to enter that world. One of the peculiarities of the fictionalizing speech act is that the "felicity conditions" upon which it

[54] Fantuzzi (2004) 170–71 suggests that the exchange of maxims between friends is a fictionalized version of such exchanges in the performative contexts of archaic lyric, iambic, and elegiac poetry. The framing would thus be analogous to the inclusion of a fictionalized performance context in the mimetic *Hymns* of Callimachus. This seems to me more convincing than the earlier suggestion by Rossi (1972) 279–93 that the poem is contamination of the bucolic genre with the poetic epistle (a form unattested at this time).

[55] For two rather different accounts of the illocutionary force of the fictionalizing speech act, see Levin (1976) and Levin (1977). The former imagines the "higher sentence" which is understood to precede such speech acts, and so give them their illocutionary power, the latter discusses in more detail the transport to a fictional domain in which this illocutionary power consists.

[56] Dolezel (1988) 489–91.

depends for its success are not vested in external circumstance as they are for other kinds of speech (the institutional authority to name a ship, or pronounce a couple man and wife), but reside, very largely, in the reader's willingness to assent to the implied invitation to partake of what is being offered. For this reason, it has been argued, an unobtrusive third-person narrator is easier to believe than a narrator who is visibly the author, or a character.[57] The less said about the source of the story the better, unless the poet has the Muse to back him up, or documentary sources of the kind favored by the narrators of Hellenistic poems.[58]

As we shall see, Theocritus saves the really jarring possibilities present in an unexpected change of narrative mode for the end of the poem. Given the build-up, in which we look back on Polyphemus from the perspective of the present, the transition to his own world is, in film terms, more like a dissolve than a cut. Nonetheless, if song is what offers relief from real-world ills (the pains of love), and if what Theocritus is offering his friend in the way of song is manifestly a fiction, Theocritus would seem to be associating poetry's healing power with its status as imaginary experience. Interestingly, then, what we find when we get to the world of the poem is a character who is himself absorbed in his own imaginary experience, as Polyphemus is rapt in picturing to himself the beauties of his beloved, the sea Nymph Galateia (11.19–21):

> ὦ λευκὰ Γαλάτεια, τί τὸν φιλέοντ' ἀποβάλλῃ,
> λευκοτέρα πακτᾶς ποτιδεῖν, ἁπαλωτέρα ἀρνός,
> μόσχω γαυροτέρα, φιαρωτέρα ὄμφακος ὠμᾶς;

O white Galateia, why do you spurn one who loves you, whiter than cream cheese to look upon, softer than a lamb, friskier than a calf, sleeker than an unripe grape?

His words endeavor to conjure, if not the actual presence of the nymph, then at least the image of that presence. He imagines objects from his own world (dairy products, lambs, calves, grapes) that simulate the tangible, physical presence of her body (its whiteness, softness, and sleek, youthful luster). Yet these qualities in her so far transcend the object to which they are compared that they suggest the limitations of comparison itself. Galateia is softer than the softest thing Polyphemus can imagine, sleeker than the sleekest, and even his initial epithet "white" is felt to be inadequate, and in need of supplementation.

---

[57] Dolezel (1988) 490, Dolezel (1998) 149.
[58] Callimachus' counterpointing of his own romantic tale of Acontius and Cydippe with Xenomedes' dusty history of the island of Ceos in which he found it is exemplary in this regard (*Aetia*, fragments 67–75).

74 Theocritus and the Invention of Fiction

Demetrius *On Style* 125 observes that such hyperbolic comparisons are generally unpersuasive because of their impossibility: "Every hyperbole is impossible; for it is not possible to be whiter than snow, or to run as fast as the wind . . . Every hyperbole therefore seems especially frigid because it resembles the impossible." He notes the fondness of the comic poets for such comparisons (126, cf. 161), "since out of the impossible they draw the ridiculous." However, he observes that they are also employed by Sappho, who brings off the risky and intractable figure of hyperbole "delightfully," ἐπιχαρίτως (127), and cites an example from her work which is strikingly similar to Polyphemus' praise of Galateia (162): "more sweetly singing than the lyre, golder than gold," πολὺ πακτίδος ἀδυμελεστέρα, χρυσοῦ χρυσοτέρα. Here Sappho's "golder than gold" avoids the frigidity of hyperbole because it incorporates the poet's own self-consciousness about the limits of comparison into the comparison itself. We sense the poet not failing in her power to find a suitable object for comparison, but rather testifying to a beauty that simply exceeds the possibilities of direct expression. Beauty is, of course, notoriously difficult to present directly. Lessing famously praised Homer for showing the effects of Helen's beauty upon the old men of Troy rather than attempting to describe it himself.[59] In Theocritus such descriptions are found in the mouths of characters rather than that of the poet. In *Idyll* 10 the infatuated Bucaeus, lagging behind in his reaping, is confronted by the more prosaic Milon, and asked to give an account of his troubles. Having explained his problem as love, Milon encourages him to sing a little to help his work, and Bucaeus begins (10.24–31):

> Μοῖσαι Πιερίδες, συναείσατε τὰν ῥαδινάν μοι
> παῖδ'· ὧν γάρ χ' ἄψησθε, θεαί, καλὰ πάντα ποεῖτε.
> Βομβύκα χαρίεσσα, Σύραν καλέοντί τυ πάντες,
> ἰσχνάν, ἁλιόκαυστον, ἐγὼ δὲ μόνος μελίχλωρον.
> καὶ τὸ ἴον μέλαν ἐστί, καὶ ἁ γραπτὰ ὑάκινθος·
> ἀλλ' ἔμπας ἐν τοῖς στεφάνοις τὰ πρᾶτα λέγονται.
> ἁ αἲξ τὰν κύτισον, ὁ λύκος τὰν αἶγα διώκει,
> ἁ γέρανος τὤροτρον· ἐγὼ δ' ἐπὶ τὶν μεμάνημαι.

Pierian Muses, sing with me the slender youth; for whatever you handle you make beautiful. Lovely Bombyca, everyone calls you Syrian, skinny, sunburnt, but I alone honey-colored. Both the violet and the lettered hyacinth are black, but nevertheless

---

[59] Lessing (1962) 111. Cf. 104–105, where he cites Constantinus Manasses' description of Helen (too long to reproduce here) to show "how foolish it is to attempt something which Homer himself so wisely left untried." The spurious *Idyll* 20.21–27 likewise illustrates the pitfalls of attempting to answer the question, "Am I not beautiful?"

these are gathered first in garlands. The goat chases clover, the wolf the goat, the crane the plow, but I am mad for you.

Bucaeus' epithets are more pictorial than those of Polyphemus; his song has been called a "description,"[60] which one could hardly say of the Cyclops' verses. Similarly, the comparison of the beloved to elements of the rustic world has an obvious "point": violets and hyacinths are dark yet highly sought after, just as Bombyca herself is, and her admirer pursues her as the animals named pursue their various objects of desire. This much is only by way of a prelude, however; as "I am mad for you" signals, Bucaeus is not content with such faint praise, and continues (10.32–37):

> αἴθε μοι ἦς ὅσσα Κροῖσόν ποκα φαντὶ πεπᾶσθαι·
> χρύσεοι ἀμφότεροί κ' ἀνεκείμεθα τᾷ Ἀφροδίτᾳ,
> τὼς αὐλὼς μὲν ἔχοισα καὶ ἢ ῥόδον ἢ τύγε μᾶλον,
> σχῆμα δ' ἐγὼ καὶ καινὰς ἐπ' ἀμφοτέροισιν ἀμύκλας.
> Βομβύκα χαρίεσσ', οἱ μὲν πόδες ἀστράγαλοί τευς,
> ἁ φωνὰ δὲ τρύχνος· τὸν μὰν τρόπον οὐκ ἔχω εἰπεῖν.

If only I possessed as much as they say Croesus once did. We would both be golden statues to Aphrodite, you having your pipes and either a rose or an apple, and I new clothes and shoes of Amyclae on both feet.[61] Lovely Bombyca, your feet are dice, your voice nightshade; your ways I truly cannot speak of.

In no bucolic poem does the love object of one of the herdsmen appear in person.[62] Rather, we see how the beloved is figured in their lover's imagination. The dramatic mode of presentation allows a more intimate portrayal of the lover's mind than narration by the poet, since the character can communicate his desire in language that (as Demetrius argues) would be risky and inappropriate for the poet himself. The final two compliments, in fact, the comparison of Bombyca's feet to dice made of knuckle bones, and her voice to a plant, are so subjective that they defy interpretation.[63] As Bucaeus'

---

[60] Cairns (1970) 42.
[61] I have adopted the interpretation of σχῆμα proposed by Gow (1952) *ad loc.* 10.35: "it is clear that the word means not, as Σ say, σχῆμα ὀρχηστοῦ, but *clothes*, and that the adj. καινάς is ἀπὸ κοινοῦ with the two nouns." Not without some misgivings, however, and I therefore cite Σ 10.34/35a, Wendel (1914) 233, in full, since it avoids having to take the adjective as Gow suggests: σὺ μὲν ἄν, φησίν, αὐλοὺς ἢ ῥόδον ἢ μῆλον εἶχες, ἐγὼ δὲ καλὸν εἶδος ὡς ἂν σχῆμα λαβὼν ὀρχηστοῦ καὶ ὑπ' ἀμφοτέραις τοῖς ποσὶν ὑποδήματα. The sequence – "pipes . . . dance step . . . feet" – is a coherent series of images, and the hasty expression as Bucaeus approaches the climax of his song seems natural enough. For σχῆμα (alone) as "dance step," cf. Aristophanes *Wasps* 1485: σχήματος ἀρχή.
[62] Stanzel (1995) 147.
[63] Gow (1952) *ad loc.* 10.36, citing the scholia on ἀστράγαλοι, notes: "The word is not elsewhere used in any metaphorical sense. Knuckle-bones are not conspicuously white, and, if they were, they would not resemble Bombyca's feet (27)." And while his commentary on "nightshade," τρύχνος, cites "the not less mysterious ὄπα λειριόεσσαν [lily-like voice] of *Il.* 3.152," this, as he notes, is merely to compare one unknown with another. The scholia refer to the plant's softness.

praise of Bombyca becomes more heated, it consists increasingly of private intuitions, and when he comes at last to imagine her actual presence as a person, rather than simply picturing to himself her absent body, he can no longer find adequate words: "your ways I truly cannot speak of." This is a strong assertion;[64] like Polyphemus, Bucaeus has reached the limits of description, the limits of his ability to conjure his beloved's presence for himself and for Milon.

Returning to *Idyll* 11, then, one advantage of the dramatic mode of presentation for the poem's example of erotic desire is clear: it allows Polyphemus to describe Galateia in his own language, and so brings the audience into a more intimate relationship with the mind of the lover and the circumscribed bucolic world he inhabits. The effect is heightened by the change in the poem's mode of presentation; Polyphemus' voice contrasts so dramatically with the voice that speaks the frame narration in large part because his distinctively subjective bucolic comparisons follow directly upon the cool quasi-medical tone of the introductory address to Nicias. Yet, as we have seen, his attempts to conjure Galateia's presence fall well short of allowing us to imagine her for ourselves. This is not because the Cyclops is inherently inept at description. As he explains Galateia's elusiveness to himself, he gives an account of his own features that is as precise as the one that Theocritus gives to Nicias (11.30–33):

γινώσκω, χαρίεσσα κόρα, τίνος οὕνεκα φεύγεις·
οὕνεκά μοι λασία μὲν ὀφρὺς ἐπὶ παντὶ μετώπῳ
ἐξ ὠτὸς τέταται ποτὶ θώτερον ὣς μία μακρά,
εἷς δ' ὀφθαλμὸς ὕπεστι, πλατεῖα δὲ ῥὶς ἐπὶ χείλει.

I know, lovely girl, why you flee. Because one long hairy brow is stretched across my whole forehead from one ear to the other, and a single eye is under it, and a wide nose above the lip.

We do not know how Polyphemus knows what he looks like. In *Idyll* 6, he has seen his reflection in the water, and perhaps that is what we are intended to imagine here; as he sits on the seashore entreating Galateia to appear, he may have caught a glimpse of his own reflection in the sea. By contrast, the sources of his knowledge of what Galateia looks like are mentioned in the poem, but these references only make it more mysterious. He has seen her face-to-face once, on a flower-picking expedition with his mother. Since then, he claims, her habit is to appear when he is asleep, only to disappear when he awakens (11.22–24). He seems not to understand what dreaming

---

[64] On μάν here, see Denniston (1950) 329–31.

is, and makes no distinction between the Galateia he has seen in the flesh and the Galateia that appears to him at night.[65] Yet, while memory and dream image have the same reality for him, only his sleeping mind is able to produce a convincing illusion of her presence. His conscious efforts to imagine Galateia lose their way in hyperbole, and so frustrate our efforts to see what they ostensibly describe, but his unconscious mind is a veritable fiction machine. Night after night, it produces an illusion whose presence is as palpable as reality. Yet, since the reader cannot enter Polyphemus' dreams any more than he can enter the ocean into which he peers by day, we once again miss the spectacular female presence that lies at the heart of the fiction. The frame narrative describes desire as a "wound in the chest," a hateful dart which the Cyprian had fixed in Polyphemus' liver. As Polyphemus tells it, Galateia's image is this wound (11.25–29):

> ἠράσθην μὲν ἔγωγε τεοῦς, κόρα, ἀνίκα πρᾶτον
> ἦνθες ἐμᾷ σὺν ματρὶ θέλοισ' ὑακίνθινα φύλλα
> ἐξ ὄρεος δρέψασθαι, ἐγὼ δ' ὁδὸν ἁγεμόνευον.
> παύσασθαι δ' ἐσιδών τυ καὶ ὕστερον οὐδ' ἔτι πᾳ νῦν
> ἐκ τήνω δύναμαι·

I fell in love with you, girl, when you first came with my mother, wishing to gather hyacinth flowers from the mountain, and I was leading the way. And having looked upon you, from that time afterwards and even now I am unable in any way to stop.

Yet it is by not making her image available that the poem imparts the workings of this hidden wound to its audience. By representing Galateia only in Polyphemus' comparisons and recollected dreams, the poem both encourages and frustrates our wish to see her for ourselves, and so communicates the Cyclops' experience of desire as an unrelieved craving to look upon an object that remains stubbornly concealed. Just as the Cyprian's shaft lies out of sight in Polyphemus' liver, yet is responsible for all he says and does, so Galateia never appears in the poem, yet is the imaginary object towards which our reading is directed. Having surprised the reader with the irruption of dramatic presence into what began as a gnomic anecdote, the poem now maps the appeal of its fiction onto the absent and the unseen, the gleaming body of the Nymph that neither we nor the Cyclops are permitted to see.[66]

---

[65] Hunter (1999) *ad loc.* 11.22–3.
[66] Cf. Lessing (1962) 104: "In this respect, also, Homer is the best model of all. He says that Nireus was beautiful, Achilles more beautiful still, and that Helen possessed a godlike beauty. But nowhere does he enter into a detailed description of these beauties. And yet the entire poem is based on the beauty of Helen." For voyeurism as an engine of narrative curiosity, Brooks (1993) 88–122 is fundamental.

The uninterrupted dramatic mode that follows the introductory address to Nicias excludes the poet's voice from the greater part of the poem; Theocritus relinquishes his ability to comment directly upon his creation until verses 80–81. While Polyphemus is speaking, authorial comment can appear only in the disguised form of irony, signals embedded in the character's speech which communicate to the audience that he is not as fully aware of his own situation as we are. These mostly take the form of unconscious allusions to Book 9 of the *Odyssey*, the events of which will take place after the scene in *Idyll* 11.[67] Thus, at verse 53 he speaks of his one eye being burned by Galateia, at 61 of "some stranger (τις ... ξένος) coming with his ship," and at 79 he calls himself a "somebody (τις) on the land." Dramatic monologue also limits the story time to the duration of Polyphemus' song. However, the "real time" of the fiction that elapses while he is singing is unobtrusively plotted against two different chronological axes. Firstly, there are the coordinates created by Polyphemus himself: his first meeting with Galateia (11.25–29), the seasonal cycle of his flocks and their produce (11.34–37), his present love and its imagined culmination in a future in which Galateia has left the ocean to cohabit with him (11.44–53). Polyphemus' experience of time matches that of Theocritus' other herdsmen; an idle present occupied by erotic yearning is set against a background of rural work. The audience, however, will compare the Cyclops' subjective experience of time with the temporal framework of the *Odyssey*, where his world is only a single episode in the forward movement of the plot, and is not experienced on what we learn from *Idyll* 11 to be his own terms. Polyphemus' distinctive temporality as a bucolic character further differentiates him from his epic and comic antecedents.

One question that necessarily suggests itself in connection with this distinctive presentation of the Cyclops is why Theocritus is offering it to Nicias as the demonstration of a propositional thought that is advanced with regard to a world outside the fictional one the Cyclops himself inhabits. The frame suggests that Polyphemus is a token in a real-world discursive exchange between the poet and his addressee, and, even if this exchange were part of the poem's fiction, it would nonetheless belong to a secondary fiction that the poem situates outside that of the dramatic monologue. Since the subject of discussion is poetry and its ability to alleviate the pain of desire, and since both writer and addressee are poets, there is a natural presumption that one or other of them is in love. However, this need not be so, and the

---

[67] Brooke (1971) 79: "The poem's structure ... is unique among the pastoral idylls in its combination of the poetic presence [of Theocritus himself] with monodic song ... But as a device it is not entirely satisfactory; the poet is unable to present his 'objective' point of view entirely within the frame and must insert himself into the song as well by means of ironic allusions to the *Odyssey*."

poem may be intended as part of a purely theoretical inquiry. Either way, we must at some point approach the long-standing problem of how it figures the role of song in relation to desire.[68] The notion that Polyphemus achieves self-knowledge through his song appears to be hopeless. For he knows everything he needs to know from the outset, including what his problem is. He is ugly, and so Galateia shuns him: "I know why you flee, lovely girl," he says (11.30), pointing to his single Cyclopean eye, with its overarching brow, just as he later refers to his unattractively hirsute condition (11.50). He also knows that he is well endowed with pastoral riches, and contemplation of them seems to do him good as he reviews them in his imagination: his cattle, the fine milk and cheese they produce, his musical skills, the abundance of baby animals he can offer as playthings, his shady cave and its cool water from the snows of Mount Etna (11.34–48). He passes all these before his mind as he sits upon the shore, and, in doing so, he turns the real world he inhabits into an imaginary object, a secondary object of desire that can take the Nymph's place. By being pictured in this way, as an imaginary presence rather than a real one, this familiar world is able to exert the same attraction over him as the absent body of Galateia. "Come forth," he says, one last time, "and having come forth forget, as I do now, sitting here, to go home" (11.64). But no sooner is the claim that he has forgotten his home out of his mouth (as if he had not spent most of his song describing it) than he comes to his senses and pledges to return to it. "O Cyclops, Cyclops, where has your mind wandered?" (11.72), he concludes, acknowledging his imaginary journey as he sets his face towards home, his lambs, and his cheese.

Polyphemus achieves his return to reality by constructing in song a fantasy double of his own pastoral existence as an alternative to erotic fantasy. In this he resembles Theocritus' other herdsmen. Lycidas in *Idyll* 7 imagines an idealized pastoral world he might have shared with Comatas; Thyrsis in *Idyll* 1 imagines himself as Daphnis. Less happily, the goatherd in *Idyll* 3 invokes his series of mythical doubles but cannot quite identify with them successfully. The pastoral world he imagines remains rooted in myth, and does not quite work as valorized double of his own experience. He is unable to transmute his own world into an imaginary object. The exchange of real for imaginary experience, however, enables Polyphemus to stand outside himself for a time, and to desist at least from reinflicting

---

[68] The problem begins with Gow (1952) *ad loc.* 11.13, who notes that Polyphemus' singing appears as a symptom of erotic affliction in a poem which asserts that singing is not a symptom of, but rather a cure for, such affliction. The course of the debate over the effectiveness of the Cyclops' song as *pharmakon* can be followed in Erbse (1965), Holtsmark (1966), Spofford (1969), Brooke (1971), Goldhill (1986), Deuse (1990), Manuwald (1990), Schmiel (1993), and Cozzoli (1994).

80   *Theocritus and the Invention of Fiction*

the wound of love; the effects of his song are evidently therapeutic, since he clearly feels better after singing than he did when he began.[69] This song, then, clearly fulfils the healing function that is claimed for it in the opening address to Nicias as far as its action upon the Cyclops himself is concerned.

There is, however, a second, and perhaps more important, way in which it instantiates (rather than simply demonstrating) this claim. For Polyphemus has not just himself as audience, but Nicias too. Many of the pastoral poems feature the performance of song as their one and only action. In *Idyll* 1 Thyrsis' performance of "The Sorrows of Daphnis," and in *Idyll* 3 the goatherd's song for Amaryllis, are the major events of the poems in which they occur. Likewise, in *Idyll* 7 the exchange of songs between Lycidas and Simichidas is the centerpiece of the poem, and Lycidas' song itself consists largely of imagining a future performance by Tityrus, who will sing to him of Daphnis and Comatas. Just as the goatherd of *Idyll* 1 professes extreme pleasure in the performance he hears, so Lycidas imagines the power of pastoral song to distract him from his love for the boy Ageanax, and concludes by wishing that he might have been able to hear the voice of Comatas himself (7.71–89). It is in hearing, rather than performing, pastoral song that its healing power resides for him.[70] By allowing Nicias, then, in *Idyll* 11, to overhear the song of a famous pastoral musician (Polyphemus "can pipe like no other Cyclops," 11.38–39, just as Lycidas is "the best of pipers among the herdsmen and reapers," 7.27–29), the poem impossibly restages the performance scenes that occur in other poems between their fictional characters across the boundary that separates fictional character from real-world reader. Listening to the Cyclops' song, we forget about Theocritus, Nicias, their world and our own, which all disappear for the duration of his monologue.[71] We are absorbed by the Cyclops' performance until we are suddenly jarred out of it by the unexpected return of the poet's voice at the end of the poem (11.80–81):

οὕτω τοι Πολύφαμος ἐποίμαινεν τὸν ἔρωτα
μουσίσδων, ῥᾷον δὲ διᾶγ' ἢ εἰ χρυσὸν ἔδωκεν.

So Polyphemus tended his desire with song, and did better than if he had paid money.

---

[69] So Hunter (1999) 220–21, citing Köhnken (1996), concludes that the song is a palliative rather than a cure for love; singing will not make desire go away for good, but will nonetheless provide temporary relief from its pain: "Song, therefore, *is* both symptom and *pharmakon*."
[70] Cf. Walsh (1985) 13.
[71] Cf. Seeck (1975) 199, on the intimacy generated by first-person narrative in *Idyll* 7: "Der Leser wird wie ein relativ enger Bekannter des Erzählers angesprochen und zum Vertrauten gemacht. Er gehört damit zu einem – echten oder fiktiven – engeren Kreis von Adressaten . . . sie interessieren sich für das kleine, ganz private Erlebnis des Erzählers."

Theocritus can speak of Polyphemus, but Polyphemus cannot speak of Theocritus; while the poet can prepare us for the appearance of his character, nothing can prepare us for this character's sudden disappearance and his replacement by the voice of the poet.[72] Making the reader aware of his absorption in the poem's fictional world has a parallel in the ecphrastic technique of *Idyll* 1, where in quick succession we enter and leave a series of miniature scenes on the surface of the goatherd's decorated bowl. Here the transition from one narrative level to another is combined with a change in mode, as the poet's voice suddenly replaces that of his character, and the self-consciousness this induces is proof of the poem's gnomic proposition. The immediacy of the poem's fictional world is manifested as the felt presence of its inhabitant, rather than simply an illusory image conjured by the poet.[73] The surprise we feel at his sudden disappearance reveals our absorption in Polyphemus' song, and so demonstrates that such song is a *pharmakon*; for, as long as it lasted, it drew the mind away from its own preoccupations. The example, then, does not just work by demonstration alone; it does not simply invite Nicias to inspect Polyphemus' state of mind at the beginning and end of his performance, and so judge the therapeutic effect of the song upon its singer. It also works as imaginative experience, drawing us in, and thereby demonstrating its power over us as listeners. *Idyll* 11 thus works upon its reader in the same way as Polyphemus' song works upon the Cyclops himself. As in *Idyll* 1, where we follow the goatherd into and out of the imaginary worlds he unfolds, so here the reader's experience is aligned with that of the poem's character; we experience a contemplative absorption in the pastoral world just as he does. The poem achieves a powerful form of mental distraction, a willing forgetfulness of the self in imaginary experience, which is all the more evident because we return to

---

[72] McHale (1987) 35: "The fictional world is accessible to our world, but the real world is not accessible to the world of the fiction ... We can conceive of the fictional characters and their world, but they cannot conceive of ours."

[73] John Ashbery's "The Instruction Manual," in Ashbery (1997) 8–10, is an excellent example of the latter. The poem begins with the poet at work in an office, summoning a vision of the city of Guadalajara as a distraction from the chore of business writing, and pointing out people and places in this imaginary city: "But I fancy I see, under the press of having to write the instruction manual, | Your public square, city, with its elaborate little bandstand! | The band is playing Scheherazade by Rimsky-Korsakov." The poet feigns losing sight of parts of his own creation, adopts a conspiratorial "we" that folds the reader into his own vision ("Let us take this opportunity to tiptoe into one of the side streets"), and points to the incomplete, yet satisfying, account of the city his poem has provided, before acknowledging that the one thing one cannot do with a fictional world is reside there: "What more is there to do, except stay? And that we cannot do. | And as a cool breeze freshens the top of the weathered old tower, I turn my gaze | Back to the instruction manual which has made me dream of Guadalajara." Here, then, the fictional world remains in the poet's give and take throughout, rather than seeming to manifest itself directly to the reader.

reality so harshly at the end of it, just as the Cyclops returns to reality at the end of his song.[74]

The didactic poem is typically dominated by the voice of the poet, who addresses a named addressee in the opening and continues to provide information and instruction in his own person throughout, without the intervention of fictional speakers. Hesiod's *Works and Days* contains little direct speech, Aratus' *Phaenomena* less, and the *Theriaca* and *Alexipharmaca* of Nicander none at all.[75] In *Idyll* 11, by contrast, the poet persuades us of a real-world truth by the judicious effacement of his own voice. Its reappearance at the end of the poem underlines the power of the poetic fiction that has taken its place, and so points to the truth of its initial claim about the power of song.

IDYLL 13: HERACLES AS LOVER

The structure of *Idyll* 13 is much like that of *Idyll* 11. In the opening verses of both poems Theocritus addresses gnomic remarks on the nature of love to his friend Nicias, then illustrates his point with an ancient lover, Polyphemus in *Idyll* 11 and Heracles in *Idyll* 13. The presentation of the example in the two poems is quite different, however. In *Idyll* 11 the prologue addressed to Nicias introduces a monologue by Polyphemus in the form of a song, and the Cyclops' speech is uninterrupted until the end of the poem; it is only in the last two verses that the poet's voice returns to comment briefly on what precedes. In *Idyll* 13, by contrast, Heracles does not speak, and the single line of direct speech in the poem comes within a simile. The poems offer a contrast in storytelling styles like the one Socrates creates artificially in Book 3 of the *Republic* by recomposing the opening of the *Iliad* in pure narrative without direct speech. In Plato's terms, the poet of *Idyll* 13 "conceals himself nowhere," while the poet of *Idyll* 11 "tries to make us feel that he is not the speaker" (*Republic* 3.392e–394b). The remainder of this chapter, then, will investigate the effects of the narrative mode (λέξις)

---

[74] For *psychagogia*, originally a word with necromantic associations, as a term for literary pleasure in the Hellenistic period, see Pfeiffer (1968) 166 and Fraser (1972) I.759. For its development in the later literary theory of Philodemus, see Wigodsky (1995) 65–68, who also provides a thorough survey of earlier usage, and Asmis (1995) 148–77. While the term may merely be part of a binarism with *didaskalia*, instruction, so that one chooses one's preferred theory of poetry's value as one or the other, it is nonetheless tempting to imagine that it found its way into this opposition because the deeper, Gorgianic, experience of poetry as a conjuring of the soul that is reflected in its etymology was still active in it. Cozzoli (1994) 107, by contrast, supposes that a Hellenistic poem can have no such effect upon its recipient, since that recipient is now a reader, and not the auditor of a live performance.

[75] *Works and Days* 54–58, 207–11, 453, 454, 503; *Phaenomena* 123–26.

chosen by Theocritus upon the message that his exemplary tale (λόγος) seeks to impart. For, as I have argued, the dramatic mode is one of the defining characteristics of bucolic poetry, and the speech of its characters is crucial in securing our paradoxical assent to their manifestly fictional world. They appear with an intimacy that is lost in narration, and so make the world of poem a living presence rather than a mere discursive topic.

Idyll 13, then, begins with a gnomic proposition about love addressed to Nicias (13.1–4):

> οὐχ ἁμῖν τὸν Ἔρωτα μόνοις ἔτεχ', ὡς ἐδοκεῦμες,
> Νικία, ᾧτινι τοῦτο θεῶν ποκα τέκνον ἔγεντο·
> οὐχ ἁμῖν τὰ καλὰ πράτοις καλὰ φαίνεται ἦμεν,
> οἳ θνατοὶ πελόμεσθα, τὸ δ' αὔριον οὐκ ἐσορῶμες·

Not for us alone did he beget Love, as we used to think, Nicias, whoever of the gods it was that did beget this child, and what is beautiful does not appear so to us first, we who are mortal, and do not behold tomorrow.

Having stated this thought, Theocritus introduces the figure who will prove its truth (13.5–6): "For even the bronze-hearted son of Amphitryon, he who withstood the fierce lion, loved a boy." Heracles is the limit case, as he is for Achilles at *Iliad* 18.117–19. Informing Thetis of his resolution to die in avenging Patroclus, he asserts: "For not even mighty Heracles escaped death . . . but fate mastered him and the fierce anger of Hera." If anyone could have escaped the mortal necessities of love and death it would have been Heracles, but even for him this could not be. Theocritus' use of Heracles is in keeping with epic precedent, and contrasts with the departure from the *Odyssey* in his portrayal of Polyphemus as a love-sick adolescent.

In *Idyll* 11 the use of dramatic monologue for the example facilitates this departure; the Cyclops reveals himself to Nicias directly as a pastoral lover, without intervention by the poet. No such intimacy is generated by *Idyll* 13. Theocritus himself narrates how Heracles adopted the pederastic role of surrogate father to his beloved Hylas (13.8–14):

> καί νιν πάντ' ἐδίδασκε, πατὴρ ὡσεὶ φίλον υἱόν,
> ὅσσα μαθὼν ἀγαθὸς καὶ ἀοίδιμος αὐτὸς ἔγεντο·
> χωρὶς δ' οὐδέποκ' ἦς, οὔτ' εἰ μέσον ἆμαρ ὄροιτο,
> οὔθ' ὁπόχ' ἁ λεύκιππος ἀνατρέχοι ἐς Διὸς Ἀώς,
> οὔθ' ὁπόκ' ὀρτάλιχοι μινυροὶ ποτὶ κοῖτον ὁρῷεν,
> σεισαμένας πτερὰ ματρὸς ἐπ' αἰθαλόεντι πετεύρῳ,
> ὡς αὐτῷ κατὰ θυμὸν ὁ παῖς πεπονημένος εἴη . . .

84 *Theocritus and the Invention of Fiction*

And as a father a beloved son, he taught him all the things which he had become noble and famous himself by learning. And he was never apart from him, neither if the middle of the day was rising, nor when Dawn of the white steeds turned back to the house of Zeus, nor when chattering chickens looked towards their bed, their mother haven shaken her wings on the smoky perch, so that the boy might be fashioned according to his spirit . . .

The greater part of this account is taken up with the hyperbolic gloss on "never" that falls between the main clause and the purpose clause that (eventually) follows. The Homeric division of the day – "either dawn or afternoon or midday" (*Iliad* 21.111) – is reworked so that its elements appear as a succession of stylistic registers; the plain "middle of the day" is followed by the elaborate "Dawn of the white steeds," which is in turn succeeded by the rustic "chattering chickens." This is a parody of epic time-keeping. In *Idyll* 11 dramatic monologue in the example means that there is an exact match between the time that elapses in the story and the time it takes to listen to the poem; we experience the same amount of time as Polyphemus for as long as he is singing his song. In narrative there is no such equivalence. Narrative duration does not match the story time it represents, and the poet is free to compress or expand the time narrated at will. This freedom is extravagantly signaled by the redundancy of the temporal markers in this passage; Theocritus spends four verses telling us what never happened.[76]

This expansive retardation contrasts with the poem's second chronological tour-de-force, the compression of Books 1 and 2 of the *Argonautica* (or an Argonautica, if we do not suppose that Theocritus is writing after Apollonius) into a three-verse relative clause (13.21–24):

σὺν δ' αὐτῷ κατέβαινεν Ὕλας εὔεδρον ἐς Ἀργώ,
ἅτις κυανεᾶν οὐχ ἅψατο συνδρομάδων ναῦς,
ἀλλὰ διεξάιξε βαθὺν δ' εἰσέδραμε Φᾶσιν,
αἰετὸς ὥς, μέγα λαῖτμα, ἀφ' οὗ τότε χοιράδες ἔσταν.

And Hylas went down to the well-benched Argo with him, which ship did not touch the gloomy clashing rocks but darted through and sped into Phasis, like an eagle, the large bay, from which time the rocks stood still.[77]

---

[76] Cf. Hamburger (1973) 159ff. on the relationship between "narrating-time" (Erzählzeit) and "narrated time" (erzählte Zeit): "the representation of time . . . was a criterion and a sort of crux for the fictional character of the reality portrayed in the novel." See also Genette (1980) 86–160 and the bibliography in Martin (1986) 230–31.

[77] Cf. the text of Hunter (1999) – αἰετὸς ὥς μέγα λαῖτμα – and his translation at *ad loc.* 13.23–24: "as an eagle [soars] over a vast expanse." While this neatly extends the narrative ellipsis to the simile, λαῖτμα in Homer, and at *Argonautica* 1.1299, even when unaccompanied by θαλάσσης, always refers to the sea and the ships or people making their way through it, and here too, I think, it refers to the element through which the Argo, not the eagle, travels.

The presence of the fictional world

Whereas verses 10–13 gloss a single word into four lines, here a sea-crossing with its attendant adventures is confined within the same compass. The artifice of the narrative is further marked by the contrast between the urgent motion of verse 23 with its two verbs and the sudden halt on "stood still" in verse 24, which involves a marked dislocation in the order of events.[78] Moreover, after this account of the Argo's successful navigation of the Clashing Rocks, at verse 25 we find ourselves back on the Greek mainland, where the Argonauts, we are told, in three lines, have not yet left home (13.25–28):

> Ἆμος δ' ἀντέλλοντι Πελειάδες, ἐσχατιαὶ δὲ
> ἄρνα νέον βόσκοντι, τετραμμένου εἴαρος ἤδη,
> τᾶμος ναυτιλίας μιμνάσκετο θεῖος ἄωτος
> ἡρώων . . .

But when the Pleiades rise, and the distant meadows feed the young lamb, when spring has already turned, then the god-like crop of heroes recalled their expedition . . .

As verses 10–13 exaggerate Homeric narration, Theocritus here all but parodies the Argonauts' adventure by recasting it as a seasonal urge, in the almanac register of Hesiod's *Works and Days* 383–84.

The story that follows will be told as narrative in its entirety. Neither Heracles nor Hylas say a word, and the only direct speech in the poem appears within a simile. After the Argonauts' arrival in the Hellespont, Hylas leaves his companions to search for water (13.28–52). As he dips his pitcher into the spring that he has discovered, the Nymphs that inhabit it take hold of his arm (13.48–52):

> πασάων γὰρ ἔρως ἁπαλὰς φρένας ἐξεφόβησεν
> Ἀργείῳ ἐπὶ παιδί. κατήριπε δ' ἐς μέλαν ὕδωρ
> ἀθρόος, ὡς ὅτε πυρσὸς ἀπ' οὐρανοῦ ἤριπεν ἀστήρ
> ἀθρόος ἐν πόντῳ, ναύτας δέ τις εἶπεν ἑταίροις
> "κουφότερ', ὦ παῖδες, ποιεῖσθ' ὅπλα· πλευστικὸς οὖρος."

Desire for the Argive boy disturbed the tender minds of them all. And he fell into the black water, as when a fiery star from the heavens falls all at once into the sea, and some sailor says to his companions, "Make the rigging light, my lads; it's a wind for sailing."

The shock of Hylas' disappearance is communicated by taking the audience outside the story world of the primary narrative and into another world

---

[78] Gow (1952) *ad loc.* 23f.: "the fixation of the Symplegades is somewhat awkwardly separated from the passage of the Argo which caused it."

that is entirely unforeseen; rather than with Hylas and the Nymphs, we find ourselves unexpectedly at sea, hearing the voice of an unknown sailor. Once again, Theocritus combines a shift in narrative level with a change in narrative mode.

Like Galateia, Hylas is now inaccessible because he is underwater. While in *Idyll* 11 the lover is so deprived of the object of his desire from the outset, in *Idyll* 13 he vanishes in the middle of the poem.[79] Like Polyphemus, Heracles calls out to his submerged beloved, although, unlike the Cyclops, he is unaware of his location (13.58–65; I omit the spurious verse 61 – see Gow *ad loc.* 13.61f.):

> τρὶς μὲν Ὕλαν ἄυσεν, ὅσον βαθὺς ἤρυγε λαιμός·
> τρὶς δ' ἄρ' ὁ παῖς ὑπάκουσεν, ἀραιὰ δ' ἵκετο φωνά
> ἐξ ὕδατος, παρεὼν δὲ μάλα σχεδὸν εἴδετο πόρρω.
> νεβροῦ φθεγξαμένας τις ἐν οὔρεσιν ὠμοφάγος λίς
> ἐξ εὐνᾶς ἔσπευσεν ἑτοιμοτάταν ἐπὶ δαῖτα·
> Ἡρακλέης τοιοῦτος ἐν ἀτρίπτοισιν ἀκάνθαις
> παῖδα ποθῶν δεδόνητο, πολὺν δ' ἐπελάμβανε χῶρον.

Three times he cried "Hylas", as loud as his deep throat could roar. And three times the boy answered, but his voice came faint from the water, and although very close, he seemed far away. When a fawn cries, a ravenous lion in the mountains speeds from its lair to a ready feast. Even so Heracles roamed in the pathless thorns seeking his boy, and covered a lot of ground.

The characters' speech is given indirectly, yet the distinctive sound of both voices is described by the poet. Heracles' is a corporeal event; it erupts from the throat, the *laimos*, more usually the site of eating than speaking, like a belch, or a roar, despite being composed of articulate language.[80] The voice of Hylas, by contrast, emerges from the water "faint," or "weak," and can no longer be traced to its origin. The literal description of the contrasting cries is supplemented by the simile that follows, which suggests the emotions that inform them. For, if "when a fawn cries" (13.62) inevitably equates the helpless young animal with Hylas, so too the equation of the "ravenous lion" with Heracles points not just to the intensity, but also to the nature, of his feelings; the image of the hungry lion changes our understanding of the erotic relationship portrayed in the poem.[81]

---

[79] Segal (1981) 47–65 explores the "archetypal associations" of the "death by water" motif in *Idylls* 1, 13, 22, and 23.
[80] Gow (1952) *ad loc.* 13.58 notes that, in remodeling *Iliad* 11.462, Theocritus has substituted *laimos* for *kephale*, "head".
[81] Mastronarde (1968) 277–78.

Apollonius explains Heracles' anger at Hylas' loss as the origin of the cult in which the present inhabitants of Mysia still seek the vanished youth (1.1348–57). His account of the disappearance differs significantly from that of Theocritus. While Polyphemus is said to hear the boy call out (1.1240), there is no particular emphasis on his voice as the Argonauts search for him, nor any mention of Heracles' repeated calling. Theocritus, by contrast, echoes the vowels of the boy's name in the verb for Heracles' cry, where they reappear in inverted form, Ὕλαν ἄυσεν, *Hulan aüsen*. Hylas has become merely the mirror image of Heracles' vocalization of desire,[82] and Theocritus draws attention to the strange separation of the boy from his voice that is so baffling for the hero: "three times the boy answered, but his voice came faint from the water, and although very close, he seemed far away" (13.60). There is a curious echo here of the ideal pastoral scene in which Lycidas imagines himself listening to Comatas (7.86–89):

> αἴθ' ἐπ' ἐμεῦ ζωοῖς ἐναρίθμιος ὤφελες ἦμεν,
> ὥς τοι ἐγὼν ἐνόμευον ἀν' ὤρεα τὰς καλὰς αἶγας
> φωνᾶς εἰσαΐων, τὺ δ' ὑπὸ δρυσὶν ἢ ὑπὸ πεύκαις
> ἁδὺ μελισδόμενος κατεκέκλισο, θεῖε Κομᾶτα.

If only you were numbered among the living in my day, so that I, pasturing your lovely sheep among the hills, might listen to your voice, and you, lying under oaks or under pines, sing sweetly, divine Comatas.

Comatas "sings sweetly," yet Lycidas does not say what he is singing about, as he does for Tityrus, whose performance he describes in the preceding verses. Lycidas imagines himself listening not to a song but to a voice. Moreover, Lycidas hears this voice as he pastures his sheep among the hills, while Comatas himself is elsewhere, reclining "under oaks or under pines."

This ideal listening scene is echoed in *Idyll* 11, where Nicias is invited to hear the voice of Polyphemus. Similarly, in *Idyll* 10 the pleasures of the voice are prominent among the attractions that Bucaeus finds in Bombyca. The objects of the pastoral lovers' desire often have "speaking" names, and while these elsewhere refer to some aspect of their physical appearance (Amaryllis, "sparkling," Galateia, "milky"), in *Idyll* 10 "delightful Bombyca," the flute player with whom Bucaeus is in love, is named after the instrument she plays; the *bombyx* may be the flute itself, a part of a flute,

---

[82] Hunter (1999) *ad loc.* 13.58: "'Hylas' has been associated with ὑλᾶν, ὑλακτεῖν . . . as a rationalisation of a ritual cry ὕλα."

or one of the sounds it produces.[83] More specifically, in fact, it is either a deep-toned flute or the lowest note played on an ordinary one,[84] the pleasing low-pitched hum for which bees are praised elsewhere.[85] This agrees with Bucaeus' mysterious description, "your voice is nightshade" (10.37). For the scholia find the meaning of the comparison in the plant's softness,[86] and the image suggests a synaesthetic accord between the feel of its leaves and the timbre of Bombyca's voice, a reflection of the low pitch of her instrument.[87]

Returning to *Idyll* 13, then, Hylas' abduction inverts a number of characteristic bucolic motifs. The shady spring with its lush vegetation is a source of peril, its Nymphs "fearsome goddesses for the country people" (13.44). Straying from the epic community of heroes, Hylas is absorbed into the landscape, where his disembodied voice enacts a grim parody of the pastoral song exchange with his lover Heracles; for this voice does not bring pleasure, but violent anxiety.[88] The reduction of body to voice that in *Idyll* 7 represents an overcoming of desire here merely indicates its unending unfulfilment.

Having described Heracles' grief, Theocritus comments (13.66–67):

σχέτλιοι οἱ φιλέοντες, ἀλώμενος ὅσσ' ἐμόγησεν
οὔρεα καὶ δρυμούς, τὰ δ' Ἰάσονος ὕστερα πάντ' ἦς.

Lovers are reckless; how greatly did he toil wandering the hills and thickets, and Jason's affairs were all secondary.

In *Idyll* 11 dramatic monologue limits the poet's commentary on Polyphemus to ironic allusions embedded in his speech; narrative allows him to reflect on Heracles directly. The poet provides both story and interpretation, judgment is inseparable from narrative, and the reader's sympathies are guided not just by explicit intervention, such as we find here, but by simile and epithet as well. The comparison of Heracles' search for Hylas to a ravening lion's pursuit of a fawn (13.62–63) controls our understanding

---

[83] Hunter (1999) *ad loc.* 10.26–27. Cf. Kossaifi (2002) 350–51.   [84] *LSJ* s.v. βόμβυξ II.
[85] αἱ δὲ καλὸν βομβεῦντι ποτὶ σμάνεσσι μέλισσαι (1.107), ὧδε καλὸν βομβεῦντι ποτὶ σμάνεσσι μέλισσαι (5.46), cf. ἁ βομβεῦσα μέλισσα (3.13).
[86] Σ 10.37, Wendel (1914) 233.
[87] For an interesting study of Sappho's innovative adaptation of Homer's epithets for the voice to characterize vocal timbre among her female friends, see Paradiso (1995), especially 106, 113.
[88] Hunter (1999) *ad loc.* 13.58–60 compares the version of Antoninus Liberalis 26, in which Hylas is assimilated to Echo, who has a prominent place in later pastoral.

of the character's inner experience just as much as being told that he is reckless.[89]

The clause that introduces Heracles as the exemplification of the gnomic proposition addressed to Nicias in *Idyll* 13 – "he loved a boy," ἤρατο παιδός (13.6) – is virtually identical to that which introduces Polyphemus in *Idyll* 11 – "he loved Galateia," ἤρατο τᾶς Γαλατείας (11.8). Moreover, the experience of the two exemplary figures is very similar. What we are told of Polyphemus, that he had "a hateful wound in his breast, which a dart from great Cypris had fixed in his liver" (11.15–16), resembles what we learn here of Heracles' suffering after Hylas' disappearance: "the harsh god was tearing his liver within" (13.71). Finally, there is a close verbal parallel of the conclusion to *Idyll* 11 – "in this way Polyphemus tended his love," οὕτω τοι Πολύφαμος ἐποίμαινεν τὸν ἔρωτα (11.80) – in the verses that end *Idyll* 13 (13.72–75):

> οὕτω μὲν κάλλιστος Ὕλας μακάρων ἀριθμεῖται·
> Ἡρακλέην δ' ἥρωες ἐκερτόμεον λιποναύταν,
> οὕνεκεν ἠρώησε τριακοντάζυγον Ἀργώ,
> πεζᾷ δ' ἐς Κόλχους τε καὶ ἄξενον ἵκετο Φᾶσιν.

In this way beautiful Hylas was numbered among the Blessed, and the heroes teased Heracles as a deserter, because he abandoned the thirty-benched Argo, and reached the Colchians and inhospitable Phasis on foot.

Yet we experience the two endings quite differently. The dramatic presentation of the example in *Idyll* 11 puts the audience in direct contact with its subject, and the measure of this engagement is the shock we feel when the poet's voice returns at the end of the poem. Suddenly we leave Polyphemus, whom we seemed to be directly overhearing, and return to the present, in which the poet is addressing Nicias; the clear demarcation between frame and example closes off the story world abruptly, and marks the separation of fictional, imaginative experience from the reality the poet shares with his addressee. In *Idyll* 13, by contrast, narrative imparts only a faint impression of the characters' inner experience. Neither Heracles nor Hylas speak, and we learn of Heracles' erotic torment in the same way as we learn of the

---

[89] On the controlling function of the epic epithet, see the well-known comments of Booth (1961) 5: "Homer 'intrudes' deliberately and obviously to insure that our judgment of the 'heroic,' 'resourceful,' 'admirable,' 'wise' Odysseus will be sufficiently favorable." Gow (1952) *ad loc.* 13.19 notes that the epithet ταλαεργός, "hard-working," that is applied to Heracles in this poem is used only of mules in early epic, and also of a slave woman at *Argonautica* 4.1062. It thus creates a resonant clash with the elaborate matronymic, "son of Alcmene queen of Midea," that appears in the following verse. The deployment of epithets juxtaposes perspectives on the hero.

Argonauts' dining arrangements (13.32–35), or the vegetation around the spring (13.40–42): the poet tells us about it himself.

At the end of the poem, however, Theocritus does not comment on the story he has just told, and no amount of tampering with the final verses can introduce a "point" here; Heracles, the subject of the example, is not even the subject of the final clause.[90] Rather than concluding the poem, like verses 80–81 of *Idyll* 11, verses 72–75 of *Idyll* 13 simply end it. They recap what we have already heard – that Hylas became an immortal – and they remind us that the story will now continue without us; Heracles had to go on to Colchis on foot. Unlike *Idyll* 11, which either brackets off the pastoral Polyphemus from the continuation of his story in other versions of his life or perhaps invites us to imagine his sentimental education as a way of linking them (the adolescent disappointed in his grand passion grows up into savage monster), this poem ends by looking ahead to what awaits Heracles and the Argonauts when they reach "the Colchians and inhospitable Phasis" (13.75): the seduction of Medea, the flight from Aeëtes, and the tragedy at Corinth. If, then, at the end of the poem we glimpse the first link in a chain of events in which other mortals will repeat Heracles' experience of desire as though it were something new, the narrative mode of *Idyll* 13 has also allowed us to experience the truth of its gnomic proposition: "Not for us alone did he beget Love, as we used to think, Nicias, whoever of the gods it was that did beget this child, and what is beautiful does not appear so to us first, we who are mortal, and do not behold tomorrow." The poet links myth with actuality by narrating a story of human desire that stretches without a break from the time of epic to the present moment, in which he is talking to Nicias. Only the omniscience of the epic narrator can allow a reader to see that his own desire is in fact the repetition of an experience that has been enacted time and time again since the beginning of the world. For only those who know what is, what has been, and what will be can have a true perspective on human affairs – the gods, and their stand-in on earth, the epic poet.

For Plato, poetic narrative is true or false, not fictional. While the epic poet may hide behind his characters in telling his story, he, just as much as the poet who speaks in his own voice, can and should be questioned about the knowledge he claims in his narration, its sources, and its status as truth or falsehood.[91] In *Idyll* 13 Theocritus has it both ways. While the opening address to Nicias constructs a discursive situation in which one real-world

---

[90] Hunter (1999) *ad loc.* 13.75 notes various attempts to "improve" the ending by making it more forceful.
[91] Gill (1993) 38–87.

person apparently addresses another, the poem's truth claim depends upon him insensibly adopting the prerogatives of the epic poet as the poem progresses, telling us what no one in real life could possibly know.[92] Most readers (unlike Plato) will not be put off by this; as Aristotle suggests, we will judge the fiction not as a true account of past events but by how usefully it models some aspect of reality. We are helped in this case by having the poet tell us in its opening exactly what real-life universal the poem will be attempting to demonstrate, so its success or failure as mimetic fiction can easily be judged. In *Idyll* 11 the situation is more complicated. While the poet makes a truth claim in the opening here too, and his character's actions to some extent demonstrate its validity, this poem invites our assent to its propositional statement not primarily by telling us a story but by showing us a world. The power of the poem is grounded not so much in the cognitive appeal of stories as a map of real-life experience as in the power of fictional presences to induce our assent to, and engagement with, an imaginary world. *Idyll* 11 is, like the other bucolic poems, better described as fully fictional than as mimetic; its power resides in itself, in the world it contains, not in that world's ability to model a reality other than its own.

---

[92] Booth (1961) 3. Hamburger (1973) 137 characterizes omniscience in "epic" (third person) narration as the absence of a genuine statement subject: "the absence of the real I-Origo and the functional character of fictional narration are one and the same phenomenon." Cf. Dolezel (1998) 149: "Where does the narrative's authentication authority originate? It has the same grounding as any other performative authority – convention. In the actual world, this authority is given by social, mostly institutional, systems; in fiction, it is inscribed in the norms of the narrative genre."

CHAPTER 3

Becoming bucolic

In the last chapter I argued that, in their concern to present characters who are real presences to the reader, Theocritus' bucolic poems are continuous with the performed drama of classical and Hellenistic theater. In particular, the poems that I examined make use of various kinds of framing device that cause the reader to experience the transition to the story world in a self-conscious way. Inducing an awareness of the poet's control of the boundary between story world and the reality of the reader thus becomes a crucial element in the poems' resistance to being taken simply as an intellectual object at the disposal of the reader. Like the opening address to the Muses in the Homeric poems, the framing of the story enables the audience's consensual transition from their own world to a world that is other than their own. Rather than limiting itself to a purely textual existence, the result of the belated position in a song culture that has become unexpectedly literate, Hellenistic literary drama insists upon its ability to confront the reader with the uncanny presence of a world that is other than his own. Indeed, the poems exploit a fact about fictional worlds that becomes all the clearer when these worlds originate on the page – literary beings can manifest themselves to us, but we cannot manifest ourselves to them. Rather than sapping the felt presence of fictional beings, textuality in fact highlights the strange authority of their appearance, the fact that the agency in this encounter seems to lie with them. It is as if they seek us out, and, confronting us with the difference between their story world and our own, call upon us to reflect on this difference.[1]

In this chapter, then, I want to argue that to be a bucolic character means to have a character that is shaped by its relationship to an imagined world, the fictional world of bucolic poetry itself, which is projected in

---

[1] So Steiner (1989) 142–43, taking his point of departure from the archaic torso in Rilke's famous poem, whose message is "change your life," argues that the question any art work asks of us is "What do you feel, what do you think of the possibilities of life, of the alternative shapes of being which are implicit in your experience of me, in our encounter?"

bucolic song and encountered in the fictional experience of listening to it. In particular, I wish to consider how bucolic identity is bound up with performance and impersonation. As I argued in the last chapter, the singers of Theocritus' monologue poems do not seem to be in communication with their intended audience. Rather, as they sing, they become their own audience, telling stories in which they fashion an imaginative escape from the desire that led them to sing in the first place. The goatherd of *Idyll* 3 introduces mythical paradigms that lead not so much to the persuasion of his beloved as to the imagination of the experience of his legendary predecessors. Polyphemus envisions a pastoral world that he shares with Galateia, who has left the ocean to become his wife. These characters are able to achieve a temporary distraction from their present suffering by invoking a more perfect version of their own bucolic existence. Comatas in *Idyll* 5 is more confident about his ability to reenact his own bucolic vision; he begins his song with Lacon with "the Muses love me more than the singer Daphnis" (5.80–81), and, after his victory, he promises a butting goat (5.150): "if I don't castrate you, may I be Melantheus instead of Comatas." By imagining his kinship with Daphnis, he is able at the same time to distance himself from an imagined antitype, the treacherous goatherd of the *Odyssey*, who is defeated (and put to death) by Odysseus. Thyrsis, the famous pastoral singer of *Idyll* 1, impersonates a still more famous pastoral singer as he performs "The Sorrows of Daphnis;" he too is able to successfully reenact a legendary counterpart for his fellow herdsmen. Finally in *Idyll* 7 Lycidas, who is for Simichidas the archetypal herdsman singer, looks forward to hearing of his predecessors from another singer, Tityrus, and wishes that he could have been the audience of Comatas.

To have heard bucolic song, then, is to have been inspired with a desire to emulate its leading characters, and dramatic impersonation is one way in which this desire for reenactment expresses itself. By imagining themselves as Daphnis or Polyphemus, the herdsmen try out roles from the repertory of bucolic myth, and so stage their own imaginative involvement with the bucolic world of which they are a part. As I shall argue in the next chapter, it is clear from *Idyll* 16 that the Ithacan books of the *Odyssey* provided Theocritus with suggestive examples of rustic characters in disguise. Further evidence for the influence of this Homeric material on the development of Theocritus' bucolic characters is provided by Comatas' disparaging reference to the goatherd Melantheus. But Theocritus has turned the Homeric rustics' disguise into deliberate theatricality; while Homer's characters are revealed in the course of the poem to be other than what they seem, Theocritus' herdsmen consciously experiment with personae. Even the most heart-felt song is a kind of role play. The goatherd of *Idyll* 3 leaves his animals at the opening of the poem to serenade Amaryllis, Polyphemus abandons his flocks to go to the seashore and sing to Galateia. Real herdsmen sing while they are working, but the songs of the *Idylls* are always a performance.

In this chapter, then, I shall look at two poems in which character is inextricably linked to imaginative role play. *Idyll* 6 presents an exchange of bucolic songs between Daphnis and Damoetas. However, the only way we know that the exchange is between these two characters is that Theocritus tells us so in the frame narration that precedes the songs themselves. Within the world of the poem, Daphnis speaks as a friend of Polyphemus, and Damoetas responds to him in the persona of the Cyclops. Without the frame narration, in other words, there would be no way for a reader to tell that the characters are not simply Polyphemus and his advisor, as they appear to be from their own words. In *Idyll* 12, a poem that has received very little critical attention, a speaker who has much in common with the characters of the bucolic poems imagines how his own unhappy love affair would look to observers from the distant future, reimagining it in erotic categories derived from the distant past. Like the goatherd of *Idyll* 3, he looks for roles to reenact, and doubts his ability to fulfil them. However, at the end of the poem he turns away from the present completely, and begins an imaginary conversation with men who lived far away and long ago. He is able to achieve freedom from suffering by imagining himself in a fictive identity, and *Idyll* 12 therefore makes an interesting comparison with the bucolic poems in this respect.

IDYLL 6

Idyll 6 is in many ways the most enigmatic of the bucolic poems. The poem begins with Theocritus addressing a friend, much as he does in the opening of *Idyll* 11 and *Idyll* 13 (6.1–5):

> Δαμοίτας καὶ Δάφνις ὁ βουκόλος εἰς ἕνα χῶρον
> τὰν ἀγέλαν ποκ', Ἄρατε, συνάγαγον· ἧς δ' ὁ μὲν αὐτῶν
> πυρρός, ὁ δ' ἡμιγένειος· ἐπὶ κράναν δέ τιν' ἄμφω
> ἑσδόμενοι θέρεος μέσῳ ἄματι τοιάδ' ἄειδον.
> πρᾶτος δ' ἄρξατο Δάφνις, ἐπεὶ καὶ πρᾶτος ἔρισδεν.

Damoetas and Daphnis the cowherd once drove their herd together into one place, Aratus. One of them was red-haired, the other was just getting his beard. Both sat down at a certain spring and in the heat of a summer day they sang thus. And Daphnis began first, because he first proposed a contest.

There is much here that resembles *Idyll* 11: the address to Aratus, the presentation of bucolic lovers in their youthful prime, who are made to sit down and sing for the poem's addressee, the explicit formulation of the poet's invention – "they sang thus" – with which their songs are introduced. Yet the differences are also immediately apparent; Theocritus gives no indication of why he is writing this poem to Aratus, and there is consequently no sense that the bucolic characters are being introduced as an example or a response to a behavior in the real world that Theocritus shares with his friend.[2]

It has frequently been argued that in narrative fiction the narrator's own evaluative stance towards the story he tells points to its significance for the reader.[3] Presenting a story, whether narrative or dramatic, as the illustration of a gnomic proposition, as Theocritus tells the stories of Polyphemus and Heracles in *Idyll* 11 and *Idyll* 13, is perhaps the most obvious way to ensure that the reader gets their point. Here narrative is most obviously "a situation-bound transaction between two parties . . . an exchange resulting from the desire of at least one of these parties," such that narrative meaning is "a function of the situation in which narratives occur."[4] In drama, however, where there is no narrator to guide us, the point of the story will be less obvious. Yet, as Ross Chambers has observed of *Othello*, storytelling situations within a dramatic work will often suggest our response to the play in which they appear. As Desdemona's father recognizes the "mighty magic" of the tales Othello tells his daughter, so we see his own vulnerability to the seductive fictions of Iago, and are able to construe various models and anti-models of storytelling within the play.[5] Likewise, in *Idyll* 1 the goatherd's responses to the visual fiction of the decorated bowl and the dramatic performance of "The Sorrows of Daphnis" key our response to the fictional world in which they occur. While the point of dramatic fiction may be less obvious, it may nonetheless be legible in the dramatic situation if we attend to the outcome of any storytelling situations within it.[6]

If, then, Theocritus does not explicitly offer the fictional world of *Idyll* 6 to Aratus as the exemplification of a gnomic proposition, what is the dramatic situation that it produces in which we might discover its point? What are the consequences of the story for characters and reader? What we find when we reach the world of the poem is a surprise. We leave the

---

[2] Cf. Fantuzzi (2004) 170–71, who notes *Idylls* 6's variation of the structuring device of *Idylls* 11 and 13.
[3] See, for example, Brooks (1984) 35, 236 for modern prose fiction, Labov (1972) on "point" in oral storytelling, and my comments on *Idyll* 13 in the previous chapter.
[4] Prince (1988) 7.   [5] Chambers (1984) 219.
[6] Prince (1988) 7, commenting on the work of Chambers, notes that he "has insisted on the importance of reading narrative meaning as a function of the situation in which narratives occur and on the equal importance of reading *in* narratives the situation they produce as giving them their point."

frame narration in the expectation of a song contest between Daphnis and Damoetas, but the first words that we hear from Daphnis make little sense as a fulfilment of this promise (6.6–9):

> βάλλει τοι, Πολύφαμε, τὸ ποίμνιον ἁ Γαλάτεια
> μάλοισιν, δυσέρωτα καὶ αἰπόλον ἄνδρα καλεῦσα·
> καὶ τύ νιν οὐ ποθόρησθα, τάλαν, τάλαν, ἀλλὰ κάθησαι
> ἁδέα συρίσδων.

Galeteia throws apples at your flock, Polyphemus, and calls you a wretched lover and a goatherd. And you do not look at her, you wretch, but sit sweetly playing your pipe.

Not only is Daphnis apparently addressing Polyphemus and not Damoetas (a situation that no other bucolic poem could have prepared us for); what he is saying to him contradicts everything we know about the Cyclops from *Idyll* 11.[7] Now it is the nymph who is in love with him and has left the sea to solicit his affections, while Polyphemus is either indifferent to her charms or master of his own desire to such a degree that he is able to feign indifference to her. Daphnis thus fictionalizes the Cyclops in his own performance for Damoetas, just as Theocritus fictionalizes him for Nicias in *Idyll* 11. By setting his character's imaginative reinvention of Polyphemus against his own, Theocritus does away with the uniqueness and authoritative status of his own bucolic Cyclops. What he did to Homer, he has Daphnis do to him. Moreover, it is not just Polyphemus who is raised to another power of fictionality by this second reinvention. Daphnis himself, who in Thyrsis' impersonation of him in *Idyll* 1 appeared as a tragic hero, overpowered, as it seems, by some hopeless infatuation, here appears as the witty advocate of a light-hearted *carpe diem* approach to desire, who mocks Polyphemus for not availing himself of the opportunity for pleasure that Galateia is offering him (6.15–19). His character, too, is quite different in the two poems in which he appears as himself and as the object of another character's impersonation.

It has been argued that Theocritus intended the Daphnis of *Idyll* 6 to be understood as a different character than the Daphnis of *Idyll* 1, and that the poet is simply careless in his use of names because he published his poems individually, and did not envisage them being read together in a collection.[8] Regardless of the details of publication, this claim seems to

---

[7] Several scholars have argued that *Idyll* 6 is written after *Idyll* 11, and presupposes knowledge of it; see Ott (1969) 72–76, Köhnken (1996), and Hunter (1999) 244. Daphnis' performance certainly creates a Cyclops who is older and more self-assured than his counterpart in *Idyll* 11, so that the dramatic setting of *Idyll* 6 has to be later.
[8] Wendel (1899) 2–4.

me unlikely. *Idyll* 6 quite deliberately toys with the idea of the Cyclops – the possibility of a Cyclops still more surprising than those of *Idyll* 11 or Philoxenus (it is the variety of the tradition that is invoked, not merely that of his own corpus). *Idyll* 6, in other words, is a poem that is about the malleability of characters in a fictionalized literary tradition, so that to imagine that Theocritus could have been unaware of this possibility in the case of Daphnis (that the Daphnis of *Idyll* 6 could have been mistaken for the Daphnis of *Idyll* 1, or vice versa, depending on which appeared first) seems to be highly implausible (and likewise in the case of Comatas, who, like Daphnis, appears as himself in *Idyll* 5, and as the subject of someone else's song in *Idyll* 7).[9]

By contrast, the irony that the poem exploits is that we learn less about a character when he appears in his own person than we do when he appears as the object of another character's impersonation. When we think of Daphnis, we think first of all of *Idyll* 1, not of *Idyll* 6, though in the former Daphnis is not actually present in the poem at all, but is made manifest solely through Thyrsis' impersonation of him. Conversely, when he does appear in person in *Idyll* 6, his character consists of the ability to make another bucolic character the object of his own impersonation. Daphnis is more palpable, more present when he is projected by someone else's impersonation than when he appears in his own person. Fictionalizing self-projection is thus the most characteristic form of subjectivity in the bucolic poems – it is by pretending to be others that the characters are most truly themselves.

Damoetas is also witty and self-assured when he takes on the persona of Polyphemus (6.21–28):

> εἶδον, ναὶ τὸν Πᾶνα, τὸ ποίμνιον ἁνίκ'ἔβαλλε,
> κοὔ μ'ἔλαθ', οὐ τὸν ἐμὸν τὸν ἕνα γλυκύν, ᾧ ποθορῶμι
> ἐς τέλος (αὐτὰρ ὁ μάντις ὁ Τήλεμος ἔχθρ' ἀγορεύων
> ἐχθρὰ φέροι ποτὶ οἶκον, ὅπως τεκέεσσι φυλάσσοι)·
> ἀλλὰ καὶ αὐτὸς ἐγὼ κνίζων πάλιν οὐ ποθόρημι,
> ἀλλ' ἄλλαν τινὰ φαμὶ γυναῖκ' ἔχεν· ἁ δ' ἀίοισα
> ζαλοῖ μ', ὦ Παιάν, καὶ τάκεται, ἐκ δὲ θαλάσσας
> οἰστρεῖ παπταίνοισα ποτ' ἄντρα τε καὶ ποτὶ ποίμνας.

---

[9] Kossaifi (2002) 355–56 suggests that, "en donnant un nom identique à deux personnages opposées, le poète veut parfois montrer les facettes différentes d'un même concept." Thus, for example, Tityrus in *Idyll* 3 looks after the sheep of the nameless goatherd as he sings for Amaryllis, while in *Idyll* 7 he is a singer himself, thereby revealing the reciprocity of bucolic song, which requires its herdsmen to be both performers and audience. Cf. the discussion of Daphnis in the post-Theocritean *Idyll* 8 as a combination of traits belonging to the Theocritean Daphnis in Fantuzzi (1998), to which I will turn in my conclusion.

I saw her, by Pan, when she was throwing apples at the flock, and she did not escape my attention, or my one sweet eye, with which I pray I may see until the end (but may the prophet Telemus who prophesied evil to me take it home with him instead, and keep it for his children). For myself, to tease her back, don't look at her, but say I have another woman, and she hears it and is jealous, o Paean, consumed with desire, and from the sea peeks longingly at my cave and my flocks.

What were unconscious allusions to the *Odyssey* in the Cyclops' mouth in *Idyll* 11 become conscious references when Damoetas impersonates Polyphemus. He refers to the prophecy of the seer Telemus, who, as the Cyclops recalls after his blinding, had predicted it (*Odyssey* 9.507–12). Moreover, rather than being willing to sacrifice his one eye, a source of his ugliness as he saw it in *Idyll* 11, for Galateia, Damoetas' Polyphemus views it as the instrument of his power over the Nymph and, like his gleaming teeth, a source of beauty when he views himself reflected in the ocean (6.34–38). He is likewise able to feign to Galateia what he imagined for himself at the end of *Idyll* 11, that, because of his vast pastoral holdings, he would be an object of desire for women on the land. However, while in *Idyll* 6 he is not naïve as he is in that poem, he is still bucolic; to avoid the evil consequence of seeing his own reflection, he says: "I spat three times into my chest, as the old woman Cotyttaris taught me" (6.39–40). The rustic magic, and the old woman who is its source, recall *Idyll* 3: Agroeo the sieve diviner and the premonitions of the future from symptoms in his own body by which the goatherd anticipates the appearance of Amaryllis.

The performances of Daphnis and Damoetas embed resistance to authoritative interpretations of the bucolic characters in the collection itself. There can be no final understanding of their character, because their character is essentially labile and performative. It is manifested in song rather than found through introspection; possible selves, like possible worlds, are, in Kripke's terms, stipulated, not discovered.[10] No matter then that this is not the real Polyphemus (or the real bucolic Polyphemus). For if this is the real Daphnis, he is present only in his performance of a part, and is less substantial in his own person than when he is impersonated by Thyrsis in *Idyll* 1. What, then, is Aratus to make of this exchange? As I observed earlier, "point" in narrative may be got either from the narrator's reflection on the events of his story or from the characters' own responses within it. Here we get both, for after Damoetas is done with his impersonation of the Cyclops Theocritus comments (6.42–46):

[10] Kripke (1980) 43–44.

Becoming bucolic

Τόσσ'εἰπὼν τὸν Δάφνιν ὁ Δαμοίτας ἐφίλησε·
χὠ μὲν τῷ σύριγγ', ὁ δὲ τῷ καλὸν αὐλὸν ἔδωκεν.
αὔλει Δαμοίτας, σύρισδε δὲ Δάφνις ὁ βούτας·
ὠρχεῦντ'ἐν μαλακᾷταὶ πόρτιες αὐτίκα ποίᾳ.
νίκη μὲν οὐδάλλος, ἀνήσσατοι δ'ἐγένοντο.

With these words Damoetas kissed Daphnis, and the former gave the latter a pipe, and the latter gave the former a beautiful flute. Damoetas plays the flute, and Daphnis the cowherd plays the pipe. Immediately the calves danced in the soft grass. Neither won, they were both undefeated.

As at the end of *Idyll* 1, the goatherd is visibly delighted with the performance he has just witnessed. Moreover, as Thyrsis' performance in *Idyll* 1 draws out the similarity of Daphnis both to himself and his audience the goatherd, so here too the outcome of the exchange of songs is to blur the difference between the two herdsmen. Damoetas gives Daphnis a *syrinx*, Daphnis gives Damoetas an *aulos*, and they play these instruments not to discover a competitive edge, but in harmonious consort. The exchange suggests equivalence, and even their animals participate in this happy outcome as they dance to the music in the soft grass. The almost comic exuberance of the dancing calves forces us to attend to the poem's fictionality and to the importance of fictionality in the self-projection of its dramatic characters.

Even if Aratus is the friend of Theocritus whose unhappy love for a boy is alluded to in *Idyll* 7, the message he has for him here is anything but obvious.[11] For the poem hardly contains a program for action. Like *Idyll* 11, it seems to suggest the importance of imaginative experience in human communication, particularly insofar as that experience takes the form of role play. The herdsmen's own response to one another's adoption of an imaginative persona is the only clue we have in responding to the poem, and their delight must largely stem from their success in shedding their own identities for the duration of their songs. This interpretation is further suggested by the concluding narration, where Theocritus tells us that, after they had become Polyphemus and his advisor, they gave one another musical instruments and began to play on them. This is like a reprise of the exchange of songs insofar as, when they play, they become virtually indistinguishable from one other – the loss of self in the musical performance parallels the assumption of a fictional identity in the songs. If there is a message here, it would seem to be that the pleasures of bucolic

---

[11] Bowie (1996) suggests that the poem is Theocritus' guarded declaration of feeling for him. If so, it is so unemphatic one could hardly imagine it being greeted with a great deal of enthusiasm. See also the reservations of Hunter (1999) 244.

song and bucolic impersonation are their own reward, even without the pain of erotic desire that in *Idyll* 11 makes this distraction desirable.[12]

The bucolic characters thus shift between dramatic levels, depending on whether they are imagined by the poet or by other characters. Polyphemus appears as Theocritus' example in *Idyll* 11 and Simichidas' example in *Idyll* 7, but as the object of Damoetas' impersonation in *Idyll* 6. Comatas appears as himself in *Idyll* 5, and as the object of Lycidas' wish in *Idyll* 7. However, it is particularly instructive in this respect to consider Daphnis in the authentic and the spurious *Idylls*. Daphnis appears as the object of Thyrsis' impersonation in *Idyll* 1, as the subject of a song that Lycidas will hear at his rustic symposium in *Idyll* 7, and as a singer who teases his friend Damoetas as if the latter were Polyphemus in *Idyll* 6. In *Idyll* 1, then, Daphnis is at one remove from the poem's first dramatic level, in *Idyll* 7 at two removes, while in *Idyll* 6, in which he appears as a character, he does not speak as himself, in order to address his friend at the level of dramatic fiction for which the introductory verses have prepared us, but through a secondary persona he has adopted. Whether he speaks as impersonator or object of impersonation, the name "Daphnis" points to the theatrical nature of bucolic song, and the fictionalizing self-projection it encourages. In *Idyll* 8, by contrast, Daphnis and Menalcas appear as boys, while in *Idyll* 9 they compete in a song contest; in *Idyll* 27 a youthful Daphnis seduces a girl. All three poems invent new episodes in the life of Daphnis, but the role play of the authentic *Idylls* has disappeared; Daphnis is simply a character, and his name merely a sign of the pastoral genre. The projection of inner experience into imaginative role play seems therefore to be a defining feature of bucolic character in the authentic *Idylls*, particularly insofar as it provides a means of escape from the traumatic experience of unfulfiled desire. It will be interesting, therefore, to consider the part of such therapeutic role play in *Idyll* 12, which shares many unacknowledged similarities with the pastoral poems.

IDYLL 12

Idyll 12 is one of the least studied poems in the Theocritean corpus. A detailed account of its narrative structure and technique will, however, reveal a particularly intriguing example of the Theocritean role poem, with

---

[12] Marco Fantuzzi has suggested to me by email that the final lines of Daphnis' song – "What is not beautiful, Polyphemus, has surely often looked beautiful to love" (6.18–19) – is in fact the poem's gnomic proposition, here moved from the frame, where it appears in *Idyll* 11 and *Idyll* 13, to the dramatic exchange. From this perspective, the value of assuming a fictional identity is clear, for the impersonator can thereby see himself through the eyes of another.

a number of interesting resemblances to the pastoral *Idylls*. The *Idyll* is a monologue by an unnamed speaker, expressing delight at the return of his "beloved boy" (12.1) after an absence of two days. The opening verses greet his beloved – "you have come, dear boy, after two days and nights you have come" (12.1–2) – in a way that recalls Sappho 48 – "you have come, and I was longing for you" – and has its literary origin in Eumaeus' greeting of Telemachus at *Odyssey* 16.23–29: "You have come, Telemachus, sweet light . . ."[13] This greeting is, however, followed by a series of comparisons which are lacking in Sappho and Homer (12.3–9):[14]

ὅσσον ἔαρ χειμῶνος, ὅσον μῆλον βραβίλοιο
ἥδιον, ὅσσον ὄις σφετέρης λασιωτέρη ἀρνός,
ὅσσον παρθενικὴ προφέρει τριγάμοιο γυναικός,
ὅσσον ἐλαφροτέρη μόσχου νεβρός, ὅσσον ἀηδών
συμπάντων λιγύφωνος ἀοιδοτάτη πετεηνῶν,
τόσσον ἔμ' εὔφρηνας σὺ φανείς, σκιερὴν δ' ὑπὸ φηγόν
ἠελίου φρύγοντος ὁδοιπόρος ἔδραμον ὥς τις.

As spring is sweeter than winter, as the apple is sweeter than the sloe, as a ewe is woollier than its lamb, as a maiden is better than a thrice-married woman, as a fawn is friskier than a calf, as the clear-voiced nightingale is the most songful of all winged creatures, even so your appearance made me glad, and like a traveler when the sun is scorching I ran beneath a shady oak.

The speaker begins his encomium with two unremarkable comparisons: "as spring is sweeter than winter, as the apple is sweeter than the sloe . . ." The next, however, appears to reverse the priority of youth over age that one would expect in the praise of the beloved: "as a ewe is woollier than its lamb . . ."[15] And while what follows – "as a maiden is better than a thrice-married woman" – appears to restore it, some questions are raised by the

---

[13] Attempts have been made to identify this opening with the kinds of welcoming speech outlined by Menander Rhetor in his second treatise. Thus Giangrande (1971) 38 refers to it as an *epibaterios logos* (Menander 377.31–388.16), while Cairns (1972) 18 calls it a *prosphonetikos logos* (Menander 414.32–418.4). For Menander, however, both are types of public political oratory conducted in prose. The *epibaterios* is "either (i) an address to one's native city on return, or (ii) an address to a city one visits, or (iii) an address to a visiting governor," while the *prosphonetikos* is a small-scale encomium of a ruler (Russell and Wilson [1981] *ad loc.* 377.32–378.4). Thus, while both types of speech may ultimately derive from poetic greetings such as those in Homer and Sappho, I accept the conclusion of Russell and Wilson (1981) xxxiii–xxxiv that the similarity of expression in *Idyll* 12 is better understood as imitation of a familiar poetic *topos* rather than as "a clear generic announcement" (Cairns [1972] 25). Cf. Wilamowitz (1924) II.141, on Lycidas' song in *Idyll* 7: "Es lehrt gar nichts und kann nur verwirren, wenn man das Lied ein προπεμπτικόν nennt; man läuft Gefahr, die Rhetorik heranzuziehen, die hier nichts zu suchen hat."

[14] Sappho 48 proceeds directly to the effect of the beloved's arrival – "you cooled my heart which was burning with desire" – and Eumaeus, having expressed his fear that he might not see Telemachus again, continues: "but come now, enter, dear child, so that I may delight my heart looking at you inside" (16.25–26).

[15] Cf. Kelly (1979) 58.

choice of epithet. Gow points out that τρίγαμος, "thrice-married," in Stesichorus *PMG* 223, and τριάνωρ, "having three husbands," at Lycophron 851, refer to Helen.[16] Whether or not one understands a specific allusion, "thrice-married" suggests a much more nuanced appreciation of the relative claims of innocence and experience than, for example, "riper than a pear," which is used of a boy whose charms are fading at *Idyll* 7.120.[17] For while the virgin girl reflects the attractiveness of the "beloved boy," the suggestion of Helen in the older woman to whom she is compared prevents the comparison from appearing entirely to the speaker's disadvantage. As in the previous assertion of the ewe's superiority to its lamb, the speaker appears sensitive to the ways in which the juxtaposition of young and old mirrors his own relationship with his youthful lover. Thus, as if shying away from his own reflection in an image that pits youth against age, his next comparison effaces this difference altogether, and the two young animals are all but indistinguishable: "as a fawn is friskier than a calf . . ." In the final comparison the speaker switches from comparatives to a superlative: "as the clear-voiced nightingale is the most songful of all winged creatures . . ." Here too there seems to be a hint of self-praise, given that the speaker is in the role of "clear-voiced singer," and his greeting as a whole suggests that it has been composed with one eye on its author all along.

The series of images has provoked considerable disagreement among the poem's commentators. Gow was offended by its "apparent lack of emotional restraint,"[18] while for Giangrande it marks the vulgarity of an ignorant rustic with a tendency "to grotesquely overdo things, to overcompensate, as it were, for his lack of articulateness and genuine education."[19] For Cairns the hyperbole marks the poem's generic affiliations,[20] while Hunter has emphasized its dramatic function in conveying the speaker's emotional excitement.[21] It will be helpful therefore to look at another occasion in the *Idylls* when a speaker employs a similar series of rustic images. Thus Polyphemus, conjuring up, if not Galateia herself, then at least her image, begins his song (11.19–21):

> ὦ λευκὰ Γαλάτεια, τί τὸν φιλέοντ' ἀποβάλλῃ,
> λευκοτέρα πακτᾶς ποτιδεῖν, ἁπαλωτέρα ἀρνός,
> μόσχω γαυροτέρα, φιαρωτέρα ὄμφακος ὠμᾶς;

O white Galateia, why do you spurn one who loves you, whiter than cream cheese to look at, softer than a lamb, friskier than a calf, sleeker than an unripe grape?

---

[16] Gow (1952) *ad loc.* 12.5.
[17] For the connection of this image to the invective of Archilochus, see Henrichs (1980).
[18] Gow (1952) II.221.　　[19] Giangrande (1971) 43.　　[20] Cairns (1972) 25.
[21] Hunter (1996a) 189–90.

When the two series are compared, their functions are clearly different. Polyphemus' hyperbole is an attempt to describe Galateia directly, and is a spontaneous characterization of what he finds attractive in her. The speaker of *Idyll* 12, on the other hand, uses the comparisons not to praise or describe his beloved but to calculate his own feelings in response to his arrival: "As spring is sweeter than winter . . . even so your appearance made me glad." Moreover, as I argued in the previous chapter, the qualities that Polyphemus discovers in Galateia in the end defy his powers of description, and so suggest the limits of comparison itself. One might also compare Bucaeus' song at *Idyll* 10.36–37, where the attempt to praise his beloved results in a feeling of inadequacy, and silence: "Lovely Bombyca, your feet are dice, your voice nightshade; your ways I truly cannot speak of." Thus, while the comparisons in *Idyll* 12 resemble the language of bucolic infatuation in their content (fruits, birds, baby animals), the speaker's use of them sets him apart from Polyphemus and Bucaeus; while they strain metaphor to breaking point to express the intensity of their admiration, he offers a more self-conscious modulation of its laudatory powers: he never loses sight of his own reflection in his praise, and his final image is more about himself than his "beloved boy."

After the series of encomiastic metaphors the poem changes course (12.10–11):

> εἴθ' ὁμαλοὶ πνεύσειαν ἐπ' ἀμφοτέροισιν Ἔρωτες
> νῶιν, ἐπεσσομένοις δὲ γενοίμεθα πᾶσιν ἀοιδή·

If only equal loves breathed upon us both, and we might become a song for those who come after.

Who are these people who will come after him, and what kind of memorialization is craved here? Given the pederastic context, Gow preferred to see here a reference to Theognis 251 (Theognis and Kyrnos), rather than *Iliad* 6.354–58 (Helen and Paris),[22] and the pathos of this allusion has been explored at length by Hunter.[23] Here, then, I want merely to examine how the speaker of *Idyll* 12 has recourse to a voice other than his own when he approaches the topic of immortality. Theognis speaks of fame that he, as author, has already conferred upon his beloved (237): "I have given you wings." Moreover, the consequences of this immortality are expressed as a series of future indicatives that apply to the beloved alone and which culminate in the lines (251–52) to which *Idyll* 12.11 alludes: "You will be a song for those who come after." Theognis thus appears as a bestower of fame rather than in need of it himself, and his address to Kyrnos assumes a body

---

[22] Gow (1952) *ad loc.* 12.11. [23] Hunter (1996a) 190–92.

of poetry in which the speaker has already been immortalized as poet, and his addressee as lover. The speaker of *Idyll* 12, on the other hand, cannot make promises about the future that derive their performative authority from references to his own work. He can only wish that he and his partner might be remembered by others for the quality of their affection: "If only equal loves breathed upon us both, and we might become a song for those who come after." Rather than reflecting on the power of his own speech to confer fame on his "beloved boy," he can merely imagine the kind of thing that people might say about them both in the future if their relationship were different (12.12–16):

> "δίω δή τινε τώδε μετὰ προτέροισι γενέσθην
> φῶθ᾽, ὁ μὲν εἴσπνηλος, φαίη Ὠμυκλαϊάζων,
> τὸν δ᾽ἕτερον πάλιν, ὥς κεν ὁ Θεσσαλὸς εἴποι, ἀίτην.
> ἀλλήλους δ᾽ ἐφίλησαν ἴσῳ ζυγῷ. ἦ ῥα τότ᾽ἦσαν
> χρύσεοι πάλιν ἄνδρες, ὅτ᾽ ἀντεφίλησ᾽ ὁ φιληθείς."

"These were two splendid men amongst our ancestors, the one 'inspirer,' as one speaking in the Amyclean dialect would say, the other what a Thessalian would call 'listener.' They loved one other with equal yoke. There were indeed then golden men again, when the beloved loved in return."

While Theognis 237–54 looks sideways, as it were, deriving its authority from the corpus of the Theognis' poems, the speaker of *Idyll* 12 moves vertically between past and future to give shape to his fantasy. He uses the archaic εἴσπνηλος, "inspirer," and ἀίτης, "listener," to reimagine himself and his lover, but sets these archaic terms in the mouth of a speaker from the future.[24] Looking back to the present of *Idyll* 12, the latter will see not the asymmetrical attraction of an older lover and his youthful beloved but a relationship from which physical desire has been entirely effaced.

While the speaker cannot confer a future he can reimagine the present, and the terms in which he chooses to do so find an interesting echo in

---

[24] The speaker's manifest desire for lexical rarity is as immoderate as his other appetites. However, his particular choices (Amyclean and Thessalian) remain obscure. Given the interest in curious local pederastic festivals evinced by the end of the poem, a connection with the Amyclean cult of Hyacinthus may have motivated his decision to describe the term εἴσπνηλος as Amyclean rather than simply Laconian (Gow [1952] *ad loc.* 12.13f. points out that the two are less than twenty stades apart). For in one version of the myth Zephyrus causes the death of the beautiful youth whose favors he shared with Apollo by blowing (πνεῖν) the latter's discus off course – a story of pederastic jealousy much like the speaker's own, with the ironic complication that it takes place in the very golden age in which he feels their relationship would have been free of such problems. The attribution of ἀίτης to a Thessalian speaker is more puzzling, since the word has no known connections with Thessaly or any other dialect.

Idyll 7. In the song which he performs for the narrator Simichidas the goatherd Lycidas describes the torment of his desire for Ageanax (7.52–56), and then imagines a rustic symposium he will celebrate upon the latter's arrival in Mytilene (7.63–4). There he will hear songs on pastoral subjects, and these lead him to wish that he could share an ideal present with the singer Comatas (7.86–89):

> αἴθ' ἐπ' ἐμεῦ ζωοῖς ἐναρίθμιος ὤφελες ἦμεν,
> ὥς τοι ἐγὼν ἐνόμευον ἀν' ὤρεα τὰς καλὰς αἶγας
> φωνᾶς εἰσαΐων, τὺ δ' ὑπὸ δρυσὶν ἢ ὑπὸ πεύκαις
> ἁδὺ μελισδόμενος κατεκέκλισο, θεῖε Κομᾶτα.

If only you were numbered among the living in my day, so that I, pasturing your lovely sheep among the hills, might listen to your voice, and you, lying under oaks or under pines, sing sweetly, divine Comatas.

The polarity of lover and beloved with which the song began has been transmuted into a relationship between singer and audience, and it is clear that in this ideal world Lycidas would prefer the role of listener. *Idyll* 12 uses the same imagery in its progression from desire to idealization. The speaker's prayer seemed initially to be a plea for reciprocity: "would that equal loves breathed upon us both" (cf. "with equal yoke"). His lexical fantasy, on the other hand, imagines a relationship between an active "inspirer" and a passive "listener" similar to that between Comatas and Lycidas. However, while the lovers' roles will be as distinct as the dialects in which they are preserved, the speaker of *Idyll* 12, as we shall see, imagines himself as the "inspirer," and his beloved as his "charming listener" (12.20).

In both *Idylls* erotic dissatisfaction leads to literary invention, and this movement accounts for the structural similarity noted by Legrand: "Entre elle [*Id.* 12] et les chansons de l'idylle VII, il existe une parenté. Ici et là, le thème sentimental est indiqué plutôt qu'il n'est traité, et sert de prétexte à toute sorte de développements parasites."[25] Lycidas' song in *Idyll* 7 begins as an expression of his desire for Ageanax, but this desire is displaced by the embedded narratives of Tityrus, Daphnis, and Comatas. In *Idyll* 12 the speaker's response to his infatuation is to invent a song that will be sung about him by men of the future, and this brief fantasy derives its imaginative appeal from the distinct accents of Thessalian and Amyclean it contains. Lycidas and the speaker of *Idyll* 12 thus attempt to escape their present pain by inventing other voices, which they imagine themselves hearing even as

[25] Legrand (1925) 80.

they incorporate them in their own speech, and these fictions in both cases involve an idealized image of their composers.[26]

Unlike Theognis, then, the speaker of *Idyll* 12 cannot confer immortality with his own voice, and so he prays for the kind of love that could give him an afterlife in song (12.17–21):

> εἰ γὰρ τοῦτο, πάτερ Κρονίδη, πέλοι, εἰ γάρ, ἀγήρῳ
> ἀθάνατοι, γενεῆς δὲ διηκοσίῃσιν ἔπειτα
> ἀγγείλειεν ἐμοί τις ἀνέξοδον εἰς Ἀχέροντα·
> "ἡ σὴ νῦν φιλότης καὶ τοῦ χαρίεντος ἄιτεω
> πᾶσι διὰ στόματος, μετὰ δ' ἠιθέοισι μάλιστα."

If only, father Zeus, if only, ageless gods, this might be, and someone, two hundred generations from now, might announce to me in inescapable Acheron: "The present love of you and your charming listener is upon everyone's lips, and especially those of unmarried youths."

The mention of the underworld seems once again to recall Theognis 237–54, where the poet promises Kyrnos that he will not be deprived of fame, even when he goes "down into the much-lamenting house of Hades, under the depths of dark earth" (243–44). Here too, however, there are characteristic changes. Firstly, the lover will not simply descend into Hades while the fame produced by the speaking voice remains upon earth. Instead, the speaker imagines himself in the underworld, where an anonymous messenger will deliver a report of his continuing fame in the world above. Moreover, this vivid future scene also belongs to the speaker's continuing attempt to reimagine his present. In verse 12 the person from the future uses the deictic δίω . . . τώδε, "these two," to refer to the lovers not as they actually are, but as the speaker of *Idyll* 12 would like them to become, and here too "the present love of you and your charming listener," spoken by the visitor to

---

[26] De Jong (1987) 77–78 observes a similar phenomenon in the *Iliad*. In a study of *tis*-speeches she notes that on two occasions Hector imagines an anonymous future speaker, whose potential speech is embedded in his own, speaking an "oral epitaph" for himself (6.460–61) and for an opponent (7.89–90). On the first occasion he imagines the speaker looking at Andromache who is still alive, and recalling that she was Hector's wife, on the second looking at the tomb of a warrior, and recalling that Hector was the man who killed him. The oral epitaph differs from an actual epitaph in that "it is spoken by passers-by, whereas real epitaphs are spoken by the stone and addressed to passers-by," and that "the content of the 'epitaph' reveals more about the character speaking than about the person it is supposed to talk about." The situation envisaged by the speaker of *Idyll* 12 is rather less concrete. Since the anonymous future speaker refers to the lovers in the past tense, he is not looking at them in person, as Hector's first speaker is looking at Andromache. On the other hand, neither does he refer to a memorial like the tomb that Hector's second speaker sees. The speaker of *Idyll* 12 has therefore put the "epitaphic demonstrative" – τώδε, "these two" (12) – into the mouth of his future speaker without any indication of how it got there.

Hades, refers to an affection that does not yet exist, since it is the object of the speaker's wish in verses 10–11. Formally, the speaker of the *Idyll* has again voiced his reconstruction of the present as embedded direct speech by an anonymous future speaker, and here too the invention expresses his desire to be not the composer, but the theme, of erotic song. Finally, it is obvious that, despite his plea for reciprocity, it is his own fame that concerns him most; the report to the underworld will be delivered "to me," not "to us" (12.19).

After the bookish fantasy of these embedded narratives the speaker returns to reality with the observation that such matters are in the hands of the gods (12.22–23), and that by reverting to erotic encomium he will at least not be convicted of falsehood (12.23–24): "but in praising your beauty I will not grow pimples on my slender nose" (*pseudea*, or pimples, being the sign of a liar).[27] The bathetic image contrasts with the idealized lovers that his archaizing imagination created, the "inspirer" and "listener," donor and recipient of a pure, disembodied breath. Unlike Lycidas, who is able to transmute his erotic yearning into the desire for pastoral song, the speaker's imagination is not yet strong enough to distract him from his lover entirely, and the fantasies of verses 12–21, which rework his present situation, do not offer lasting escape. So he lapses back into the emotional "arithmetic"[28] with which the poem began (12.25–26):

ἢν γὰρ καί τι δάκῃς, τὸ μὲν ἀβλαβὲς εὐθὺς ἔθηκας,
διπλάσιον δ' ὤνησας, ἔχων δ' ἐπίμετρον ἀπῆλθον.

If you hurt me sometimes, you immediately set it right, so you confer a double benefit, and I depart with a profit.

As with the pimples on the nose, the language here is remarkably mundane; ἐπίμετρον, "profit," is elsewhere confined to prose,[29] and it is a measure of the speaker's ultimate imaginative success that his accounting imagery will appear transfigured in the poem's conclusion.

His final fantasy is a description of the festival of Diocles in Megara, which is appended to the hesitant strivings that precede it as an exultant apostrophe of the Megarians themselves, without any kind of transitional motif or syntactical connection; the speaker is no longer even addressing his ostensible audience. Just as in the series of images with which the poem begins, however, what starts off as the praise of an addressee soon begins to look very much like an encomium of the speaker himself (12.27–31):

[27] Gow (1952) *ad loc.* 12.23f.   [28] Walsh (1990) 19.   [29] Gow (1952) *ad loc.* 12.26.

Νισαῖοι Μεγαρῆες, ἀριστεύοντες ἐρετμοῖς,
ὄλβιοι οἰκείοιτε, τὸν Ἀττικὸν ὡς περίαλλα
ξεῖνον ἐτιμήσασθε, Διοκλέα τὸν φιλόπαιδα.
αἰεί οἱ περὶ τύμβον ἀολλέες εἴαρι πρώτῳ
κοῦροι ἐριδμαίνουσι φιλήματος ἄκρα φέρεσθαι·

Nisaean Megarians, excellent with the oar, may you dwell in good fortune, since you honored superlatively your Attic guest, boy-loving Diocles. Every year in early spring a host of youths compete around his tomb to win the prize for kissing.

No mention is made of Diocles' having sacrificed his own life on the battlefield to save that of his lover (which is what the Diocleia commemorated), and, in the speaker's vision, he is honored simply as an older lover. Similarly, he transfers the blessing that is conferred upon the victor in poems celebrating athletic achievements from the competitor to the judge (12.34–37):

ὄλβιος ὅστις παισὶ φιλήματα κεῖνα διαιτᾷ
ἦ που τὸν χαροπὸν Γανυμήδεα πόλλ᾽ ἐπιβῶται
Λυδίῃ ἶσον ἔχειν πέτρῃ στόμα, χρυσὸν ὁποίη
πεύθονται, μὴ φαῦλος, ἐτήτυμον ἀργυραμοιβοί.

Blessed is he who judges those kisses for the boys. Surely he calls often upon bright-eyed Ganymede that he may have a mouth equal to the Lydian stone with which money-changers test true gold to see if it is false.

His reference to the Lydian stone, or *basanos*, marks a fantastic distance from the victory poems of Pindar and Bacchylides, where it is the guarantee that the poet's voice is speaking the truth; it is the touchstone, in other words, of a mouth that is singing, not kissing. The speaker thereby invests the festival with the same aura of unreality that pervades his embedded songs. However, while the account of the festival may be questionable from an antiquarian perspective, its erotic exuberance is undeniable. There is no resolution of the relationship between lover and beloved; after a greeting, a series of comparisons, a pair of wishes, and a prayer, the speech simply ends with an image of rapture: an umpire comparing kisses from a throng of anonymous young men. One might compare the end of *Idyll* 7, where, after addressing unanswered questions to the Castalian Nymphs about the experience he has just undergone, Simichidas expresses a wish that he may once again plant his winnowing fan before the altar of Demeter, whose statue smiles over the end of the poem. These fantasy endings contrast with the pastoral *Idylls*' tendency to close on a quiet or even bathetic note (*Idylls* 1, 3, 4, 11). Yet, by identifying in fantasy with the judge of the kissing competition, the speaker at last accepts the role of agent rather than object of commemoration, and this acceptance yields his most successful composition, as attachment to his beloved is effaced in an ecstasy of his own imagining. In the words of Legrand, "il en vient à oublier lui-même son bien-aimé, à commettre envers lui une infidélité de pensée, puisqu'il envie l'arbitre qui, à Mégare, reçoit et apprécie les caresses des concurrents."[30]

Earlier I cited Legrand's observation regarding the similarity between *Idyll* 12 and the songs of *Idyll* 7: "Le thème sentimental . . . sert de prétexte à toute sorte de développements parasites."[31] These "parasitic developments" can now be seen as the means by which the composer is able to escape his "sentimental theme." For just as in *Idyll* 7 the embedded narratives of Lycidas' song eventually involve him in an imaginative world that frees him of his desire for Ageanax, so here too "infidelity of thought" leads the speaker away from his lover and into the world of his own imagination. Nevertheless, while *Idyll* 12 offers many points of resemblance to the pastoral poems in its themes, imagery, and narrative complexity, one crucial question remains in determining its relationship to them: who speaks the poem? Is the voice purely textual, a persona of the poet himself, like Theognis 237–54, or should we imagine a dramatic character? The rustic imagery of verses 3–9 associates the speaker with pastoral lovers like Bucaeus and Polyphemus, and the pimples of verse 24 are found again at *Idyll* 9.30. Since this poem is a pastoral by someone other than Theocritus, the imitation would suggest that its writer thought *Idyll* 12 was pastoral too.[32]

There are some difficulties, however, in assigning it to a fictional character, a Polyphemus or a Bucaeus. The first of these is the Ionic dialect in which it is written, since the other dramatic poems, both rural and urban, are in Doric; the poem thus stands out from the Doric character poems, though the choice of Ionic itself remains obscure.[33] The second is that in other *Idylls* that consist wholly or in part of character monologue there are clear indications of the fictional identity of the speaker, and of the poem's dramatic setting. In *Idyll* 3 the goatherd identifies himself as such by his references to his flock and his companion (3.1–5), and his song is performed before the cave of Amaryllis (3.6). Similarly, in *Idyll* 11 Polyphemus is named in both the frame narrative and his own self-address (11.8, 72, 80), and he sings on a high rock by the seashore (11.17–18). Moreover, in both these poems it is clear that the addressee is absent, not simply because, as in

---

[30] Legrand (1925) 80.   [31] Legrand (1925) 80.
[32] Not so the scholiast, who in the Hypothesis describes the poem as spoken by the poet to his beloved (*Id.* 12 arg., Wendel [1914] 249). Cf. Gow (1952) II.221: "The Idyll is a monologue addressed by the poet to a boy whose two days' absence has seemed all too long."
[33] Cf. Gow (1952) II.221: "It is impossible to guess why a piece of such content should be written in Ionic hexameters."

Idyll 12, there is no reply, but because the speaker tells us so. The goatherd of *Idyll* 3 complains that the Nymph will not leave her cave (3.6), and Polyphemus that Galateia will not leave the sea (11.42, 63). We are therefore given plenty of details with which to imagine the scene of the performance. In *Idyll* 12, by contrast, there is no indication of a dramatic setting, no mention of the speaker's identity, and no sign of whether or not the boy is present to hear the speech addressed to him. While one might imagine him as a silent listener, like Simaetha's servant Thestylis in *Idyll* 2, or Tityrus in *Idyll* 3, the presence of these non-speaking characters is signaled by the speaker, and they offer opportunities for increased dramatization of the monologue.[34] Similarly, while no one expects a reply to songs like those in *Idylls* 3 and 11 (if the singer were not separated from the object of his desire he would have no reason to sing), an extended greeting without a response reads as a very peculiar kind of performance; it appears to be conducted for its own sake rather than for its natural function of greeting the new arrival.[35] While it is in keeping with the speaker's all too obvious concern for his own fame that we cannot tell whether his addressee is present or not, the absence of direct reference by which we might understand his presence extends to the physical setting as well, and should not, I believe, be explained simply as the solipsism of the dramatic character Theocritus has created. Rather, the unique combination of formal features – a fictional first-person speaker in the Ionic dialect without a narrative frame and with no indications of a dramatic setting within the speech itself – points to an intriguing curiosity in the cabinet of *Idylls*. For *Idyll* 12 lies midway between the textual drama of the Aeolic poems, with their range of addressees – the distaff of *Idyll* 28, the faithless boy of *Idyll* 29, and the poet's own heart in *Idyll* 30 – and the fully developed *mise en scène* of the dramatic poems.

In *Idyll* 3 the goatherd's song before the cave of Amaryllis appears to be a kind of private role play, in which he indulges temporarily while his animals

---

[34] On the use of the unspeaking addressee in mime, see Wiemken (1972) 22, Albert (1988) 80–83, and my Chapter 2.

[35] For Walsh (1990) 19–20, the poem departs from the rhetorical agenda signaled in the opening because it is spoken some time after the boy's arrival. As the speaker has already been relieved of his desire, he no longer has to conciliate or seduce, and his speech is free "to follow [his] unconstrained, autonomous thoughts." An interval between the speaker's gratification at the boy's return and the moment when the poem is delivered requires understanding the aorists in the opening – ἤλυθες (12.1), εὔφρηνας (12.8) – as simple past tenses. However, while Walsh (1990) 19 n. 53 criticizes Gow for "unaccountably" translating them as perfects – "Thou art come . . . so hast thou gladdened me" – the latter was presumably thinking of Telemachus' return at *Odyssey* 16.23, where, since he has just arrived, a perfect is required to render Eumaus' greeting, ἦλθες. Given that *Idyll* 12 contains no indication of the occasion of the speaker's delivery of his speech, I do not believe that one can decide between the different dramatic situations envisaged in these two versions.

are watched over by a friend. Only the reader of the poem witnesses his solitary performance. As he adopts a persona for the duration of his song, so he uses myth within it as a vehicle for his own imaginative experience. Rather than an attempt to persuade an addressee, his examples are a form of role play, mythical figures whom he longs to reenact. The speaker of *Idyll* 12 would also be the hero of his own tales. The poem is difficult to place because it exhibits features of the pastoral dramatic poems without projecting a fully realized setting through the speaker's words; it falls midway between genuine drama and poems spoken by a persona of the poet himself. Yet the shift from erotic distress to the freedom of imaginative self-absorption is shown quite clearly by the speaker's apostrophe of an imaginary ancient audience at the end of the poem. Like the bucolic characters, he purifies his own world of its shortcomings and so makes it an object to which he can aspire in his imaginary experience. In the next chapter I will look at the importance of this experience in the depiction of poetic apprenticeship and poetic autobiography in *Idyll* 7. In this poem, as many commentators have pointed out, there appears to be a deliberate attempt on the poet's part to counter the characterization of poetic experience as a form of distraction that not only lacks therapeutic value but is positively harmful to psychic well-being that Socrates presents in the *Phaedrus*. Before that, then, it will be well to conclude this chapter with a brief consideration of how far the poems I have discussed depart from the account of the relationship between mimetic experience and psychic health that is outlined in the *Republic*, Plato's fullest treatment of this subject.

In Book 10 (604b–605c), Plato contrasts two possibilities for a soul that is dealing with painful experience, on the one hand therapy (ἰατρική), on the other lamentation (θρηνῳδία). Lamentation, Socrates argues, belongs to the unreasoning part of the soul, and leads us to dwell on the painful experience in our memory in such a way that we relive its pain. In this respect it is the opposite of the therapy that philosophy provides, which analyzes the underlying causes of the pain, and so leads us to recognize that, as he has earlier claimed, "nothing in mortal life is worthy of great concern." Poetry that offers mimetic portrayals of suffering characters hinders this therapeutic process because these imitations "implant an evil constitution in their audience." Recurring here to the argument that was introduced in Book 3 (395c–d), when the distinction between mimetic poetry (poetry employing the direct speech of characters) and diegetic poetry (poetry in the voice of the poet) was first introduced, Socrates claims that fictional creations have power over our real lives because they leave behind in the soul residues of the mimetic character to which that soul responded with imaginative identification. These may seem harmless enough, but in the course of time they build up to the point where the soul's original appearance is as unrecognizable as that of the sea god Glaucus, who is so thoroughly encrusted with the detritus of his undersea world that his original shape is no longer apparent (611d). More dangerous still, not only do we easily forget that these residues are in fact alien to ourselves (401b–c), their presence may induce us to repeat the behavior of the mimetic character with which we first identified if suitable triggers are present in our real life, so that we will end up by responding to authentic pain with inauthentic behavior, without even being aware that we are doing so. The only remedy, Socrates argues, is to strip away these alien accretions so that the soul can embark upon the project of philosophical knowledge unhindered by these impediments.

It should be clear from the foregoing that Plato conceives of a relationship between an active poetic representation and a passive audience. Identification is something that just happens to us when we are exposed to mimetic literature, and its residues simply end up in our souls whether we like it or not. He never discusses the possibility of an elective relationship between particular listeners and particular mimetic characters, or even the possibility of elective affinity, the possibility that, even if they do not fully choose to identify with particular characters, particular listeners may nonetheless be predisposed towards some characters rather than others. The process by which the soul becomes burdened with mimetic residues seems to be as unwilled and as ineluctable as the process by which an object submerged in the sea is overwhelmed by marine parasites. The bucolic characters, by contrast, appear to be fully in command of their mimetic choices. They are freely chosen models for their behavior rather than virus-like intruders that subvert it. They allow the herdsmen to aspire to, and attain, states of themselves other than the present state of pain in which they find themselves. The poems, in other words, offer a vision of self-development that is based not upon the philosophical project of self-knowledge but upon the literary project of self-projection.[36] They show the necessary presence of fiction in any vision of selfhood in which the self posits a version of itself in imagination to which it aspires in reality, by demonstrating how identification with an imagined (and hence, from the perspective of the present,

---

[36] Or self-staging as Iser (1993) 303 calls it: "Staging is the indefatigable attempt to confront ourselves with ourselves, which can be done only by playing ourselves. It allow us, by means of simulacra, to lure into shape the fleetingness of the possible and to monitor the continual unfolding of ourselves into possible otherness." As he argues (24), pastoral is paradigmatic of literary fictionality in this respect because it "thematizes the act of fictionalizing, thereby enabling literary fictionality to be vividly perceived."

fictional) future self inevitably figures in any version of self-growth.[37] Pastoral rejects the idea that an original self can be present to itself as an object of knowledge as a dream of philosophy, and offers instead its own vision of a self that, through its encounters with fictional counterparts, is endlessly en route to its imagined possibilities.

[37] So Moran (1994) 75–106 in an important paper argues that the general problem of fictional emotions that has been a concern for philosophers is in fact a pseudo-problem insofar as the imaginative projection that is proper to our engagement with fictional worlds is in fact just the kind of intuitive projection that is involved in our real-world experience of modal operations, memory, sympathy, and so forth.

CHAPTER 4

From fiction to metafiction

Aristotle, as we have mentioned, thought of dramatic poetry as poetry from which the poet's own person was excluded, and praised Homer for approaching as closely as is possible in epic to this condition of drama. While other poets are constantly intruding into their poems, Homer, after a brief prologue, brings in a succession of dramatic characters who advance the plot through their interaction with one another (*Poetics* 24). Conversely Longinus, while fully acknowledging the dramatic quality of the *Iliad*, would read its drama not as an exclusion of the poet's self but as the form in which the vigor and plenitude of Homer's creative genius found their natural expression when the poet was at the height of his power. He contrasts this with the love of storytelling that marks the *Odyssey* and which is, he suggests, characteristic of the mellowing of Homer's power in old age (*On the Sublime* 9.13). The form of both poems may be understood as a projection of the poet's psychic life. While Aristotle sees drama as the goal to which all poetry should aspire, Longinus sees all poetry as, in effect, species of lyric that give concrete embodiment to the inner world of their writer in a variety of formal guises. Drama is simply the form this expression takes when the writer's need to externalize his inner life is most urgent and vigorous.

Longinus' position had long been anticipated by the Hellenistic poets. Consider these verses of Hermesianax (fr. 7 Powell):

> Αὐτὸς δ'οὗτος ἀοιδός, ὃν ἐκ Διὸς αἶσα φυλάσσει
> ἥδιστον πάντων δαίμονα μουσοπόλων
> λεπτὴν ᾗς Ἰθάκην ἐνετείνατο θεῖος Ὅμηρος
> ᾠδῇσιν πινυττῆς εἵνεκα Πηνελόπης,
> ἣν διὰ πολλὰ παθὼν ὀλίγην ἐσενάσσατο νῆσον,
> πολλὸν ἀπ' εὐρείης λειπόμενος πατρίδος·
> ἔκλεε δ' Ἰκαρίου τε γένος καὶ δῆμον Ἀμύκλου
> καὶ Σπάρτην, ἰδίων ἁπτόμενος παθέων.

And the Bard himself, whom the justice of Zeus maintains to be the sweetest spirit of all the race of singers, divine Homer, worked up slender Ithaca in his songs for the sake of shrewd Penelope, on whose account he traveled to that little island, suffering greatly, leaving his own wide homeland far behind. And he celebrated the family of Icarius, and the people of Amyclas, and Sparta, drawing on his own experiences.

Hermesianax' catalogue poem *Leontion*, a long fragment of which is preserved by Athenaeus, consists of a series of miniature biographies of the Greek poets that playfully explore the notion treated so seriously by Longinus that a poet's work can be considered as a fictional analogue of his own experience. So here it is Homer himself who makes the long journey to Ithaca for the love of Penelope that in the *Odyssey* appears as the voyage of his hero Odysseus. This is by no means the most outlandish of Hermesianax' tales; Hesiod's poems, we learn, are the outcome of his infatuation with the Ascraian girl Ehoia, whose name is derived from the opening formula of the *Catalogue of Women* (ἢ οἵη). Hermesianax makes no attempt to make his stories credible; indeed, the gap between their evident erudition and the blatantly fantastic use to which this erudition is put is perhaps the first thing about his poem that calls for explanation.[1] If Hemesianax knows as much about poets and poetry as his work would seem to indicate, why is it that this knowledge is used to construct a series of narratives that give the impression of having been written by someone who knew nothing about either?

The lives of the Greek poets have often been treated as if they were produced by naïve projection of details from the poetry.[2] No one, however, would, I think, mistake Hermesianax' biographies for a truth claim: they are simply too fantastic for that. Rather than falsehood, then, what we see here is a deliberate and transparent fictionalization of the relationship between poet's life and poet's work.[3] The Homeric poems are understood to be in some sense a fictionalization of Homer's own experience, but

---

[1] C. L. Caspers, in a paper to appear in the proceedings of the Seventh Groningen Workshop on Hellenistic Poetry, argues convincingly for the "fundamentally allusive nature of Hermesianax' biographical constructs," and hence for the enhanced appreciation of the poem that comes from studying it in the light of its intertextual affiliations. I thank him for sharing this paper with me in advance of its publication, and for his felicitous translation of ἰδίων ἁπτόμενος παθέων.

[2] So Lefkowitz (1981) viii. Pelling (1990) 219 wonders why "no tradition of systematic mendacity seems to have developed" in political biography as it did in the biography of cultural figures. The answer, I would suggest, is that there is no mystery to be accounted for in the former case; as Aristotle tells us, all men are political by nature; not all of them are poets, however.

[3] Cf. Bing (1993) 629 on the "bizarre fairyland, beguiling but weird," to which we are transported by Hermesianax.

Hermesianax does not attempt to give a true account of the relationship between the two; rather, he tells a story that in its manifest fictionality draws attention to the mystery of poetic creation. By inventing a narrative in which the experiences of Odysseus have become those of Homer himself, Hermesianax, in his blatant mystification of the relationship between a poet's life and his poetic work, points to the fact that we cannot give a reasonable explanation of this relationship, even though we may guess that the two are, in some way, related. For what experiences could possibly have given rise to the fantastic invention that is the *Odyssey*? The fictional story, on the other hand, recaptures the wonder of poetic creation that for an earlier time was expressed by locating the source of poetic stories with the Muses.

Hermesianax' poem is a useful introduction to Theocritus' *Idyll* 7 because many of its themes recur in a more nuanced way there. For the poem presents itself as the autobiography of a poet, or, to be more precise, the autobiographical account of a moment of decisive importance in the life of a poet. As we shall see, however, reality effects coexist with elements of manifest fiction, so that it is impossible to understand the poem as straightforward autobiographical narration. Rather, like Hermesianax' poem, it belongs to a special genre of poetic biography, which tells of poetic inspiration by mingling biographical detail with transparent invention. In *Idyll* 7 a speaker named Simichidas recalls how he traveled from the city of Cos to a harvest festival at the country estate of some friends. On the way he and his traveling companions met a goatherd named Lycidas, and the two of them exchanged songs before their paths diverged. Lycidas tells of his love for a boy, but soon turns from erotic to pastoral themes. He imagines the songs that will be sung for him at a rustic symposium he is to host, and recalls the famous bucolic singers of long ago. Simichidas' song remains within the present, but it is full of pastoral details as it cautions his friend Aratus against unrequited love. Lycidas gives Simichidas a staff as a token of his esteem, and the two parties go their separate ways. In the last part of the poem Simichidas gives an account of his surroundings at the festival that is both rapturous in tone and exceptionally rich in descriptive detail. He concludes by comparing the wine he drank there with wine drunk by Heracles and Polyphemus, and wishes that he might be allowed to experience the festival again in the future.

Idyll 7 thus recaps all the major themes of the bucolic poems. Lycidas is a none too realistic herdsman who wishes to emulate his legendary counterparts; in his song, longing for an ideal pastoral world takes the place of erotic desire. The song that Simichidas sings recalls the rustic imagery with which lovers express their desire in other bucolic poems. His careful evocation of his surroundings at the end of the poem is a more expansive version of the deictic gestures that bring to life the fictional worlds of *Idyll* 1 and *Idyll* 3. His use of Polyphemus and Heracles as imaginative equivalents for his own experience is like the use of such mythical examples by Theocritus' fictional herdsmen. Yet there are several features of the poem that prevent the reader from understanding it as simply an invented tale. The story is set on the island of Cos rather than in an undefined fictional place. Simichidas and Lycidas discuss real Hellenistic poets, and Simichidas' songs are said to have reached "the throne of Zeus," generally understood to be a reference to the court of Ptolemy Philadelphus, who was born on and patronized the island, as Theocritus recalls in his encomium for the king (*Idyll* 17.58–72). Finally, while the other pastoral poems use the present tense of literary drama, *Idyll* 7 is a retrospective account of an event that happened at some time in the speaker's past; its form purports to be an account of lived experience, which ancient commentators took to be that of Theocritus himself.[4]

Like its poet narrator, Simichidas, *Idyll* 7 is a poem "fabricated for the sake of truth" (7.44). In it Theocritus stages an encounter between a youthful poet who is all too likely to be taken for himself and a figure who looks very much like one of his own poetic creations. Since the older bucolic singer gives the younger one a staff, as the Muses gave a staff to Hesiod, this encounter looks very much like an inspiration scene. Theocritus seems to have dramatized his own involvement with bucolic poetry in the form of an encounter with a figure from that world who embodies its imaginative appeal in a particularly compelling fashion. In the other poems the bucolic world is a self-contained fictional universe, although Theocritus uses its appeal to produce a real-world effect upon Nicias in *Idyll* 11, much as Polyphemus uses it to influence himself. In *Idyll* 7, however, when Simichidas reflects upon his rustic symposium at the end of the poem, he is emulating not just Polyphemus and Heracles, whom he takes as his examples, but also Lycidas, who proposed just such an occasion for himself earlier in the poem, a rustic feast at which he would listen to tales about Daphnis and Comatas, powerfully imagined representatives of the bucolic world that he himself inhabits. Lycidas thus inspires Simichidas with the same desire to project a world of bucolic characters to which he can aspire in his imagination that animates his own psychic life. The bucolic fiction

---

[4] Cf. Puelma (1960) 144: "Im Gegensatz zu manchen anderen, deutlich als imaginär gekennzeichneten autobiographischen Berichten alexandrinischer Dichter hat Theokrit seinem Selbsterlebnis der 'Thalysien' einen ausgesprochen 'historischen' Anstrich gegeben."

embodied in Lycidas is, in the fiction of *Idyll* 7, given power over the image of the real-world poet Simichidas in the autobiographical account of his own development. What in the other poems is represented as an autonomous fictional world appears in this poem as a model for behavior in a world that is a mimetic image of historical reality.

Theocritus suggests the implications of his fictional creation by showing its transformative effect upon the image of its creator. The poem shows the transformation of the young poet Simichidas from the composer of erotic poetry with a superficial pastoral flavor into a poet capable of projecting his inner life into imagined dramatic characters whose fictional experiences are themselves capable of inspiring emulation in others. In generic terms this could be described as the union of an erudite erotic elegy with a superficial rustic flavor (the kind that Hermesianax fr. 7.77–78 associates with Philetas) with the conventions of Sicilian mime as represented by Theocritus' fellow Syracusan Sophron. *Idyll* 7, however, is less concerned with demonstrating its cunning redeployment of generic models than with impressing upon us the effects of a certain kind of mimetic desire – the desire to refashion one's life after literary models. The text that is interrogated, transformed, and ultimately turned inside out in this regard is not a work of poetry, but Plato's *Phaedrus*. The poem contests Socrates' suggestion that the self-forgetfulness involved in imaginative experience is a kind of stultification, and that, by aspiring to repeat this experience in real life, we depart without purpose from the useful pursuit of self-knowledge. It does so by employing the same curious structure that Plato employs: a walk in the country by city folk, an exchange in this unfamiliar setting of literary compositions that reflect upon the relationship between writing and desire, then a telling demonstration of what the kind of life the interlocutors aspire to might actually look like.[5] Needless to say, the life of the imagination to which Simichidas aspires bears little resemblance to Socrates' perpetual intellectual vigilance. Yet it is in this reversal of Socrates' disparaging account of the value of poetic seduction that Theocritus' espousal of mimetic desire finds its clearest expression. As we have seen in the other bucolic poems, identification of the self with mimetic models is, within the world of these poems, a form of self-projection, an inevitable component in the process by which one evolves towards an imagined future. *Idyll* 7 demonstrates how this is also true for the poet: by having Simichidas engage in the very kind of mimetic self-fashioning that defines the bucolic characters, he allows the poems in which they appear to

---

[5] On the structure of the *Phaedrus*, see Ferrari (1987) 25–26. Hunter (2003) 233–34 points to a structural similarity between *Idyll* 7 and the *Phaedrus* insofar as they tell of "naïve enthusiasts [Phaedrus and Simichidas] who encounter an ironic wisdom beyond their understanding."

From fiction to metafiction 119

be read as metafiction, that is to say, as instances of the poet's self-projection, much as Hermesianax would read Homer. *Idyll* 7 therefore has a unique value for the understanding of bucolic poetry, for it allows us to see the literary drama of the other poems as a kind of lyric, an imaginary stage on which the poet's inner world takes shape.[6] The relationship between the empirical self and its fictional counterparts is expressed as another fiction, a narrative that preserves the mystery of this self-fictionalizing projection by casting it as an inspiration scene. This experience cannot be predicted in advance, nor can the forms that result from it be anticipated before the inspiration that gives them concrete shape. As a means of clarifying this process, I will compare Theocritus' achievement in *Idyll* 7 with that of the twentieth-century poet who went furthest in developing the lyric poem as a means of giving independent life to possible versions of the creative self, Fernando Pessoa. For, in his invention of a series of heteronymic poets whose work is stylistically autonomous from his own, Pessoa gives a striking account of inspiration as the emergence of other selves within the empirical self of the writer.

Idyll 7 begins with a voice that is hard to place within the kinds of dramatic structure employed by Theocritus' bucolic poetry. In contrast to literary drama, in which fictional characters speak about their situation in the present tense, or the poems in which Theocritus frames this drama with some sort of introductory address to a friend, the speaker here tells a story about his own life that took place some time ago (7.1–2):

ἦς χρόνος ἁνίκ' ἐγών τε καὶ Εὔκριτος εἰς τὸν Ἅλεντα
εἴρπομες ἐκ πόλιος, σὺν καὶ τρίτος ἄμμιν Ἀμύντας.

Once upon a time Eucritus and I were on our way to the Haleis from the city, and Amyntas was with us as a third.

The discursive situation is strange – the poem addresses us intimately, as if we knew who Eucritus, Amyntas, and the speaker were, and this information did not have to be repeated. Likewise, if we know that the river Haleis and the spring Burina (7.4–9) are on the island of Cos, we will know that this is where the poem takes place. It is almost as if we were within the world of the poem, and already familiar with its characters and setting. Yet the speaker refers to this world as a world of "once upon a time," a world to which he no longer belongs, although he does not say how or why he has come to be separated from it.[7] Again, in the verses that follow,

---

[6] As we shall see in the next chapter, *Idyll* 3 was already read this way in antiquity.
[7] Gow (1952) *ad loc.* 7.1: "the Greek implies only that the epoch referred to is closed, or the state of affairs no longer existing, not that it belongs to the distant past."

we are placed in a position of unwarranted intimacy; the speaker simply tells us that he and his friends made the journey because Phrasidamus and Antigenes were offering a harvest festival (7.3–4), but he does not give any details about their relationship to himself.[8]

The unspecified "once upon a time" (7.1) that locates the story in relation to the present contrasts with the precision of detail within the story itself. When the travelers "had not yet gone half way, and the tomb of Brasilas had not appeared" to them (7.10–11), they meet with the goatherd Lycidas, a "Cydonian man" (7.12). After the speaker has given Lycidas' name and origin, his description continues (7.13–19):

> ἦς δ' αἰπόλος, οὐδέ κέ τίς νιν
> ἠγνοίησεν ἰδών, ἐπεὶ αἰπόλῳ ἔξοχ' ἐῴκει.
> ἐκ μὲν γὰρ λασίοιο δασύτριχος εἶχε τράγοιο
> κνακὸν δέρμ' ὤμοισι νέας ταμίσοιο ποτόσδον,
> ἀμφὶ δέ οἱ στήθεσσι γέρων ἐσφίγγετο πέπλος
> ζωστῆρι πλακερῷ ῥοικὰν δ' ἔχεν ἀγριελαίῳ
> δεξιτερᾷ κορύναν.

He was a goatherd, and no one could not have known it looking at him, since he looked exactly like a goatherd. On his shoulders he had the dark skin of a shaggy, thick-haired goat still smelling of rennet, and around his chest an old tunic was fastened with a wide belt, and he held a crooked staff of wild olive in his right hand.

The structure of the thought seems clear enough: Lycidas is said to look just like a goatherd, and a picture is given which explains this assertion. Yet the straightforward propositional content of the words is belied by their Homeric resonances. Verses 13–14, "no one could not have known it looking at him," rework an expression in which one god recognizes the actions of another,[9] while verse 14, "he looked exactly like . . .," is standard when a

---

[8] Furusawa (1980) 96–97 argues that the naming of genuine and identifiable heroic ancestors for Phrasidamus and Antigenes points to the historicity of these two, and indeed of the poem as a whole – fictional descendants could not be added to historical antecedents in a way that would be acceptable to a contemporary audience, for such a combination would be understood as false, not fictional. She thus picks out the problematic blend of reality effect and fiction that lies at the heart of the poem, while rejecting as impossible the very quality that, as we shall see, made *Idyll* 7 so suggestive a model for later writers of pastoral fiction, namely its combination of real history with manifest fiction. Krevans (1983) 201–20 approaches the problem in a different way, arguing that the poem contrasts a named geography that recalls not actual places, but rather literary history, with the anonymous geography of bucolic poetry that arises from direct or natural inspiration, rather than evolving out of earlier poetry. Such a distinction between immediate and learned poetry is impossible to maintain, however – the named, real-world geography of Cos is in fact the very site of bucolic inspiration and exchange, and Lycidas, the master of bucolic song, explicitly compares his composition with trends in Hellenistic poetics even as he sings of his imagined counterparts, Tityrus and Comatas.

[9] *Il.* 1.536–37 (Hera realizing that Zeus had been with Thetis), *Od.* 5.77–78 (Calypso recognizing Hermes).

god adopts a disguise.[10] Lycidas, perhaps, is not a goatherd, but someone, or something, who looks just like one.[11] Unlike the disguised gods of epic, however, Lycidas is never revealed as anything other than what he seems. If he is wearing a mask, the mask remains firmly in place. The suggestions of divinity that surround him are, moreover, not facts imparted by an omniscient narrator, as they are in the Homeric passages on which they are modeled, but the response of one participant in the story to another.[12]

In addition to these echoes of Homeric epiphany scenes, there are resemblances between Simichidas' meeting with Lycidas and Odysseus' meeting with the goatherd Melantheus at *Odyssey* 17.204–16. In both poems the encounter occurs on the road, a spring is described, and the goatherd greets the travelers with mockery – here Lycidas teases Simichidas for rushing to the feast in the midday heat, "when even the lizard sleeps in the dry stone wall, and the crested larks do not go forth" (7.21).[13] Theocritus comments explicitly on the Ithacan books of the *Odyssey* in *Idyll* 16, the *Encomium of Hieron*. Along with the leaders of the Lycians, the sons of Priam, and Cycnus, he observes that the rustic characters of the *Odyssey* also owe the preservation of their names to Homer (16.54–57):

ἐσιγάθη δ' ἂν ὑφορβός
Εὔμαιος καὶ βουσὶ Φιλοίτιος ἀμφ' ἀγελαίαις
ἔργον ἔχων αὐτός τε περίσπλαγχνος Λαέρτης,
εἰ μή σφεας ὤνασαν Ἰάονος ἀνδρὸς ἀοιδαί.

The swineherd Eumaeus would have been forgotten, and Philoetius busy with the herded cows, and courageous Laertes himself, if the songs of the Ionian had not favored them.

The transition from Trojan princes to Ithacan herdsmen is surprising in a series of examples offered to a ruler as proof of the commemorative power of poetry until we recall the importance of disguise in the rustic scenes of the *Odyssey*. Eumaeus is the son of a king who, as a boy, was abducted by pirates and brought to Ithaca, where he has served Odysseus' family

---

[10] Cf. Gow (1952) *ad loc.* 7.14, Hunter (1999) *ad loc.* 7.13.
[11] Gow (1952) II.129–30, rejecting the "bucolic masquerade" proposed by earlier scholars, who saw Lycidas as a contemporary poet in disguise, lists the candidates proposed. More recently, Lycidas has been interpreted as a god in rustic costume; Lawall (1967) proposes a satyr, Williams (1971) Apollo, Brown (1981) Pan, while Hunter (1999) *ad loc.* 7.10–11, 21 sees traces of Hermes.
[12] Gow (1952) *ad loc.* 7.14: "The passage seems adequately explained by the assumption that Simichidas is striking in advance the amused and quizzical tone which Lycidas assumes in his opening speech." Cf. Seeck (1975) 199: "Im Gegensatz zum allwissenden Typ des Erzählers, der das Geschehen völlig durchschaut und die innersten Regungen und Gedanken der Personen kennt, besitzt der Ich-Erzähler nur ein subjektives Teilwissen . . . So erfahren wir zwar nicht, was hinter dem Lächeln des Lykidas steckt."
[13] See Ott (1972) 147–48 for a tabulation of verbal and thematic echoes.

loyally ever since (15.403–84). Philoetius too (20.185, 254), like Eumaeus (14.22, 121; 15.351, 389; 16.36; 17.184), is a "leader of men." Their humble dress conceals a nobility acknowledged only in Homer's narrative. They occupy a middle position between Odysseus himself, who even as a beggar "looks like a kingly ruler" (20.194), and the wicked goatherd Melantheus, in whom appearance and reality are one.[14]

From here it is only a step to the aristocratic foundlings and piratical abductions of the Greek novel; in *Daphnis and Chloe* the pastoral decor is merely a temporary costume for lovers who will eventually be restored to their rightful position in society. Yet in the Ithacan scenes of the *Odyssey* there are deeper and more disquieting disguises. The island itself is disguised by Athena so that Odysseus, after all his efforts to return, is unable to recognize his home (13.187–216). Athena herself appears to him disguised, as a shepherd who looks like the delicate son of a king (13.221–23), and Odysseus responds to her disguise by pretending to be a fugitive from Crete (13.256–86) and telling the first of his self-fictionalizing tales. Athena then changes Odysseus' appearance to ensure that he passes unrecognized, although she appears unseen by Telemachus to remove the disfigurement for the duration of the recognition scene between father and son (16.172). Odysseus' disguise is restored at 16.454, although his scar ensures that he can be identified by Eurycleia (19.467–73) and Eumaeus (21.221–27). Yet Penelope refuses to acknowledge him until he reveals his knowledge of their house's secret architecture (23.173–230). Dramatic suspense in this unmasking, the last and most important of all, hinges on the fact that Penelope seems not to recognize her husband even when his rags are removed (23.175–76): "I know very well what kind of man you were when you left Ithaca on your long-oared ship." After twenty years away from home, Odysseus' transformation, we fear, may be deeper than his disguise.

It is not simply the rusticity of the Ithacan books of the *Odyssey* to which *Idyll* 7 responds, then, but their combination of rusticity and disguise. The Lycidas that Simichidas encounters is not just a goatherd, but "some worthy (ἐσθλόν) wayfarer" (7.12). As Gow observes, this epithet, which occurs nowhere else in the Doric poems, occurs five times in this poem, where it describes the hosts of the festival (4), Lycidas (12), the poet Sicelidas (39), bucolic songs (93), and Simichidas' friend Aristis (100).[15] Yet the disguised

---

[14] Cf. Parry (1972) 21–22, who argues that the use of apostrophe to introduce the speeches of Eumaeus helps to communicate a special sense of his character as "the type of the loyalty which Odysseus' good kingship in Ithaca has won from those worthy of appreciating it," and distinguishes him from the other loyal servants, like Philoetius, who are developed less fully.

[15] Gow (1952) *ad loc.* 7.12.

nobility, which is a fact in the *Odyssey*, is only a suggestion in *Idyll* 7. We never learn why the speaker of the poem calls Lycidas worthy, and the epithet adds to the enigma of his appearance. If Lycidas is playing a role, he is identified with it completely. While Athena as a herdsman looks like the delicate son of a king, and Odysseus as a beggar resembles a kingly ruler, Lycidas, in his shaggy goatskin and wretched tunic, not only looks like a goatherd, he smells like one too (7.15–17).

Yet, when Simichidas invites this evil-smelling rustic to an exchange of songs by comparing his own work modestly with that of Sicelidas and Philetas, Lycidas responds with a disquisition on Hellenistic poetics (7.43–48):

> "τάν τοι," ἔφα, "κορύναν δωρύττομαι, οὕνεκεν ἐσσί
> πᾶν ἐπ' ἀλαθείᾳ πεπλασμένον ἐκ Διὸς ἔρνος.
> ὥς μοι καὶ τέκτων μέγ' ἀπέχθεται ὅστις ἐρευνῇ
> ἶσον ὄρευς κορυφᾷ τελέσαι δόμον Ὠρομέδοντος,
> καὶ Μοισᾶν ὄρνιχες ὅσοι ποτὶ Χῖον ἀοιδόν
> ἀντία κοκκύζοντες ἐτώσια μοχθίζοντι."

"I will give you," he said, "my staff, since you are in all respects a shoot fashioned for truth by Zeus. How hateful to me is the builder who strives to fashion a house equal to the peak of Mount Oromedon, and the cocks of the Muses who, laboring in vain, crow against the Chian bard."

A goatherd who speaks like this must surely be a poet in disguise, or a manifest fiction. What light, then, does Lycidas' song throw upon his identity? He introduces it with an invitation – "come let us now begin the bucolic song," ἀλλ' ἄγε βουκολικᾶς ταχέως ἀρξώμεθ' ἀοιδᾶς (7.49) – that recalls the refrain of Thyrsis' "Sorrows of Daphnis" in *Idyll* 1 – "beloved Muses, begin the bucolic song," ἄρχετε βουκολικᾶς, Μοῖσαι φίλαι, ἄρχετ' ἀοιδᾶς (1.64). And, like Thyrsis, Lycidas will also sing of desire (7.52–62):

> Ἔσσεται Ἀγεάνακτι καλὸς πλόος ἐς Μιτυλήναν,
> χὤταν ἐφ' ἑσπερίοις Ἐρίφοις νότος ὑγρὰ διώκῃ
> κύματα, χὠρίων ὅτ' ἐπ' ὠκεανῷ πόδας ἴσχει,
> αἴ κα τὸν Λυκίδαν ὀπτεύμενον ἐξ Ἀφροδίτας
> ῥύσηται· θερμὸς γὰρ ἔρως αὐτῷ με καταίθει.
> χἀλκυόνες στορεσεῦντι τὰ κύματα τάν τε θάλασσαν
> τόν τε νότον τόν τ' εὖρον, ὃς ἔσχατα φυκία κινεῖ,
> ἀλκυόνες, γλαυκαῖς Νηρηΐσι ταί τε μάλιστα
> ὀρνίχων ἐφίληθεν, ὅσοις τέ περ ἐξ ἁλὸς ἄγρα.
> Ἀγεάνακτι πλόον διζημένῳ ἐς Μιτυλήναν
> ὥρια πάντα γένοιτο, καὶ εὔπλοος ὅρμον ἵκοιτο.

There will be good sailing to Mitylene for Ageanax when, with the Kids in the west, the south wind chases the wet waves, and Orion sets his feet upon the ocean, if he saves Lycidas, who is roasting because of Aphrodite. For hot love for that boy is scorching me. And halcyons will calm the waves of the sea, the south wind and the east, which stirs the seaweed in the lower depths, halcyons, most beloved of birds to the green Nereids, and all those who take catches from the sea. May all things be favorable to Ageanax as he seeks passage to Mitylene, and may he arrive at the harbor with good sailing.

As Thyrsis begins by contrasting the scene of Daphnis' death with landscapes of distant mountains and streams (1.66–69), so Lycidas sets his lover's journey within its full astronomical and geographical framework. In his imagination, Lycidas follows Ageanax from his departure to his safe arrival in Mytilene. Ring composition sets the imagined journey apart from what follows, as he goes on to picture the parallel future that he will inhabit: "On that day I will wreathe my brow with anise or roses or a crown of white flowers, and I will draw Pteleatic wine from the bowl as I lie by the fire" (7.63–66). Lycidas imagines a kind of rustic symposium at which he will eat and drink, remembering Ageanax (7.69). He imagines the music that will accompany this symposium: two shepherds will play the flute, and Tityrus will sing of how Daphnis loved Xenea and at his death was mourned by hills and trees, and how Comatas was imprisoned in a cedar chest by an evil king and fed with honey by bees (7.72–85).

Intense expression of desire gives way to the vision of a pastoral listening scene that resembles those we have observed in other poems; as Ageanax arrives in Mytilene, Lycidas imagines himself hearing about the legendary singers of the past from one of their present-day counterparts. As he imagines himself hearing this song, he begins to separate himself in his imagination from the boy who was its cause. He then thinks of a greater pleasure still, an imaginary present in which Comatas lives, and he himself is his audience (7.86–89):[16]

> αἴθ' ἐπ' ἐμεῦ ζωοῖς ἐναρίθμιος ὤφελες ἦμεν,
> ὥς τοι ἐγὼν ἐνόμευον ἀν' ὤρεα τὰς καλὰς αἶγας
> φωνᾶς εἰσαΐων, τὺ δ' ὑπὸ δρυσὶν ἢ ὑπὸ πεύκαις
> ἁδὺ μελισδόμενος κατεκέκλισο, θεῖε Κομᾶτα.

If only you were numbered among the living in my day, so that I, pasturing your lovely sheep among the hills, might listen to your voice, and you, lying under oaks or under pines, sing sweetly, divine Comatas.

---

[16] Cf. Kelly (1983) 113: "No longer will his verbs be future or past but, as the grammarians say, present contrary to fact. In this world of the imagination, time can be negated and events inverted: instead of being buried alive, the now dead singer comes back to life."

From fiction to metafiction

By following his projection of Tityrus' future performance with regret for an imaginary world in which he would have been able to listen to Comatas in person, Lycidas suggests that the effect of such songs is to create a yearning in their audience to belong to the world that they portray. Lycidas does not dramatize the appeal of this world merely by singing about it, but by showing its effect upon him as a listener, even when that listening is a form of auto-suggestion. In this purified version of his own pastoral existence "even the goats are 'beautiful,'"[17] and longing for it displaces his grief over his lover's departure.[18]

Lycidas introduces his imagined stories of Daphnis and Comatas with the indefinite temporal expression, ὥς ποκα, "once" (7.73, 78); he imagines a pastoral world distinct from his own, peopled by fabulous herdsmen with enchanting powers of song. Simichidas likewise begins his story of a meeting with one such herdsman, ἇς χρόνος ἁνίκ,' "once upon a time" (7.1). The sense of separation from a more desirable life is the same in both. Moreover, as Simichidas responds to Lycidas' appearance with marked recollections of Homer (7.13–14), so Lycidas represents Comatas' plight with an equally obvious Homeric echo: the goatherd falls victim to "the wicked folly of his master," κακαῖσιν ἀτασθαλίαισιν ἄνακτος (7.79).[19] The stylistic mannerism that introduces Lycidas in Simichidas' narrative recurs when Lycidas speaks of Comatas, and marks the reframing of the figure of the herdsman singer: as *Idyll* 7 contains Lycidas, so his song contains Tityrus, whose imagined song in turn contains Daphnis and Comatas. There is, moreover, a curious echo of this formal device in the theme of enclosure in the Comatas story. Like Daphnis, he is shut up in a cedar chest where he is fed by bees "because the Muse had poured sweet nectar

---

[17] Lawall (1967) 94.
[18] Serrao (1977) 217: "È stato giustamente osservato come tutti i carmi teocritei di argomento amoroso terminino con un motivo rasserenatore, e come Teocrito proponga l'azione e la confidanza del canto come unico rimedio per le pene di amore. I *boukoliasmòi* inseriti nel nostro carme sono idilli in miniatura e seguono le norme degli altri idilli teocritei: Lykìdas sotto l'azione del canto si libera gradualmente dalla sua passione amorosa e riacquista lo stato di *hasychìa*. Il mito di Komàtas con cui Lykìdas fa terminare il suo carme, appunto perché non presenta nessun rapporto con l'argomento centrale, sta a significare che il canto ha esercitato il suo effetto e l'autore ha raggiunto la sua catarsi." Cf. Walsh (1985) 13: "Lycidas happily contemplates a series of good things which lead him farther and farther from the immediate present until he forgets the boy with whom his poem began." For Seiler (1997) 114–30, the content of Lycidas' song is likewise sublimation of desire through the creative process. However, his insistence that a generalized intertextuality is the means by which sublimation is achieved and expressed seems to me to miss the distinctive form it takes in Theocritus' bucolic fiction – the identification of the herdsman singer (and, as we shall see, his poet) with the objects of his own bucolic imagination.
[19] See *Od.* 12.300, 24.458. Cf. Hunter (1999) *ad loc.* 7.79, a "grand 'heroisation' of the fate of the goatherd."

on his mouth" (7.82): "O blessed Comatas, you did indeed suffer these delights, you too were shut up inside the chest, you too labored out the fertile season of the year feeding on the honeycomb of bees" (7.83–84). His imprisonment is a mixture of pleasure and pain; the chest is "spacious" (7.78) and made of "sweet cedar" (7.81), and within it he "suffered the delight" of an imprisonment in which he was fed on honey. Comatas, in fact, receives the reward for his song that the goatherd wishes upon Thyrsis in *Idyll* 1: "May your mouth be filled with honey" (1.146). This mixture of toil and sweetness echoes the two aspects of bucolic song stressed by Lycidas in the prelude to his song and in the stories that he imagines: the laboriousness of composition (7.51) and the sweetness of the singing voice (7.89). Once again, framing tale and embedded narrative reflect one another.

The figure of the herdsman singer recurs in increasingly diminutive stories: the meeting with Lycidas occupies forty-one verses (7.10–51), the symposium at which Tityrus will perform eleven (7.61–72), the stories of Daphnis (7.73–77) and Comatas five apiece (7.78–82), and the recapitulation of the latter three (7.83–85). While it is nowhere else as complex as in *Idyll* 7, this process of embedded miniaturization can be seen in other *Idylls*. In *Idyll* 1, the goatherd's speech contains the description of the decorated bowl, with its three framed scenes, in the last of which a child is weaving a cage for crickets (1.52).[20] Since the goatherd compares Thyrsis to a cicada (1.148),[21] it is natural to see the boy's desire for the cricket's song as analogous to the goatherd's desire for "The Sorrows of Daphnis": the longing for song lies at the heart of the fictional world of the bowl, just as it lies at the heart of the fictional world of the poem. In both cases, the reader's imagination is directed towards a voice that sums up the attractions of the pastoral world, but is figured within it only as a suggestive absence. As the boy's cage remains empty, so Thyrsis' voice is the material presence that cannot be enclosed within the poem's structure of words.

In *Idyll* 7, the series of reframings leads ultimately to Lycidas' imagination of the voice of Comatas, which is able to replace his longing for

---

[20] Cf. Haber (1994) 24 on *Idyll* 4: "The governing structure of the idyll – and it is one that recurs throughout the Idylls – could be described as a series of diminishing mirrors. As we progress from Herakles to Aigon to Korydon . . . we are continually confronted with diminished versions of what we have left behind." Cf. 168 n. 38: "In addition . . . one might consider the following two series: the goatherd, the boy with the cage for the cicadas, the cicadas (*Idyll* 1); Daphnis and Damoetas, Polyphemus, Polyphemus' dog (*Idyll* 6; here the concern with 'mirror images' is made explicit [35–41])."

[21] Cf. Cairns (1984) 104, "an explicit symbol for the singer." Cf. 7.41, where Simichidas compares Philetas and Sicelidas to crickets.

Ageanax with a greater longing for pastoral song. The diminutive reframing produces a series of increasingly concise reflections of a single event: the listening scene between the pastoral singer and his audience. This series can properly be understood as a form of *mise en abyme*, the recursive repetition of the structure or content of a framing text within that text itself. Lucien Dällenbach has argued for the self-reflexive, and hence explanatory, function of such structures. The *mise en abyme* sheds light on the primary narrative because the reduced scale of the copy exaggerates the distinctive features of its original. It stylizes its model, and so "distinguishes what is essential from what is only contingent." In this way it provides "a kind of internal dialogue and a means whereby the work can interpret itself."[22] The *mise en abyme* therefore reveals just as clearly as Thyrsis' impersonation of Daphnis in *Idyll* 1 that bucolic song is both a manifestation and a vehicle of what René Girard has called mimetic desire, the attempt to replicate in one's own life the desires one has found expressed in a work of literature.[23]

It is in showing the effectiveness of mimetic desire as a kind of therapy that the poem offers the most striking critique of its Platonic model. For while there are many superficial similarities between the pastoral experience of the *Phaedrus* and that of *Idyll* 7 – the walk in the countryside by city dwellers, the exchange of speeches on the topic of love, the particularly close attention to the details of their surroundings on the part of Socrates and Phaedrus, the curious bipartite structure of this dialogue, which is so like *Idyll* 7[24] – it is in the dramatization of mimetic desire that the poem engages most closely with the content of its philosophical anti-model. For Phaedrus wishes to be a lover not because he truly loves but because he would imitate the idea and expression of love as he has found it formulated in the speech of Lysias. In this way he shows himself to be like the cicadas, whose story Socrates tells him (259a–d) – these were the Muses' first human audience who, under the spell of their song, forgot about their own lives to such an extent that

---

[22] Dällenbach (1989) 55–56. Pucci (1998) 177 discusses the listening scene between Odysseus and the Sirens in the *Odyssey* as the Homeric text's self-conscious reflection upon the themes of enchantment and literary desire.

[23] Discussing the Paolo and Francesca episode in Dante's *Inferno*, Girard (1978) 3 notes how Dante emphatically underlines the fact that the lovers' adulterous kiss is performed in imitation of Lancelot and Guinevere, who they have just been reading about, and observes: "The hero in the grip of some second-hand desire seeks to conquer the *being*, the essence, of his model by as faithful an imitation as possible." I am referring therefore to the more limited idea of mimetic desire as imitation of literature rather than the generalized model of human desire as essentially mimetic that Girard develops from it. The idea appears first in Girard (1966), and is refined and developed in Girard (1978).

[24] These resemblances were observed by Murley (1940) 281–95. Hunter (1999) 145–46 notes Theocritus' transformations of Plato's narrative technique. For the role of topography in articulating the two-part structure of the *Phaedrus*, and focusing our attention at crucial moments in its argument, see Ferrari (1987) 3, 25–28.

they neglected to feed themselves and, so dying, were transformed into the insects whose meaningless yet seductive murmur fills the country air. Moreover, when Socrates demonstrates the shortcomings of Lysias' speech, Phaedrus abandons his love as suddenly as his admiration for the author who inspired it. The "pendulum swing of sudden contempt" with which he rejects Lysias, until that moment the object of his emulation,[25] points to the inauthentic character of his feelings. Rather than arising autonomously in himself, they were grafted in him artificially by a work of literature. When these feelings, and the mimetic desire that gave rise to them, are revealed as inauthentic and assumed, both are rejected in favor of the pursuit of reality through philosophical dialogue which occupies the remainder of the dialogue. In *Idyll* 7, by contrast, it is the inauthentic, the mimetic, that is, paradoxically, the most real. It is Lycidas' mimetic desire to be like Daphnis and Comatas that makes him who he is, not his genuine, but trivial, desire for Ageanax, which he is able to displace through song. Lycidas, as we have seen, is defined by his consummate resemblance to a herdsman, and he achieves this perfection of his role by imitating others.

The reflection of Simichidas' narrative in Lycidas' song clarifies the goatherd's role in the poem: Lycidas is to Simichidas as Comatas is to Lycidas, and as Lycidas endeavors to emulate Comatas, so Simichidas will endeavor to emulate Lycidas. What, then, of Simichidas himself? What does his reaction to Lycidas' song tell us about him, and how does his own song fit into the structures of mimetic desire that we have seen to be constitutive of bucolic song? His immediate response is self-praise: (7.91–95):

"Λυκίδα φίλε, πολλὰ μὲν ἄλλα
Νύμφαι κἠμὲ δίδαξαν ἀν' ὤρεα βουκολέοντα
ἐσθλά, τά που καὶ Ζηνὸς ἐπὶ θρόνον ἄγαγε φάμα·
ἀλλὰ τόγ' ἐκ πάντων μέγ' ὑπείροχον, ᾧ τυ γεραίρειν
ἀρξεῦμ'· ἀλλ' ὑπάκουσον, ἐπεὶ φίλος ἔπλεο Μοίσαις."

"Lycidas my friend, the Nymphs have also taught me many fine things while I was tending my flocks in the hills, which fame has brought perhaps even to the throne of Zeus. But this is by far the most superior, with which I will honor you now. Listen then, since you are a friend of the Muses."

Whether the "throne of Zeus" here refers literally to the heavens[26] or to the court of Ptolemy Philadelphus,[27] the speaker clearly has a high opinion of his own work, and the poem that he will perform is intended as a proof of this prowess. While Simichidas is already a poet, and a pastoral poet too,

---

[25] Ferrari (1987) 28.   [26] Σ 7.93a, Wendel (1914) 102.   [27] Gow (1952) *ad loc.* 7.93.

his response to Lycidas is defensive, competitive even. While the objects of Lycidas' emulation – Daphnis and Comatas – belong to a world he cannot hope to enter, the object of Simichidas' emulation confronts him in person, so that competitive rivalry may overshadow imitation, just as it does in a song contest proper, as each of the rival herdsmen strives to instantiate bucolic excellence more fully than the other.[28]

The exchange of songs between Lycidas and Simichidas echoes those of other pastoral poems (*Id.* 5, 10), as Simichidas suggests by his use of "let us sing bucolic songs," βουκολιασδώμεθα (7.36), to introduce it. The exchange is not quite a contest, however, and the performances complement, but do not respond directly to, one another.[29] Simichidas signals his familiarity with bucolic song by beginning his own contribution to the exchange with obvious rustic imagery: the divinities of erotic desire have sneezed for him (a favorable omen) because he, poor thing, "loves Myrto as much as goats love spring" (7.96–97). The sneeze as love omen, like the wish with which the poem ends – that an old crone may spit on him and Aratus to ward off evil – have their parallels in the goatherd's rustic love tokens in *Idyll* 3.28–39 – a plant smacked against the arm, sieve divination, eye twitching – and the pimples on the nose to which the speaker of *Idyll* 12 appeals (12.24). Likewise the comparison of his desire with goats in spring recalls the rustic comparisons of Polyphemus in *Idyll* 11, Bucaeus in *Idyll* 10, and the anonymous speaker in *Idyll* 12. Yet there is something studied in these motifs, as is clear from the way he introduces himself in the third person in his own song – "the Erotes sneezed for Simichidas." Simichidas is self-consciously representing himself as a figure of bucolic song, rather than actually being a bucolic singer. His song takes for granted his own fitness as a subject of such song, rather than exploring the possibility that he might belong to its world, as Lycidas explores his identification with Daphnis and Comatas, and as Simichidas himself, at the end of the poem, will explore the similarity of his own experience at the festival with archetypal pastoral scenes. His complacent assumption of the bucolic mode is clearer still in his invocation of Pan, whom he enjoins to help his friend Aratus by bringing him the object of his desire. The goatherd of *Idyll* 1 refuses to play his pipes because this threatening god may be nearby. Simichidas,

---

[28] Girard (1978) 3: "The nearer the mediator, the more does the veneration that he inspires give way to hate and rivalry."

[29] Serrao (1977) 210 tabulates how Lycidas responds point by point (7.43–50) to Simichidas' *invitation* to sing (7.35–41), although, since both songs are prior creations rather than spontaneous effusions, this excludes the exact correspondence one would look for in a song contest proper (215). Furusawa (1980) 10–11 sees the progress from erotic suffering to emotional tranquility as the common theme of the songs of Lycidas and Simichidas, and hence the ground of the poem's unity.

however, speaks as though he could summon and dismiss him at will. So, having heard of an Arcadian ritual in which boys flog an image of the god in times of scarcity, Simichidas threatens him with this punishment if he does not heed his wishes, or with exile to the coldest place on earth in the winter, and the hottest in the summer (7.103–14). The threats demonstrate the superficiality of Simichidas' relationship to bucolic song; while Lycidas' reverence for Daphnis and Comatas matches that of the anonymous goatherd for Pan and of Thyrsis for Daphnis in *Idyll* 1, Simichidas has yet to develop a deeply felt relationship with this world, expressed through identification with its leading characters. His invocation of Pan reveals no knowledge of his bucolic character, and seems to be included not because of any real belief in its potential efficacy, but rather as a demonstration of his familiarity with obscure points of geography and cult. So too in calling upon the Erotes, whom he now compares to "reddening apples," to appear from "the sweet stream of Hyetis and Byblis, and Oecus, the high seat of blond Dione" (7.115–17), he mixes obvious bucolic motifs with learned topographical references. Then, as he asks these divinities to wound with their bows the boy Philinus, with whom his friend Aratus is in love, Simichidas calls him "riper than a pear," imagining the cries of women who mock him for his fading charms. The rustic comparison, elsewhere a means by which the lover explores his almost inexpressible infatuation with his beloved, becomes, in Simichidas' mouth, a piece of invective instead.[30] Finally, he suggests to Aratus that they no longer wear out the night on the doorstep of his beloved but let another "be choked in that wrestling." Having thus invoked the customs of urban serenade and the urban landscape of the wrestling school, Simichidas ends with a wish for peace, the guarantee of which will be having an old woman spit on them, "to keep what is unpleasant away" (7.120–27).

Simichidas, as we know, is from the town (7.2), and it would be all too easy to dismiss his claim that the Nymphs taught him his song while he was tending his flocks in the hills (7.92) as the sentimental delusion of an urban

---

[30] Henrichs (1980) 7–27 points to the origin of Simichidas' abuse in the poetry of Archilochus, and Hunter (2003) 228 has likewise emphasized that "it is certainly the iambic mode that is evoked by Simichidas' liberal use of (to us at least) obscure proper names, the sense that the poem is full of in-jokes, the joking prayer to Pan, and the persistent detached irony that is so remote from the true pathos that is productive of elevation." To this I would simply add that if iambic poetry is being recalled here, then it is iambic poetry reimagined through the lens of its bucolic counterpart, the acerbic style of the Comatas of *Idyll* 5, who is as attuned to the physical shortcomings of his rivals as any iambic poet, and no less knowing than Simichidas in his manipulation of bucolic motifs and archetypes. It seems to me incorrect therefore to see Theocritus' urban poetry as the model for Simichidas' song, as do Kühn (1958) 67–68 and Ott (1969) 167.

visitor.[31] However, as a stylistic medley the song has obvious affinities with the song of Thyrsis in *Idyll* 1, and its tendency to invective is paralleled in the abusive style of Comatas in *Idyll* 5, two characters whose bucolic credentials are hardly in doubt. It is not so much, then, that Simichidas' song is spurious bucolic, but rather that it is immature; as comparison with Thyrsis and Comatas reveals, it is marked as such not by what is present in it but by what it lacks, the sense that one's identity as a bucolic singer depends upon identification with, and reenactment of, other powerful bucolic singers who are present to the imagination as models for one's own experience. While already a poet in *Idyll* 7, Simichidas is still a young poet. His songs may have reached "the throne of Zeus" (7.93), but he has not yet attained the personal relationship to archetypal bucolic paradigms exhibited by the song of Lycidas.[32] And it is in this spirit that Lycidas responds to his song, confirming the gift of the staff that he had offered him earlier as a promising young starter on the right path of poetry (7.128–29):

> τόσσ' ἐφάμαν· ὁ δέ μοι τὸ λαγωβόλον, ἁδὺ γελάσσας
> ὡς πάρος, ἐκ Μοισᾶν ξεινήιον ὤπασεν ἦμεν.

So I spoke. But he, laughing sweetly as before, gave me his stick as a token of friendship in the Muses.

This gift has been compared with the Muses' gift of a staff to Hesiod at the beginning of the *Theogony*, and the meeting with Lycidas has therefore been called an initiation into bucolic poetry that enables Simichidas to experience and describe the festival so richly in the remainder of the poem.[33] Simichidas does not explicitly connect the staff with the gift of song, as Hesiod does, since he is already a poet of some accomplishment, nor is the disparity between him and Lycidas in the art of song so great that one might speak of genuine initiation here, as one can with Hesiod and the Muses. However, the gift clearly acknowledges a kind of kinship on the part of Lycidas, a recognition that the younger poet will belong to the ranks of

---

[31] So Giangrande (1968).
[32] Cf. Hunter (2003) 230: "Lycidas ... finds personal, exemplary comfort in the bucolic and aipolic heroes of his own world – Daphnis and Komatas – and what is important, as it had traditionally been in the poetic representation of myth, is how their stories, their *pathe*, act as paradigms for his own experience." For an interpretation of Simichidas' song as an ironic demonstration of the limited abilities of the youthful poet as seen from the perspective of the writer of *Idyll* 7, see Van Groningen (1959).
[33] Puelma (1960) 155–56; *Theogony* 30–31: "And they cut and gave me a staff, a shoot of flourishing laurel, a wonder. And they breathed into me an inspired voice, so that I might celebrate things that will be and have been." Cf. Pearce (1988) 300: "the last part of the poem expresses the result of the encounter between Lycidas and Simichidas."

bucolic singers, of whom he himself is an outstanding example.[34] In the remainder of this chapter I will consider some of the ways in which Lycidas' esteem for his younger contemporary is borne out by the end of the poem.

Having parted from Lycidas, Simichidas and his companions arrive at the estate of Phrasydamas, where they recline with delight "on beds of deep rushes and newly cut vine leaves" (7.133–35). At this point Simichidas gives a lengthy description of his surroundings (7.135–47):

> πολλαὶ δ' ἄμμιν ὕπερθε κατὰ κρατὸς δονέοντο
> αἴγειροι πτελέαι τε· τὸ δ' ἐγγύθεν ἱερὸν ὕδωρ
> Νυμφᾶν ἐξ ἄντροιο κατειβόμενον κελάρυζε.
> τοὶ δὲ ποτὶ σκιαραῖς ὀροδαμνίσιν αἰθαλίωνες
> τέττιγες λαλαγεῦντες ἔχον πόνον· ἁ δ' ὀλολυγών
> τηλόθεν ἐν πυκιναῖσι βάτων τρύζεσκεν ἀκάνθαις·
> ἄειδον κόρυδοι καὶ ἀκανθίδες, ἔστενε τρυγών,
> πωτῶντο ξουθαὶ περὶ πίδακας ἀμφὶ μέλισσαι.
> πάντ' ὦσδεν θέρεος μάλα πίονος, ὦσδε δ' ὀπώρας.
> ὄχναι μὲν πὰρ ποσσί, παρὰ πλευραῖσι δὲ μᾶλα
> δαψιλέως ἁμῖν ἐκυλίνδετο, τοὶ δ' ἐκέχυντο
> ὄρπακες βραβίλοισι καταβρίθοντες ἔραζε·
> τετράενες δὲ πίθων ἀπελύετο κρατὸς ἄλειφαρ.

Many poplars and elms murmured over our heads, and nearby the holy water from the cave of the Nymphs babbled as it fell. Black cicadas conducted their chatter on the shady branches, and the tree frog muttered from afar among the dense thorns of the brambles. Larks and finches were singing, the dove was moaning, and buzzing bees flew round about the springs. Everything was very fragrant of the rich harvest, and fragrant of the fruit. Pears rolled in abundance by our feet, and apples by our sides, and the young trees hung down to the ground laden with plums. And the four-year seal was removed from the top of the wine jars.

The passage is a full representation of sensory experience, which progresses from sound – "murmured," "babbled," "chattered," "muttered," "sang,"

---

[34] Some scholars, by contrast, have seen Lycidas' gift as ironic, like his laughter, a mock-investiture in which he teases the city poet for his rustic song. Cameron (1995) 412 cites Homeric usage of the phrase ἁδὺ γελάσσας (7.42, 128) in support of the idea that Lycidas' attitude to Simichidas is one of ironic disparagement. However, as Cameron acknowledges (416), a completely ironic attitude on the part of Lycidas is difficult to reconcile with his giving a gift in the first place. Moreover, seeing a *hostile* pun in presenting the staff to Simichidas, since he is "a shoot thoroughly fashioned for truth by Zeus," πᾶν ἐπ' ἀλαθείᾳ πεπλασμένον ἐκ Διὸς ἔρνος (7.44) – "'I'll give you my staff because you're a chip off the old block' – namely as wooden as the staff, stupid!" (417) – contradicts the Homeric precedent cited in support of his interpretation of ἁδὺ γελάσσας: of the four occurrences of "shoot," ἔρνος, in Homer, three indicate a nurturing relationship (*Il.* 17.53, farmer and olive sapling; 18.53 [= 18.437], Thetis and Achilles; *Od.* 14.175, Eumaeus and Telemachus), while the other is a complimentary comparison (*Od.* 6.163, Odysseus to Nausicaa). Similarly, in *Idyll* 28, a poem to accompany the gift of a distaff to the wife of Nicias, Theocritus refers to his friend as a "holy plant of the Graces, whose voices are desire," Χαρίτων ἱμεροφώνων ἱερὸν φύτον (28.7).

"moaned," "buzzed"[35] – to smell – "everything was very fragrant of the rich harvest, and fragrant of the fruit" – and taste – "the four-year seal was removed from the top of the wine jars." The mass of sensations has led some commentators to see the description as a generic landscape, even a combination of seasonal events impossible in nature.[36] The coincidence of grain harvest (θέρεος, 143) and fruit crop (ὀπώρας, 143) was, however, standard ancient practice,[37] and, rather than an impossibility, is another of the poem's reality effects. Moreover, the vocabulary of the description is anything but conventional; a large proportion of the nouns, and in particular the botanical terms, are elsewhere confined to scientific or technical authors, and the Hellenistic poets who utilized them.[38] The specificity of Theocritus' botanical language has in fact long been recognized,[39] and the technical register of the nouns here contrasts with the more traditional poetic language of the verbs that accompany them: δονέοντο, "murmured," κελάρυζε, "babbled," λαλαγεῦντες, "chattering," τρύζεσκεν, "muttered," ἄειδον, "sang," ἔστενε, "moaned." As Simichidas names the elements of the scene, he fills the poem with technical vocabulary; as he attempts to communicate what he felt, he integrates these terms into a representation of the full expressive range of the human voice; the conflict of vocabularies points to the unexpected confluence of fictional and lived experience in this moment.[40]

In contrast to the listening scenes in which we are invited to imagine the voice of a single human singer which sounds like falling water, a nightingale, a cicada, or a swan (*Id.* 1.7–8, 136, 148; *Id.* 5.29, 136–37), the passage asks us to imagine the voice of nature itself: poplars, elms, water, cicadas, frogs, larks,

---

[35] I have followed the suggestion of Gow (1952) *ad loc.* 7.142 in translating ξουθαί, which elsewhere may also refer to color and movement: "the context here points strongly to sound."
[36] Schönbeck (1962) 114–15.
[37] Gow (1952) II.127; Hunter (1999) *ad loc.* 7.143. So too Furusawa (1980) 120–27 argues for the "der Wirklichkeitscharakter der Thalysienszene."
[38] οἰναρέα is a *hapax*, cf. οἰναρίς Hp. *Mul.* 2.206, οἴναρον X. *Oec.* 19.18, Thphr. *HP* 9.13.5, Babr. 34.2, οἰναρέος Ibyc. 1.6, Hp. *Mul.* 2.195, οἰναρίζειν Ar. *Pax* 1147; ὀρόδαμνος *AP* 9.3, Thphr. *HP* 9.16.3, Call. *fr.* 139, Nic. *Th.* 863, *Al.* 603; βάτος *Od.* 24.230, Aen. Tact. 28.6, Hp. *Mul.* 2.112, Ar. *fr.* 754, Thphr. *HP* 1.5.3; ἀκανθίς Arist. *HA* 616b31; ὄχνη (tree) *Od.* 7.115, 11.589, 24.234, Thphr. *HP* 2.5.6, (fruit) *Od.* 7.120, Nic. *Th.* 513, Rufus Medicus *Ren. Ves.* 14.6; βράβιλον Antyllus Medicus ap. Orib. 10.20.4, Gal. 6.612. Gow (1952) *ad loc.* 7.139 judges the ὀλολυγών to be a frog rather than a nightingale by comparing Thphr. *fr.* 6.42, Arat. 948, Arist. *HA* 536a11, Plut. *Mor.* 982E, Ael. *NA* 6.19, 9.13, Pliny *NH* 11.172. In this context one might wonder whether αἰθαλίωνες as applied to the cicadas is merely a descriptive epithet, or likewise belongs to the scientific register.
[39] By Lindsell (1937) first, cf. Lembach (1970). The former argues that the medical and botanical vocabularies in the *Idylls* are related, and suggests that Theocritus' familiarity with both may stem from an acquaintance with the medical school of Cos.
[40] Cf. Hamon (1981) 15: "[la description] risque d'introduire dans le texte des vocabulaires 'étrangers,' et notamment le lexique spécialisé des diverses professions qui s'occupent de l'objet décrit."

finches, doves, bees. These singers do not perform in the orderly sequence of a song contest, but all around, and all at once. Nature is, however, carefully stylized in Simichidas' account; chiasmus (ὄχναι μὲν πὰρ ποσσί, παρὰ πλευραῖσι δὲ μᾶλα), repetition (ὧσδεν . . . ὧσδε), and highly mannered word order (περὶ πίδακας ἀμφί)[41] give form to his sense that nature itself has here taken on an almost human voice. Literary artifice is a prominent theme in Lycidas' prologue to his song. He compares the wasted effort of those who "labor in vain," constructing large-scale works in competition with Homer, with the trouble he has taken over his own modest effort. The artifice of Simichidas' voice here – his heterogeneous vocabulary and the density of stylistic and mimetic effects he employs – is a surprise after the straightforward narration that precedes it, and is the first unambiguous indication that the Simichidas who narrates the poem is a rather different poet from the one who appears within it. Like the herdsmen of *Idyll* 1, he is now able to hear human music in the sounds of trees and streams, and to imitate what he has heard there.

In the effort to combine accurate deixis with the feeling of lived experience the poem's curious form once again makes itself felt; Simichidas reports an event in his past with the intensity it would have if it were occurring in the fictional present of literary drama. The poem ends, however, with emphatic reminders that the period of his life that it records is over. Concluding his description of the festival with the wine that was served there, Simichidas seeks mythical parallels for his experience (7.148–57):

> Νύμφαι Κασταλίδες Παρνάσιον αἶπος ἔχοισαι,
> ἆρά γέ πᾳ τοιόνδε Φόλω κατὰ λάινον ἄντρον
> κρατῆρ' Ἡρακλῆι γέρων ἐστάσατο Χίρων;
> ἆρά γε πᾳ τῆνον τὸν ποιμένα τὸν ποτ' Ἀνάπῳ,
> τὸν κρατερὸν Πολύφαμον, ὃς ὤρεσι νᾶας ἔβαλλε,
> τοῖον νέκταρ ἔπεισε κατ' αὔλια ποσσὶ χορεῦσαι,
> οἷον δὴ τόκα πῶμα διεκρανάσατε, Νύμφαι,
> βωμῷ πὰρ Δάματρος ἁλωίδος;

Castalian nymphs, who inhabit the slopes of Parnassus, did old Chiron set a cup such as this before Heracles in the stony cave of Pholus? Did nectar such as this persuade that shepherd by the Anapus, the mighty Polyphemus, who hit ships with mountains, to dance about the sheepfolds with his feet, such a drink as you then mixed beside the altar of Demeter of the Threshing Floor, Nymphs?

---

[41] Hunter (1999) *ad loc.* 7.139, 142, 143, 144.

Hunter suggests that the question addressed to the Nymphs "'bucolizes' the epic practice of questioning the Muses,"[42] and compares *Iliad* 2.484–93: "Tell me now Muses who have your homes on Olympus . . . who were the leaders and chiefs of the Danaans." In contrast to the Catalogue of Ships, however, Simichidas is not asking for divine assistance in recalling a fact, but reflecting on the nature of the experience he has just described; he does not ask what wine was drunk by Heracles and Polyphemus, but whether it was such as he drank at the Thalysia. Homer's question is the performer's guarantee that what he is about to tell his audience is true. Simichidas, by contrast, does not answer his own question, and so invites us to look closely at the question itself.[43] His first example recalls how Heracles, in the performance of his labors for Eurystheus, was entertained by the centaur Pholus, who opened a cask of wine that had been given to him by Dionysus. Simichidas does not mention that the aroma of this wine led the other centaurs to attack them, and so resulted in the deaths of Pholus and Chiron.[44] The second tells how Polyphemus danced around his sheepfolds under the influence of wine. Simichidas does not mention that the wine was given to him by Odysseus, and so led to his blinding. In both examples, Simichidas focuses on the pleasure the wine brings at the moment of its consumption and suppresses its unpleasant consequences. Yet in the tale of Heracles and Pholus the attraction of the other centaurs to the wine of Dionysus is the very thing that reveals its marvelous nature, and, in telling the story of the Cyclops, Simichidas calls him "the mighty Polyphemus, who hit ships with mountains," recalling what he does after his blinding. Both examples reveal the speaker's knowledge of the story as a whole and show his tentative engagement with the myth as an imaginative equivalent of his own experience.

Here, then, is a second change in the voice of Simichidas. While the song he represents himself as performing in the past of the poem lacks the play with imagined models that is characteristic of bucolic song, in reflecting on that past at the moment of writing he now thinks, like a true bucolic singer, that his own experience at the festival may have been a reenactment

---

[42] Hunter (1999) *ad loc.* 7.148–55, and *ad loc.* 7.148. For the Nymphs as bucolic Muses, and the problematic counter-example of Thyrsis, who invokes the Muses repeatedly as patrons of bucolic song in the refrain of the "Sorrows of Daphnis," see Fantuzzi (2000) 142–47.

[43] Cf. Walsh (1985) 17–18: "[Simichidas] begins to report the activity of his imagination, speaking as much to himself as to any other auditor . . . Even if he really wanted answers to these questions, none could be given."

[44] Apollodorus 2.5.4. Fantuzzi (1995) 27 notes that the story formed a part of Stesichorus' *Geryoneis* and was the subject of at least two comedies.

of the very models that were absent from his song at the time. He has not yet achieved the mastery of a Comatas or a Lycidas in this respect, for these characters are able to instantiate for others the very archetypes they imagine for themselves. Simichidas is more like the goatherd of *Idyll* 3; he is trying out the relationship between myth and personal experience, but he does so without a great deal of confidence. His examples are still questions, and we can entertain a variety of answers to them. Simichidas imagines the pleasure of Heracles and Polyphemus in the wine they drank as a kernel of identity with his own experience at the festival. Yet this kernel of pleasure contrasts with the catastrophic outcome of the episode as a whole; their pleasure proved very short-lived. One might compare the more extended use of Heracles and Polyphemus in the examples of *Idyll* 11 and *Idyll* 13; allusions to the *Odyssey* recall the impending destruction of the pastoral Cyclops at the hands of Odysseus, of which he himself is unaware, while *Idyll* 13 ends with a suggestion of the labors that lie ahead of Heracles, unknown to the hero himself. Simichidas' questions likewise evoke what lies beyond the moment of comparison, and we wonder how the festival relates to the rest of his life. Did pleasure precede misfortune, as it did in the stories of Heracles and Polyphemus?[45] This uncertainty makes the prayer with which Simichidas ends the poem – that he be allowed to return to the festival some time in the future – all the more poignant (7.155–57):

ἇς ἐπὶ σωρῷ
αὖτις ἐγὼ πάξαιμι μέγα πτύον, ἁ δὲ γελάσσαι
δράγματα καὶ μάκωνας ἐν ἀμφοτέραισιν ἔχοισα.

On her heap may I fix the great winnow once again, and may she smile holding sheaves and poppies in her hands.

In the first verse of the poem Simichidas' "once upon a time" suggests that he is now a different person from the one who appears in the story. In the last verse, his wish to repeat the experience he has just described suggests its importance to him. How, then, are we to relate the moment at which the story is told to the moment at which it took place? For it is the use of retrospective first-person narration that sets *Idyll* 7 apart from the other

---

[45] Cf. Fantuzzi (1995) 28: "Both questions which Theocritus asks the Nymphae imply in fact a negative answer – Phrasidamus' symposium has obviously nothing to do with those mythical wines which provoked such violence." For Fantuzzi, the function of examples in Theocritus' bucolic poetry is "deconstruction of the traditionally exemplary features of mythical characters" (20), and in this poem, in which the poet speaks in his own voice, "he avoids the responsibility of the 'failure' by the interrogative form, which, half in jest half in earnest, stresses the problematic nature of paradigms which seem to be positive, but hardly can be" (28). On this reading, then, Simichidas keeps an ironic distance from his mythological stories even as he tests his own imaginative identification with them.

bucolic poems. When people tell their own story, whether in fiction or real life, "convergence is the rule" – story time usually ends in the moment of narration.[46] The *Odyssey* offers a rather convoluted proof of this rule. In Book 12 Odysseus is recounting his adventures to Alcinous. In doing so he is also giving the "back story" of the *Odyssey* to the poem's audience. However, when he reaches the island of Calypso, a problem arises, because from this point on the audience of the poem has already heard the story from Homer. The poet therefore has Odysseus recall that he told Alcinous the latter part of his story (up to his arrival at his house) the previous evening (*Odyssey* 12.450–53):

> τί τοι τάδε μυθολογεύω;
> ἤδη γάρ τοι χθιζὸς ἐμυθεόμην ἐνὶ οἴκῳ
> σοί τε καὶ ἰφθίμῃ ἀλόχῳ· ἐχθρὸν δέ μοί ἐστιν
> αὖτις ἀριζήλως εἰρημένα μυθολογεύειν.

But why should I tell you this? For in fact I told it yesterday in the hall to you and your noble wife. It is a hateful thing to me to tell again what has been clearly said.

In the *Aeneid* the solution is simpler – when Aeneas (in Book 3) reaches the end of the story of his travels, he tells Dido (3.714–15): "This was my last labor, this the end of my long journey; from here a god drew my wandering self to your shores."

It has in fact been argued that this convergence is essential for autobiographical writing. It is the autobiographer's sense that he is different from the person he used to be that leads him to write in the first place, and it is the need to explain how this change came about that gives his narrative its shape:

> It is the internal transformation of the individual – and the exemplary character of this transformation – that furnishes a subject for narrative discourse in which "I" is both subject and object . . . The narrator describes not only what happened to him at a different time in his life but above all how he became – out of what he was – what he presently is.[47]

Starobinski's analysis holds good not just for the confessional type of prose narrative that he is speaking of here, but also for the autobiographical narratives of the Greek poets. Hesiod, for example, to have composed the *Theogony*, must have had the encounter with the Muses that he narrates in its opening, in which the goddesses give him a staff and inform him that

---

[46] Genette (1980) 221, citing examples from the modern novel.
[47] Starobinski (1980) 78–79. Cf., in the same volume, Mandel (1980) 65: "In ratifying the past, the autobiographer discloses the truth of his or her being in the present."

from now on he will be a poet capable of recording the kind of information about the gods and the world that the poem contains. A transformation that we might imagine to have occurred over time is told as a single decisive event that has its outcome in the poem we are reading. So too, in the Mnesiepes inscription, the way in which Archilochus becomes a poet is not a lengthy process of education and training, but is the result of single encounter with the Muses, whom he meets while driving his cows into town.[48]

From this perspective, then, *Idyll* 7 both invites and rebuffs autobiographical readings.[49] The poem written in the first person, it is full of allusions to the historical world in which Theocritus lived, and records an important, and perhaps even decisive, moment in a poet's sense of self. However, the story time does not end in the moment of narration, and the speaker refrains from explicitly addressing the changes in himself at which the poem hints. Simichidas the narrator never comments on Simichidas the character, and *Idyll* 7 avoids the convergence between the narrator and the character who is a younger version of himself; past and present are simply juxtaposed by the act of narration. Moreover, the absence of a common name shared by author, narrator, and protagonist might seem to deny the poem the status of autobiographical writing altogether, for it is in the identity of these three figures that the "autobiographical pact" between writer and reader has been located.[50]

How, then, are we to understand this puzzling narrative? Who is the "I" who speaks to us from this poem, and what kind of life story is he telling us? In order to answer this question, let me first briefly review the poem's structure. The events of the poem all take place within a single afternoon. There are, however, marked variations in emphasis. Half the journey, from departure to the meeting with Lycidas, is accomplished in nine verses (7.1–9). From this point until the travelers separate from Lycidas, narrative duration approximates story time very closely because he and Simichidas are talking (7.10–127). After the exchange of songs and the gift of the staff, however, the departure of Lycidas, the remainder of the journey to the house of Phrasidamus, and the arrival at the festival are compressed into

---

[48] Discussed by Lefkowitz (1981) 27, and see now Clay (2004), who locates the cult of Archilochus on Paros amid the full range of cult honors for poets in the Greek city.

[49] The most ambitious attempt to grasp the autobiographical project of *Idyll* 7 is Meillier (1993), who approaches the poem under three principal rubrics: the involvement of the poet in his own poem, the self-fictionalization in the transformation of Theocritus into Simichidas, and the construction of a personal temporality by means of which autobiographical experience is given literary form (104). The deeply insightful reading of *Idyll* 7 is connected with a highly questionable theory of the origin and order of a collection of Theocritus' bucolic poetry, but this ought not to prevent it from being better known than it seems to be at present.

[50] Lejeune (1989) 4–5.

four verses (7.130–34). The poem focuses upon two incidents, the meeting with Lycidas and the festival (7.135–155), and these incidents are juxtaposed with a minimum of intervening narration. Moreover, we never meet the hosts whose ancestry is recounted in the opening verses, and Simichidas' companions gradually fade from sight: Eucritus and Amyntas recline with Simichidas at verses 131–32, trees murmur over their heads at verse 135, and then they are not heard of again. The festival is presented not as a communal celebration but as the private aesthetic experience of the poem's speaker.[51] Changes in style and content distinguish this part of the poem from the narrative that precedes it. Moreover, the juxtaposition of this change in register with the meeting with Lycidas suggests that the two are in some way related, although nothing is said explicitly on this subject.

The key to understanding the poem's status as autobiographical narration lies, I suggest, in the bucolic poems to which it responds and whose appeal is embodied in the person of Lycidas. All ancient biographies (and autobiographies) of poets contain a large admixture of fiction.[52] Moreover, in writing this poem Theocritus has surely been influenced by the tradition of Socratic biography, in which experiments with life-writing are directed "towards capturing the potentialities rather than the realities of individual lives,"[53] as the echoes of the *Phaedrus* demonstrate. However, while these forms of life-writing no doubt "occupy an ambiguous position between fact and imagination"[54] – Hesiod may never have met the Muses, and Socrates and Phaedrus may never have taken their walk in the countryside – the separation between historical person and imagined counterpart in them is less radical than in *Idyll* 7, as Theocritus' use of an assumed name indicates. The autobiographical project of *Idyll* 7 rather owes its peculiar form to the presentation of character in the bucolic poems upon which it reflects: their use of a bucolic persona for imaginative role play, and the rejection of Platonic forms of self-analysis that this fictionalizing self-projection entails. It is against the function of role play in the bucolic poems that this version of autobiography, and its peculiar reimagining of the scene of poetic inspiration, must be understood.

Idyll 7 does not commemorate either its author or its narrator becoming a poet. Simichidas is already a poet at the time the poem is set, and while, in his own estimation, his poems do not equal those of Sicelidas or Philetas, two near contemporaries with well-established reputations, the fame of his songs "has reached the throne of Zeus." Simichidas, in other words, is

---

[51] Cf. Seiler (1997) 114–16.   [52] Lefkowitz (1981) viii and *passim*.
[53] Momigliano (1971) 46, cf. Kahn (1996) 33.   [54] Momigliano (1971) 46.

portrayed as a poet in the early years of an already established poetic career, and one who already has some kind of reputation for bucolic poetry. He is comfortable using its terms to introduce his exchange with Lycidas, and what he performs for him contains the elements of a rustic love song. Lycidas acknowledges his degree of accomplishment in this vein with the gift of the staff, but, as we have shown, there is a striking transformation of Simichidas' voice at the end of the poem that seems to stem from his encounter with this acknowledged bucolic master. What Simichidas understands at the festival is how to make a start on the kind of song that Lycidas performed earlier in the poem. This kind of song combines close attention to the singer's own pastoral world with the ability to reimagine that world by focusing on archetypal bucolic characters and situations that embody it more perfectly. From the light-hearted mocker of love who advises his friend Aratus simply to seize the day and ignore the stronger bonds of erotic desire Simichidas, at the end of the poem, is able to conceive the kind of imaginative experience that could make this desire of secondary importance in a person's psychic life. It has become possible for him to imagine his own experience at the festival as a reenactment of the experience of Heracles and Polyphemus, much as Lycidas is able to envision the rustic symposium at which he will listen to Tityrus as the near equivalent of a fictional experience in which he is the audience of Comatas. The gift of the staff thus precipitates not an initiation into poetry as such, or even into bucolic poetry, but the conception of a kind of poetry that is able to invent fictional doubles as aspirational models for one's present existence. The poetry Simichidas is able to imagine at the end of the poem contrasts with the more limited version of bucolic song he performs in it earlier. Simichidas cites Philetas and Asclepiades as models, and it seems reasonable to assume that his song is an image of the erudite erotic elegy for which they are celebrated incorporated into the hexameter poetry of *Idyll* 7, just as *Idyll* 1, for example, represents Thyrsis' song in the same meter as the spoken dialogue that surrounds it. They are obvious models for the kind of song the young Simichidas has to offer, though neither put erotic elegy in the mouths of fully realized fictional herdsmen, the development for which Theocritus has traditionally been credited by the subsequent pastoral tradition.[55] Both the song itself, then, and its literary historical affiliations contrast the youthful poet with the more imaginative successor whose emergence is commemorated, and whose works are anticipated, by the end of the poem.

---

[55] I cannot therefore agree with the suggestion of Bowie (1985) that Lycidas is derived from the poetry of Philetas. Philetas is acknowledged as the model for the poetry to which the young Simichidas aspires, but not for Lycidas or his song.

If, then, *Idyll* 7 commemorates the separation between the poet who has written the poem and the poet who is remembered in it, this is because it imagines the transformative moment that gave birth to his more imaginative successor. Like Hesiod's encounter with the Muses in the opening of the *Theogony*, the poem imagines a scene of inspiration that changes its poet forever. But who is the inspirer here? Who or what is Lycidas? He appears in the poem as the exemplary herdsman, and the song he sings gives supreme expression to the mimetic desire that animates all of Theocritus' bucolic fiction. Theocritus, it appears, has made his inspiration scene an encounter between a version of himself and a fictional dramatic character who is in fact the fruit of that inspiration.[56] Why, then, has Theocritus chosen to portray himself under an assumed name in this encounter? Lejeune, in his earliest efforts to theorize autobiography at least, argued that the absence of a single name shared by author, narrator, and protagonist ruins the notion of autobiography: "The hero can resemble the author as much as he wants; as long as he does not have his name, there is in effect nothing. Autobiography is not a guessing game; it is in fact exactly the opposite."[57] Yet the line between autobiography and autobiographical fiction is not so easy to maintain, as his own efforts to police it show. He cites Gide, Mauriac, and Sartre, who all claim that the truest, and perhaps the only, way in which the autobiography of a fiction writer can be told is as fiction.[58] This, as we have seen, is an insight that was already possessed by ancient biographers and autobiographers. The moment of inspiration, in which the distinctive self responsible for the creation of the poetic work is born, cannot be truly told as a story of everyday growth and self-development. Something more dramatic is required – an encounter with a being who is not oneself.

At this point I would like to turn again to Pessoa and the heteronymic poets among whom he divided his poetic works. As many scholars have noted, the poets Pessoa invented – Alberto Caeiro, the writer of pastoral, Ricardo Reis, the neoclassical pessimist, Álvaro de Campos, the futurist – look like ways of bestowing full ontological independence upon Pessoa's various styles of poetic writing. This is "the adventure that binds the heteronyms together."[59] It is crucially important to appreciate that the heteronymic writing is not intended to provoke our wonder at the creative genius of a single author who was able to adopt a variety of masks, all

---

[56] Cf. Meillier (1993) 115: "Lycidas se présente comme le personnage de la fiction littéraire qu'est la bucolique, confronté à un createur de cette même fiction qu'est Simichidas, jeu comparable à celui du personnage d'Icare dans le roman de Queneau."
[57] Lejeune (1989) 13.   [58] Lejeune (1989) 26.   [59] Nogueras (1985) 450.

ultimately to be recognized as the many modes of a single self, but rather to draw our attention to an empirical self that is best conceived as it is in fact experienced – as a number of fully independent beings.[60] There is no self behind the masks, no author behind the personae, only an experience of selfhood that finds itself best articulated as a series of contradictory others. Pessoa's poetry thus does not simply enlarge the domain of the empirical self of author and reader by giving it access to worlds it could not otherwise have; almost any literary experience could do this. Nor does its contribution consist in showing that the empirical self, in its social manifestations, is not the whole self; this is hardly news by the early years of the twentieth century.[61] While the minute analyses of alienation and projection recorded in Pessoa's prose masterpiece, *The Book of Disquiet*, complement the poetry in interesting ways, the experience of the poetic heteronyms is rather more disquieting. For it suggests that personal development occurs through a process of self-fictionalization so radical that it amounts to the appearance of entirely new beings within the self. Pessoa's heteronyms are not temporary disguises that can be put on and off at will but ontologically independent others that coexist with the person that bears the name "Pessoa." The multiplicity in selfhood amounts not to a Whitmanesque abundance of actionable possible selves but rather to a feeling of ontological separation in their copresence.[62] And so it is that Pessoa looms larger and larger in the landscape of early modernism. As ontological experiments have become the dominant ones in postmodern poetics,[63] Pessoa's adventures in this area look decidedly prophetic. In particular, the dramatization of the discontinuity of selfhood as the author's encounter with his own literary personae is a postmodern fictional trope that is very fully explored in Pessoa's account of his relationship with his heteronyms.[64]

This relationship is not simply ludic. Pessoa describes the emergence of the heteronyms in a letter to Adolfo Casias Monteiro, a younger contemporary:

---

[60] So Hamburger (1969) 138–47 and De Sena (1982) 19–32 distinguish Pessoa's aims and achievement from the persona poetry of Pound, Eliot, and other twentieth-century poets.
[61] Cf. Hamburger (1969) 147.
[62] Cf. Pessoa (2001) 262: "My dramas, instead of being divided into acts full of action, are divided into souls. That's what this apparently baffling phenomenon comes down to ... I subsist as a medium of myself, but I'm less real than the others, less substantial, less personal, and easily influenced by them all. I too am a disciple of Caeiro."
[63] McHale (1987) xii, 10, 148, 213–14.
[64] So Timothy Findley, in *Famous Last Words* (1981), imagines a meeting between Ezra Pound and Hugh Selwyn Mauberley (see Hutcheon [1988] 148), and Kurt Vonnegut, in *Breakfast of Champions* (1973), records a meeting between Kilgore Trout, a caricature of the straightforward science fiction writer he used to be, and that author's author, Kurt Vonnegut (see McHale [1987] 72).

In 1912, if I remember correctly (and I can't be far off), I got the idea to write some poetry from a pagan perspective. I sketched out a few poems with irregular verse patterns (not in the style of Álvaro de Campos but in a semiregular style) and then forgot about them. But a hazy, shadowy portrait of the person who wrote those verses took shape in me. (Unbeknownst to me, Ricardo Reis had been born.)

A year and a half or two years later, it one day occurred to me to play a joke on Sá-Carneiro – to invent a rather complicated bucolic poet whom I would present in some guise of reality that I've since forgotten. I spent a few days trying in vain to envision this poet. One day when I'd finally given up – it was March 8th, 1914 – I walked over to a high chest of drawers, took a sheet of paper, and began to write standing up, as I do whenever I can. And I wrote thirty-some poems at once, in a kind of ecstasy I'm unable to describe. It was the triumphal day of my life, and I can never have another one like it. I began with a title, *The Keeper of Sheep*. This was followed by the appearance in me of someone whom I instantly named Alberto Caeiro. Excuse the absurdity of this statement: my master had appeared in me. That was what I immediately felt, and so strong was the feeling that, as soon as those thirty-odd poems were written, I grabbed a fresh sheet of paper and wrote, again all at once, the six poems that constitute "Slanting Rain," by Fernando Pessoa. All at once and with total concentration . . . It was the return of Fernando Pessoa as Alberto Caeiro to Fernando Pessoa himself. Or rather, it was the reaction of Fernando Pessoa against his nonexistence as Alberto Caeiro.

Once Alberto Caeiro had appeared, I instinctively and subconsciously tried to find disciples for him. From Caeiro's false paganism I extracted the latent Ricardo Reis, at last discovering his name and adjusting him to his true self, for now I actually *saw* him. And then a new individual, quite the opposite of Ricardo Reis, suddenly and impetuously came to me. In an unbroken stream, without interruptions or corrections, the ode whose name is "Triumphal Ode," by the man whose name is none other than Álvaro de Campos, issued from my typewriter.[65]

What begins as play, a prank upon a younger poet, becomes an unsettling experience of the self-alienation that is inseparable from fictional invention. As in *Idyll* 7, this invention is given a particular date and time, one that can only figure as a source of nostalgia since the writer knows it will never be experienced with the same intensity again. Most striking, however, is Pessoa's sense that this master who has appeared in him is an independent being, so that he can hardly speak of himself as his inventor. His autonomy is acknowledged by the heteronym, and by the need that is immediately felt to fashion a disciple for him.[66] So it is that, as another younger poetic

---

[65] Pessoa (2001) 256. The letter is discussed by Paz (1995) 7–8, an introduction to Pessoa.
[66] It is interesting to note that Caeiro, the sun around whom the other heteronyms and Pessoa himself keep their courses, in the metaphor of Paz (1995) 10, was conceived by Pessoa as a bucolic poet, the author of *The Keeper of Sheep* and *The Amorous Shepherd*. Paz points out that Caeiro (and in this he is like Lycidas) is a sage, not a philosopher, insofar as his life is inseparable from his thinking, and so is paradoxically the least real of all the heteronyms because his existence denies the very distance between lived and imaginary experience (in Pessoa) of which he is the outcome.

acquaintance of Pessoa has claimed, the older poet's mystification of his inner life is "a serious way of reaching the core of the creative process," for it is only through self-fictionalization that the poet is able to attain the relationship with himself that would allow him to create mimetic poetry.[67] And so it is that Pessoa, a poet who, in his own words, "is several different poets at once, a dramatic poet who writes lyrical poems," refuses the distinction between dramatic and lyric poetry, so that lyric poetry "draws close to dramatic poetry without assuming dramatic form." The poems of his heteronyms, he claims, "are a literature that I have created and lived, sincere because it is . . . felt in the other's person; written dramatically, but as sincere (in my sense of the word) as what King Lear says, though Lear is not Shakespeare, but one of his creations."[68]

Something like the heteronym seems to have been current in the Hellenistic period, for some poets are known to have used a name resembling a patronymic to sign parts of their work, and Theocritus alludes to this practice in *Idyll* 7 with his reference to the poet Asclepiades under his assumed name Sicelidas.[69] However, the extended use of heteronymic narrative for the inspiration scene of *Idyll* 7 has special relevance for a poem in which an authentic bucolic poetry of impersonation and imagined identification is contrasted with a superficial bucolic poetry that merely cloaks the expression of erotic desire with rustic imagery. For the bucolic character is essentially labile; in any given poem, a character no sooner appears before us than he imagines himself in the role of other bucolic characters. *Idyll* 7, then, engages in a double play with this distinctive characteristic of bucolic song. Just as Lycidas projects himself into an imagined past, so that by thinking of himself as the audience of Comatas he completes his self-creation as a bucolic character, so Theocritus projects Simichidas into the past, imagining the moment at which he was the audience of Lycidas as the decisive experience in his becoming capable of the authentic bucolic poetry of which Lycidas is the embodiment.[70]

---

[67] De Sena (1982) 29. [68] Pessoa cited in Hamburger (1969) 139, 146.
[69] See Gow (1952) *ad loc.* 7.40, who also notes: "Ligyastades is said to be formed from λιγύς, and, if so, refers like Melicertes to the writer's poetical quality." Cf. Wendel (1899) 20: "veri homines suis veris nominibus appellantur exceptis ut videtur duobus, ipso Theocrito et Asclepiade poetis, qui nomina Simichidae ac Sicelidae assumpserunt."
[70] Why Theocritus chose the name Simichidas is unknown. Some ancient commentators saw a link with the epithet *simos*, "snub-nosed," which the goatherd of *Idyll* 3 applies to himself, and imagined that the anonymous herdsman of this poem was also the poet in disguise; see Σ 3.1a, 8/9a, Wendel (1914) 117, 119. This is an attractive suggestion insofar as it points to the transformation of real life in the image of pastoral fiction that is such a prominent theme of *Idyll* 7. Certainly no better explanation has been offered to date; the other suggestion found in the scholia, that Simichidas is Theocritus' real patronymic, is contradicted by the evidence that his parents were named Praxagoras

From fiction to metafiction

The heteronym Simichidas allows a version of the poet to meet Lycidas, a fictional character, in a fictional inspiration scene.[71] By showing this naïve, yet initially rather smug, younger self outwitted, yet inspired, by the embodiment of his own bucolic fiction, Theocritus creates a poem that is unlike anything else in ancient literature. Yet in doing so he remains faithful to the message of this fiction, that we change by identifying with the products of our imagination. It is, then, entirely fitting that a kind of fiction that celebrates the power of imaginary experience to transform the lives of those who engage in it should represent its founding moment as the encounter between its creator and one of his own fictional creations. As Girard observed of Proust, mimetic desire achieves its truest expression when the author shows himself to be the subject of the very experience he has portrayed in his invented characters.[72] As we have seen with Hermesianax, other Hellenistic poets invent stranger and more hilarious relationships between the poet's life and his work. If my reading of *Idyll* 7 is right, however, this poem conceives of an entirely new possibility in this regard. For the poem does not simply imagine the possibility that a work of poetic fiction might be conceived as the expression of the inner life of the poet who wrote it, but envisages the possibility that its creator might appear in it alongside his fictional characters. This possibility is not explored by Hermesianax, but, as we shall see in the next chapter, it is enthusiastically embraced by a certain line of development in Theocritus' bucolic imitators.

---

and Philinna; see Gow (1952) I.xvi, Hunter (1999) 1. Kossaifi (2002) 358–61 compares the formations Melicertes and Ligyastades and concludes that Simichidas is a programmatic formation from *simos* that emphasizes the poet's solidarity with those of his characters who achieve peace through song while at the same time gently mocking the pretensions of his self-representation as a "sonorous mouthpiece of the Muses." For Nickau (2002) 398, the name points to Simias of Rhodes.

[71] Cf. Bowie (1985) 77: "Theocritus could hardly, on a walk in the countryside, encounter a fictitious character." So too, by the use of the heteronym, Pessoa was able to invent a meeting between himself (his orthonym) and the bucolic master Caeiro in which Caeiro inspires his "inventor" Pessoa with a new kind of poetry: "Pessoa, completely shaken upon hearing Caeiro read poems from his *The Keeper of Sheep*, immediately went home to write verses of a kind he never could have produced otherwise." See Pessoa (1998) 6, 41, and Guillén (1971) 242.

[72] See Girard (1966) 38, cited in Introduction, n. 38. So too Aristotle *Nicomachean Ethics* 9.7.3–4, 1167b34–68a4 concludes that were a poet's work to come to life, he would love this work more that it would love him.

Conclusion: The future of a fiction

Εἶπέ τις, Ἡράκλειτε, τεὸν μόρον, ἐς δέ με δάκρυ
ἤγαγεν· ἐμνήσθην δ'ὁσσάκις ἀμφότεροι
ἥλιον ἐν λέσχῃ κατεδύσαμην. ἀλλὰ σὺ μέν που,
ξεῖν' Ἁλικαρνησεῦ, τετράπαλαι σποδιή,
αἱ δὲ τεαὶ ζώουσιν ἀηδόνες, ἧσιν ὁ πάντων
ἁρπακτὴς Ἁίδης οὐκ ἐπὶ χεῖρα βαλεῖ.

Someone told me you were dead, Heraclitus, and it brought me to tears. I remembered how often the two of us, chatting, put the sun to bed. You, I suppose, my Halicarnassian friend, are long since dust. It is only your nightingales that live. On them Hades, who snatches all things, will not lay his hands.[1]

Callimachus' famous epigram is a studious and poignant reflection on the possibility of a kind of personal immortality through the survival of one's literary work. The message at first seems familiar and consoling: Heraclitus is dead, but no matter, his works live on and assure him a kind of afterlife. Contrasts between literature and life structure the poem. The physical separation of friends in the real world, Callimachus in Alexandria, Heraclitus, his Halicarnassian friend, dead someplace far away, is overcome by the fiction of literary address as the poet seems to speak to his dead friend, just as his poems, his "nightingales," will speak to all those addressees that Heraclitus will never know in the eternal present of poetic communication.[2] As Plato imagined in the *Symposium*, works of art are our most authentic progeny, a reflection that gains additional poignancy here when we recall that all we now have of Heraclitus is not a collection of poems that restore him to us with some sense of the fullness of a life lived, but a single funerary

---

[1] Callimachus, *Epigram* 2, Pfeiffer (1949–53) II.81 = *AP* 7.80.
[2] On the innovative use of fictions of direct address in the poem, see Walsh (1990) 1–6. Cf. Hunter (1992a) 113–23, who points to various ways in which the poem complicates its theme of literary immortality.

Conclusion: The future of a fiction

epigram, for a wife who died in childbirth, taking with her to Hades one of the twins she was in labor with.[3]

Yet the poem's ironies are not primarily concerned with the accidents of survival. While the disappearance of all but one of Heraclitus' poems has proven Callimachus' prediction wrong, the poem in fact asks us to consider just how much of a consolation their survival, in their entirety, would really be. The poem balances a fond memory of shared conversation, the many times that, in what sounds like a colloquial expression, the two friends, "chatting, put the sun to bed," with the formalization of speech in writing, the "nightingales" that constitute Heraclitus' claim to fame and hence to a kind of personal immortality. But it is this very relationship between literary work and living person that makes the question of immortality troubling rather than consoling. While it seems clear enough that ἀηδόνες, "nightingales," stands for poems, this is anything but ordinary language. The literary person that will be available to posterity through Heraclitus' poems will hardly be the genial conversational friend that is remembered in Callimachus' epigram, but rather some stylization of him. The second self the poems contain is a source of anxiety for Callimachus even as he contemplates the possibility that this self may live forever.

We can also appreciate the irony of the poem's fictional form of address from this perspective. Callimachus knows quite well of course that his friend cannot hear him, and that it is his own anxieties about the relationship between the empirical self and its projection in literary work that he is confronting here. If the debates surrounding the structure and editions of Callimachus' *magnum opus*, the *Aetia*, have taught us anything, it is that its poet was intensely concerned that the poem as a whole should be a full portrait of the creative life of the modern poet in all his guises – scholar, dream interlocutor with the Muses and the illustrious poetic dead, raconteur of curious and erotic tales, court poet and praise poet of the Alexandrian royal family.[4] Callimachus confronts the possibility of his own immortality by fabricating a dazzling multiplicity of possible selves in preparation for the afterlife. This self-portrait is further complicated by the collection of *Iambi*, in which the poet fabricates other

---

[3] *AP* 7.465 = Page (1975) p. 113 (Heraclitus 1). Cf. the discussion of poets as parents of their works in Aristotle *Nicomachean Ethics* 9.7.3–4, 1167b34–68a4.

[4] Cf. Meillier (1993) 111: "Callimaque va même très loin. Il ne fait pas un ou plusieurs receuils, mais l'édition de ses oeuvres, c'est-à-dire la représentation de toute une carrière de poète. L'édition elle-même devient le témoignage de d'un *bios*, comme le souligne le rapprochement entre sa jeunesse et sa vieillesse dans l'*Invective aux Telchines*, qui tient lieu de pièce liminaire." For an excellent summary of the ongoing debates about the form of the *Aetia*, see Hunter (2004) 44–49.

personae – moralist, impersonator of the archaic abuse poet Hipponax, polemicist, fabulist – that add to, and complicate, the self-image presented in the *Aetia*. Callimachus avoids nostalgia for the empirical self, and its occlusion by a simplified literary persona, by fabricating an array of literary selves that are as various as the poetic genres in which they are manifest.[5]

The *Aetia* also anticipates the kind of biographical approach to a poet's work that we have seen in Hermesianax and Longinus – reading it with varying degrees of seriousness as an analogue of his social or imaginative experience – by including a number of scenes in which the author gives a more or less tongue-in-cheek account of the origin of various moments in the poem we are reading: the antiquarian research that concludes the romantic tale of Acontius and Cydippe (frr. 67–75), the meeting at a drinking party with a stranger from the island of Icus that precedes the account of this island's curious ritual customs (fr. 178), and, most famously, the words of Apollo to the youthful poet with which the poem begins and which lay out the poetics of the poem we are about to read (fr. 1). Given the fragmentary state of the poem, it is difficult to assess how the demystified account of the origins of poetic speech in the tale of Acontius and Cydippe, or in the description of the ritual practices of the Icians, coexisted with the framework of an ongoing question-and-answer session with the Muses that structured Books 1 and 2 of the *Aetia*. What seems clear, however, is that the persona of a pedantic cataloguer is deliberately constructed so as to contrast at particular moments with the wonder of the tales themselves. The fabulous love story of the long-dead Acontius and Cydippe, for example, gains extra luster by contrast with the imagined dullness of the local historian of the island of Ceos, Xenomedes, in whose work the poet has found it, and with the equally dull life of the antiquarian poet who spends his days engaged in such reading.[6] The opening of the *Aetia* situates the poem in a tradition of inspiration stories that begin with Hesiod and Archilochus, and their encounter with divinities of song; here too an account of the special ontology of poetic narratives precedes the particular examples we are about to hear, and is connected with the autobiographical account of a moment in the poet's life in which the capability for this kind of narrative was guaranteed by the encounter with a god. However, the implied self-portrait of the poet as heir to a special kind of psychic richness as a result

---

[5] For a detailed discussion of the theme of *polyeideia*, or writing in different genres – the accusation of his critics that Callimachus sets out to justify in the *Iambi* (though the accusation may have been directed at his work as a whole) – see Acosta-Hughes (2002) and Fantuzzi and Hunter (2004) 17, 460.

[6] Cf. Hutchinson (1988) 30–31.

Conclusion: The future of a fiction

of this encounter is contrasted with the vignettes the poem offers of the poet in action, where he appears both literally and intellectually a model of sobriety. The imaginative richness of the *Aetia* cannot be discovered in the poet we encounter within it, so that the traditional mystery of poetic storytelling reappears in the poem as the contrast between the engaging variety of its tales and the image of the poet who has created them.

We have observed something similar in Theocritus' *Idyll* 7. The poem is an autobiographical account of a poet's life that seems to record a decisive moment in his literary development. However, the young poet who is the subject of the narrative is definitely not an inspiring presence in the poem. He comes from the city, is somewhat ill at ease with the inhabitants of the bucolic world to which his own poems lay claim, and the song he volunteers in his exchange with Lycidas suffers by comparison with that of the authentic herdsman singer. It is not until the end of the poem that he seems to grasp what is required of a genuine bucolic poet, but even here nothing of the poet who is capable of writing the poem as a whole appears in his poem except the fact of writing itself. The glamour of creative personality is deferred to the character of Lycidas, who appears to be a product of the imagination of the genuinely creative poet whose presence is excluded from his own inspiration story. Together, then, these two poems offer a fascinating meditation on the relationship between the imagined world of a writer's work, and the origin of that world in his empirical experience. For both poets thwart easy answers to questions about the ontology of their literary worlds, Callimachus by including in his own poem an ironically simplified depiction of its relationship to its sources, Theocritus by creating a fictionalized autobiography in which the relationship between creator and created is reversed.

Interest in the relationship between poetic worlds and their authors is, as we have seen, widespread in the poetry and poetics of the Hellenistic period. However, bucolic poetry was uniquely well positioned to become the medium in which reflection on this topic could occur. For while any work of literature may be read as a projection of the inner life of its author (as Hermesianax and Longinus read Homer), there is, in bucolic poetry, a particular symmetry between represented world and real world that invites autobiographical exploration on the part of both author and reader. The defining characteristic of Theocritus' shepherds is that they are singers whose major concern in the time in which we are able to observe them is to engage in fictionalizing self-projection in the medium of song. They are thus obvious doubles of the poet himself in a way that the characters of epic, or any other genre, are not. Because bucolic poetry consists of dramatizations of characters who, like their authors, are makers of songs, we are able to see clearly that literary characters may be understood as projections of the inner life of their authors. Because these characters are shepherds, which their authors are not, we can see that such projections are fictional, that is to say, that it is by imaginative identification with invented others that the psyche gives life to its own movements. This point is clearer still when we recall that the contents of the shepherds' songs are efforts to identify with characters that they imagine as counterparts of their own inner life.

The claims of the bucolic world as a representation of the poet's literary imagination have, as we shall see, been set forth with exemplary clarity in the case of Virgil's *Eclogues*,[7] and it is no part of my intention to underestimate Virgil's achievement in this respect. However, by examining in some detail the path from the *Idylls* to the *Eclogues*, I hope to show how the reception of Theocritus' poems prepared the way for the thematization of this relationship in Virgil's work by making explicit the analogy between bucolic poet and bucolic character that is, as I have shown, already present and clearly legible in the *Idylls* themselves. In particular, I hope to show that the contrast between a simple or mimetic Theocritus and a complex, or self-reflective, Virgil that has underwritten so much of the comparison between the two poets is illusory insofar as it concerns the poet's self-representation in his poems. For the very self-consciousness about the bucolic fiction that has been taken as one of the defining characteristics of Virgil's adaptation of his Theocritean models was recognized in the *Idylls* themselves by their earliest commentators and adaptors.

A variety of interpretive approaches to the bucolic poems are apparent in the first critical and creative responses to them. The majority of the ancient scholarship preserved in the scholia tries to accommodate them within the familiar categories of Aristotelian genre theory. For Aristotle, genre is determined by correlating character type with form. Thus, the representation of men better than ourselves in dramatic form gives tragedy, the presentation of men worse than ourselves in dramatic form gives comedy, and so on (*Poetics* 3–4).[8] This synchronic view is combined with a diachronic perspective on the evolution of tragedy and comedy as a development of the dramatic potential inherent in the ritual origin of both genres: tragedy arose from the speech of the leaders of the dithyramb, comedy from the speech of the leaders of phallic song. Both ideas can found in the scholia to Theocritus. The

---

[7] See the discussion of Putnam (1970), Schmidt (1972), and Alpers (1979) below.
[8] Cf. Gill (1993) 76–77: "Each poetic form is characterized by certain generic features: it has its own specific objects of *mimesis*, and its own specific means and modes of *mimesis*."

diachronic perspective is found in section B of the Prolegomena, where the account of bucolic poetry's ritual origin is modeled upon the discussion of comedy's ritual origin in *Poetics* Chapter 3.[9] The synchronic view is found in Section D, where it is argued that the bucolic poems represent ordinary peasants in a variety of literary forms.[10] While there is not a consistent relationship between content and form in these poems as there is in the classical genres, genre theory can still be used to analyze them because their subject matter remains constant, and all forms may ultimately be regarded as either narrative, dramatic, or mixed, depending on whether or not the poet speaks in his own voice in them.[11] The Prolegomena thus treat the bucolic characters as ordinary herdsmen, even though the commentaries on the individual poems identify some of them as mythical beings – the desire for generic consistency outweighs the recognition that they are drawn from a variety of realms.[12]

The same desire for consistency can be seen in the scholiasts' unwillingness to leave any of the herdsmen without a name. They suggest that the goatherd of *Idyll* 3 is Battus of *Idyll* 4, since at 4.38–40 Battus mentions Amaryllis as the object of his affections, and this is also the name of the Nymph courted by the goatherd in *Idyll* 3. Similarly, they propose that the unnamed goatherd of *Idyll* 1 is either Menalcas or Comatas. The scholia to *Idyll* 7 even suggest that Comatas and Menalcas are one and the same, further simplifying the cast of characters. As the scholiasts are troubled by the fact that anonymous characters occupy center stage in *Idyll* 1 and *Idyll* 3, and try to fill in the names that Theocritus has left blank, so too they are concerned with the fact that characters with the same name have markedly different attributes from one poem to the next. Thus, the scholia to *Idyll* 9

---

[9] Cremonesi (1958) 109–22. The scholia consist of Prolegomena, which precede the collection, Hypotheses, which precede and summarize the individual poems, and line-by-line commentary. The Prolegomena consist of the following: the life of Theocritus (A), the invention of bucolic poetry (B), the kinds of herdsmen (C), the form of the poems (D), the meaning of the term "Idyll" (E), dialect (F), epigrams on the collection (G, H). See Wendel (1914) 1–7.

[10] Prolegomena D, Wendel (1914) 5: "As far as is possible this poetry portrays the ways of countrymen, depicting very delightfully those who are made sullen by their rusticity in accordance with their way of life." This is what Van Sickle (1976) 35 calls the "simple mimetic concept" of the poems.

[11] As discussed in Chapter 2. See, for example, *Id.* 1 arg., Wendel (1914) 23, *Id.* 5 arg., Wendel (1914) 154.

[12] The Hypothesis to *Idyll* 8, which, like *Idyll* 9, includes a dialogue between Daphnis and Menalcas, refers to Alexander Aetolus, in whose work Daphnis appeared as the tutor of Marsyas, and to Sositheus, in one of whose plays his companion Menalcas was judged the loser in a singing contest by Pan. Cf. Gow (1952) *ad loc.* 8.2, Hunter (1999) 66. The effort on the part of the scholiasts to systematize the bucolic world, and thereby make it recognizable as a synecdoche of a segment of real life, is discussed with exemplary thoroughness in Fantuzzi (forthcoming). I thank the author for sharing this work with me ahead of publication and only regret that it did not come to my attention sooner.

ponder whether the Menalcas of this poem is the same as that of *Idyll* 8, having swapped his sheep for cows, or a different Menalcas who is a cowherd, and assert, in the Hypothesis to *Idyll* 1, that the Daphnis of *Idyll* 6 is the Daphnis of *Idyll* 1. As I have argued earlier, an author as self-conscious of his reshaping of characters from the literary tradition as Theocritus shows himself to be in his creation of the Cyclops of *Idyll* 11 is unlikely to have been unaware of this issue, whether his poems were disseminated piecemeal or in a collection,[13] and the scholia are aware of it too, although they do not discuss it in any detail.

What we miss in them is any extended consideration of the reasons why the attributes of the bucolic characters of both Theocritus and his imitators should be so different from one poem to the next if they are in fact the same person. For the scholia do not reflect upon the role of impersonation in the poems, and how this gives the bucolic characters their essential lability. The Daphnis of *Idyll* 1 is an impersonation by Thyrsis, while the Daphnis of *Idyll* 6 himself impersonates the companion of Polyphemus in his dialogue with Damoetas. The shifting image we have of Daphnis in particular points to the self-fictionalizing impulse that is at the heart of bucolic song: when he appears in his own person in *Idyll* 6, all he has in common with his impersonation by Thyrsis in *Idyll* 1 is the fact of impersonation itself. Marco Fantuzzi, in an important article, has pointed out how, in contrast to the scholia, this lability is recognized by Theocritus' first creative imitators, and motivates their own continuing development of the character of Daphnis. While acknowledging the argument of earlier critics that the imitation of Theocritus in the post-Theocritean *Idyll* 8 gave rise "to an idealised, sentimental bucolic 'manner' by superimposing a mythical Daphnis and a 'living' bucolic shepherd Daphnis," Fantuzzi argues that "the author of *Id.* 8 arrived at this superimposition not only as a result of an obvious idealising short-sightedness, but probably because he was 'authorised' by a superimposition of the different characterizations of Daphnis in two of Theocritus' poems (*Idd.* 1 and 6)."[14] By contrasting the two versions of Daphnis in *Idyll* 1 and *Idyll* 6, the author of *Idyll* 8 has recognized the fictionalizing impulse of both author and character, which then becomes a model for his own idealizing fiction.

It is only a small step from seeing the bucolic characters as fully fictional beings – inventions of their author who have no reality outside their author's

---

[13] As discussed in Chapter 2, n. 7.
[14] Fantuzzi (1998) 61–62. The argument that the author of *Idyll* 8 is responsible for an idealizing bucolic "manner" because he lacks familiarity with the realities of pastoral life and labor is advanced by Rossi (1971b).

imagination – to seeing them as versions of that author, fictional projections of his own self-understanding, and this step was taken by at least some critics in antiquity. The majority of the scholia derive from the work of Theon who was active in Alexandria between 50 BCE and 20 CE, and it is tempting to ascribe the unsatisfactory synthesis of Aristotelian genre theory I have outlined above to his belated efforts to combine the work of his predecessors.[15] There is another voice in the scholia, however, that offers a more interesting solution to the problem posed by the novelty of the bucolic characters. The critic Munatius is cited eight times in the Theocritus scholia, three times on questions of prosody (1.110 a,c, 2.100b, 9.14), once for an etymology (7.138a), and once regarding the Arcadian festival of Pan to which Simichidas refers in *Idyll* 7 (7.106, 7.108b). With one exception, where he is chastised for his ignorance of quantity (2.100b), his suggestions are accepted. On three occasions, however, he is censured for his identification of characters. In *Idyll* 3 he identifies the speaker as Theocritus because the epithet *simos*, "snub-nosed," which the goatherd applies to himself, suggests Simichidas of *Idyll* 7.[16] In *Idyll* 7 he names Simichidas' companions on the walk as Phrasidamus and Antigenes, the hosts of the festival, rather than Eucritus and Amyntas (7 arg. a). In *Idyll* 17 he identifies the wrong Ptolemy (Philopator) as the recipient of the poem. The last is simply a mistake, but calling Simichidas' traveling companions in *Idyll* 7 Phrasidamus and Antigenes so blatantly contradicts the opening verse of the poem that it is unlikely to be a mere error. It seems instead to be something like an ancient version of the "bucolic masquerade" in which the characters of the poems are seen as Theocritus and his contemporaries in pastoral disguise.[17] Munatius' interpretation of *Idyll* 3 takes this idea a

---

[15] His commentary on Theocritus was preceded by the work of Asclepiades of Myrlea, his commentary on Nicander by the work of Demetrius Chloros and Antigonus; see Wendel (1920) 165, Guhl (1969) 3, 17 nn. 1a and 1b. It has likewise been suggested that his commentary on Callimachus resembled his role in the history of the Pindar scholia: synthesis and summary of his predecessors rather than original research; see Cameron (1995) 191–94.

[16] Σ 3.1a, 3.8, 3.9a, Wendel (1914) 117, 119. These suggestions are refuted by the scholia with a sharpness that suggests contemporary polemic. Since the final stratum of original scholarship in the scholia derives from the work of Theaetetus and Amarantus in the second century CE, Munatius has been identified with the critic Munatius of Tralles, who is named by Philostratus as one of the teachers of Herodes Atticus (*Lives of the Sophists* 538, 564). See Wendel (1920) 75. Intriguingly, at *Idyll* 14.53 the unhappy lover who is thinking of becoming a mercenary refers to a Simos who sailed off to Alexandria because he had fallen in love with a hard-hearted girl, and came back cured.

[17] Taking his cue from the assertion of bucolic poetry's ritual origin in Prolegomena B, Reitzenstein argued that Theocritus and his friends on Cos organized their poetic circle in imitation of a group of cowherds devoted to Artemis, and that his bucolic poetry originated in this cultic milieu. The group abandoned a formal connection with cult, at which point the personalities and poetic concerns of its members became clearly perceptible in the song contests of the *Idylls*. For his identification of the historical poets concealed in the *Idylls*, see Reitzenstein (1893) 228–39.

stage further, seeing Theocritus himself in the poem's nameless goatherd. The suggestion that the poet has portrayed himself as a rustic is rejected by the other scholiasts as inappropriate: "It is unfitting for Theocritus to be in love with a peasant girl, going as far as to spend time in the fields."[18] They do not think that it is inappropriate for Theocritus to have represented himself in his own poems as such. The Hypothesis to *Idyll* 7 states that Simichidas is the poet, and that it is Theocritus who narrates how he met Lycidas on the way to the festival.[19] It is acceptable for Theocritus to portray himself interacting with a herdsman in Simichidas' exchange of songs with Lycidas because he has been clearly identified as a city-dweller beforehand (7.2). What is unacceptable is for the poet to portray himself as a herdsman, adopting the language and manners of his own rustic characters.

Perhaps Munatius saw the impossibility of interpreting the goatherd of *Idyll* 3 mimetically, as a realistic dramatization of a real-world herdsman. Perhaps he had also read *Idyll* 12, and noticed the similarity in the language of its nameless speaker to that of the nameless herdsman of *Idyll* 3.[20] While the speaker of *Idyll* 12 is called Theocritus not just by the scholia, but also by modern editors,[21] it is only a small step from the self-fictionalizing persona of this poem to the fully fictional self-projection of *Idyll* 3, and the line between them is not only difficult to police, but perhaps not worth drawing in the first place. Likewise, in *Idyll* 11 Theocritus makes his fictional Cyclops the means by which he communicates with his real-world interlocutor Nicias, so that a fictional character is manifestly the projection of an authorial intention. Finally, in *Idyll* 7 the ontological difference that ought to keep fictional character and real-world author apart is removed entirely, so that the young bucolic poet Simichidas is able to meet the product of Theocritus' own bucolic imagination, Lycidas. This possibility, that the author of a fiction might appear, in one guise or another, in the fictional world of his own invention, clearly has tremendous potential as a means of staging the relationship between the author and his own creative imagination, and it is indeed seized upon by later bucolic poets as a way of thematizing both the power and the limits of fictionalizing self-projection.

---

[18] Σ 3.1a, Wendel (1914) 117.
[19] *Id.* 7 arg. b, Wendel (1914) 76–77; cf. arg. c: "Theocritus speaks the introduction."
[20] Gutzwiller (1991) 180–81, by contrast, argues that Munatius is reading the analogy between herdsman and poet that is established only in later bucolic poetry back into the *Idylls*.
[21] Cf. Gow (1952) II.221: "This Idyll is a monologue addressed by the poet to a boy whose two days' absence has seemed all too long." Gow refers to the speaker as "T." throughout his commentary on the poem, deploring its "conspicuous deficiencies of tact and taste," though noting the opinion of Wilamowitz that its bucolic elements are "not to be taken quite seriously when applied to the poet himself."

Conclusion: The future of a fiction

The transformation of this idea, present in Theocritus in a suggestive, embryonic form, into a central feature of the bucolic poetry of the *Lament for Bion* and the *Eclogues* of Virgil and Calpurnius Siculus will be the subject of the remainder of this chapter.

The *Lament for Bion* is the work of an unknown writer mourning in it the death of the poet Bion who flourished around 100 BCE The poem blends echoes of "The Sorrows of Daphnis" in Theocritus' *Idyll* 1, most obviously in its refrain – "begin the grief, Sicilian Muses, begin" – with imitation of the *Lament for Adonis* of Bion himself. In the latter the goddess Aphrodite mourns the death of her lover Adonis, and hills, rivers, and flowers, Hymen, the Graces, and eventually the Fates come to share in her distress. The extravagant emotional tone of the *Lament for Adonis* is quite different from Thyrsis' song in *Idyll* 1, but the narrative premise of the two is similar: a pastoral hero is grieved by nature and a series of divinities. The novelty of the *Lament for Bion* is apparent by comparison; it is a real historical poet who is commemorated in the poem, and who is mourned in the lamentation scenes within it. Initially his mourners are mythical beings – Apollo and Aphrodite, as well as Nymphs, satyrs, and a host of lesser gods – and natural phenomena: streams, rivers, trees, flowers, birds, and animals. So far, then, the poem is in keeping with its models. Next, however, the poet presents a scene in which the dead Bion is lamented by his own poetic creations (58–63):

> κλαίει καὶ Γαλάτεια τὸ σὸν μέλος, ἅν ποκ' ἔτερπες
> ἑζομέναν μετὰ σεῖο παρ' ἀιόνεσσι θαλάσσας·
> οὐ γὰρ ἴσον Κύκλωπι μελίσδεο. τὸν μὲν ἔφευγεν
> ἁ καλὰ Γαλάτεια, σὲ δ' ἅδιον ἔβλεπεν ἅλμας,
> καὶ νῦν λασαμένα τῶ κύματος ἐν ψαμάθοισιν
> ἕζετ' ἐρημαίαισι, βόας δ' ἔτι σεῖο νομεύει.

Galateia too weeps for your song, whom you used to delight as she sat beside you on the shore. For you did not play like the Cyclops. The lovely Galateia shunned him, but you she looked upon with more delight than the sea, and now, having forgotten about its waves, she sits upon the lonely sands, and tends your flocks till this hour.

In this remarkable scene, the fictional Galateia is portrayed as having listened to the poetry of the historical Bion while he was alive, and, now that he is dead, as continuing to lament her own inventor. The poem goes on to claim that Bion, in his own life (80–81), "piped as a cowherd and sang while he herded; he made pipes and milked the sweet heifer." Scholars have noted that this is the first time in the bucolic tradition that a historical poet is called a herdsman.[22] Bion can, however, only be called a herdsman because the author of the *Lament* has created a world in which the poet he is commemorating associates with and is lamented by his own bucolic characters. He lives in the same world as them.[23] Finally, in an extension of the mourning scene unprecedented in the poem's models, the poet presents a series of Greek sites that lament the death of Bion more than they did the deaths of their own native poets: Ascra, Boeotia, Lesbos, Paros, and Mytilene grieve more than they did for Hesiod, Pindar, Alcaeus, Archilochus, and Sappho respectively (86–97). Having created a poetic world in which gods, fictional beings, and historical cities can lament together, the poet turns to gnomic reflection on the nature of his own grief – men, unlike plants, will not spring again from the earth once they are buried in it (99–107) – recalls Bion's mysterious death – he seems to have perished by consuming a poison (*pharmakon*) that he had asked to be prepared for him (109–12) – and concludes by claiming that if his song had the same power to charm the underworld divinities as Bion's had, he would have sung the present poem to them in Hades (113–26).

The author of the *Lament for Bion* emphasizes his own, and the dead Bion's, allegiance to the bucolic poetry of Theocritus. He calls himself "no stranger to bucolic song, which I learned from you [Bion] as an inheritor of the Doric Muse," and perhaps refers to Bion as "a Theocritus to the Syracusans" (93–96).[24] However, in making the bucolic poem a world in which ontologically problematic contact between the realms of myth, bucolic literature, and historical reality can be staged, he clearly moves well beyond the model that authorizes his experiments in this regard. In doing so, he foregrounds the power of the bucolic poet as fiction maker to appropriate entities from all of these worlds to create the world of his bucolic poems.[25] In the actual world, it is impossible for a poet to meet a character

---

[22] Van Sickle (1976) 27, Alpers (1996) 153.
[23] Manakidou (1996) 48 observes that in this poem "a poetic creation of Bion is presented mourning for his loss," but does not comment further.
[24] The text is very problematic here. At line 93, the manuscripts of the poem have ἐν δὲ Συρακοσίοισι Θεόκριτος, and Gow (following Musurus) prints a lacuna before it. The line marks the transition from the lament of the Greek cities that mourn their native sons less than they do Bion (who is referred to in the second person) to the continuation of bucolic poetry by his successors. Wilamowitz accordingly proposed εἰ δὲ Συρακοσίοισι Θεόκριτος, "you, Bion, are [a, another] Theocritus to the Syracusans." The suggestion is difficult, however, and it is perhaps easier to imagine an omission that claimed something like "even Theocritus was mourned less among the Syracusans than you were, Bion." In either case, the poem stresses that Bion exemplifies bucolic poetry as well as, or even better than, its inventor, Theocritus, and so the poet himself hopes to live up to the tradition as its inheritor.
[25] For an exemplary demonstration of this point that draws upon Dolezel (1998), see Kania (2004). Cf. now the discussion of the *Lament* in the conclusion to the section entitled "Myth" in Bernsdorff (forthcoming).

from his own poetry if this character is invented, although, as the prologue to Hesiod's *Theogony* indicates, his encounters with gods whose stories are told in myth may be recorded in his poems in a way that eludes definitive redescription as either literary trope or autobiographical testimony.[26] For it is generally believed that some kind of interaction between these beings and ordinary mortals is possible. Contact between actual and fictional entities is not, however, conventionally accepted, although in bucolic poetry it can be staged. As I have argued, Theocritus, in *Idyll* 7, masks the ontological and cognitive difficulties of such contact by inventing the heteronym Simichidas to stage his own encounter with the fictional being Lycidas. The author of the *Lament for Bion* is far less reticent in this respect. He quite unabashedly asserts Bion's coexistence with his fictional creations, and leaves his readers to work out the consequences.[27] One answer to the problem of their sharing a world is to reply that this world is fictional; all its agents are therefore equally fictional, and the Bion it portrays has a nonessential relationship with his historical counterpart.[28] Yet the poem presents itself as a lament for a real-world poet, with whom its composer has a real-world relationship as apprentice and successor. Moreover, it is not just the author who laments the poet but a series of real historical cities that are more grieved by his death than they were by the deaths of their most celebrated native authors. Like Theocritus' *Idyll* 11, the poem's bucolic fiction is intended to produce a real-world effect – in this case, grief for the dead poet – which it could hardly do if the Bion who appears within it could not be identified with his real-world counterpart. The poem calls into question the ontological separation of the "purely fictional" even as it revels in its own ability to create a world we can only understand as such.

In this respect, the *Lament for Bion* is a worthy successor to *Idyll* 7. In that poem Theocritus' bucolic fiction comes full circle, and the heteronym of its maker is shown to emulate his invented characters, aspiring to a purified version of a pastoral world he himself has inhabited, just as they

---

[26] See the discussion in the previous chapter. Lowe (2000) 263 notes the permeability of the boundary between myth and reality as crucial to the operation of myth in Old Comedy.
[27] The *Lament* poet's extravagance is clear when one compares him with Hermesianax in this regard; while, as we saw in the previous chapter, Hermesianax invents imaginative stories in which the narratives of well-known poems are read as fictional analogues of events in their authors' lives, he never attempts a scene in which an author is in love with one of his own creations. Cf. Caspers (forthcoming), who imagines just such a possibility on the part of Hermesianax only to dismiss it as inconceivable in practice: "It would have been an absurdity unparalleled even in fr. 7 to have suggested that the historical poet Philoxenos was in love with the nymph Galateia."
[28] So Kania (2004) 13, who also observes, however, that "the poet is not unaware of the irony entailed in using a carefully constructed fiction to sing the praises of a real poet and real poetry" (21).

do. Here too entry into the bucolic world is presented as the attainment of the bucolic poet who has been able to emulate his predecessors successfully. As Theocritus is no longer simply the historical poet of that name but a bucolic archetype that has been successfully emulated by his successor, Bion, so Bion in turn has become such a model for the author of the poem, who is "no stranger to the bucolic song" that he learned from him as his pupil (93–97). As the majority of the bucolic *Idylls* imagine the transformation of the herdsmen in the image of their own song, so this poem, like *Idyll* 7, imagines the transformation of the historical poet in the image of his own fiction. The emulation that is characteristic of bucolic poetry is not just poem-internal.[29] Rather, the problematic contact between historical and fictional worlds makes it clear that bucolic poetry is the place where the recursive relationship between literary fiction and historical reality may be staged and investigated. As the bucolic poets are assimilated to their own fictional creations, they become models for bucolic imitation in much the same way as the fictional beings their poems contain. If, therefore, in the *Lament for Bion* the dead poet is represented as a herdsman, he has simply experienced the same transformation as Theocritus' fictional characters: by singing of bucolic singers he became one himself.[30]

The ease of this transformation is taken for granted in the bucolic poems of Theocritus; while the goatherd of *Idyll* 3 may have some difficulty in convincing himself (and us) of his resemblance to his self-elected models, the majority of the herdsmen blend without difficulty into their imagined doubles, Thyrsis with Daphnis, Lycidas with Comatas, Daphnis and Damoetas with Polyphemus and his friend. Their self-transformation is as effortless as the act of singing, the imitation as convincing and compelling as the staging of Polyphemus that Theocritus offers his friend Nicias in *Idyll* 11. Likewise, in the *Lament for Bion* the freedom to have whatever kind of imaginative life one desires is simply taken for granted as the premise of the bucolic fiction. As we shall see, it is the very ease of the bucolic assimilation of self to model, the free extension of selfhood through fictional self-projection, that will be questioned in Virgil's version of pastoral.

The bucolic *Idylls* demonstrate in exemplary fashion the process by which, through identification with the products of the imagination, the

---

[29] As in the intertextual approaches of Hubbard (1998) 37 and Berger (1984) 39.
[30] Cf. Schmidt (1972) 111: "Es ist ein überprüfbares Faktum, daß die antike Bukolik die einzige literarische Gattung ist, die durchgehend von Dichtern handelt und zwar gerade sowohl insofern sie selbst Bukolik ist als auch insofern diese Dichter Dichter sind. Diese Dichter sind als Hirten Hirtendichter, d. h. Bukoliker. Der Dichter, der sie dichtet, ist ebenso ein Bukoliker, also dasselbe wie seine Dichter. Schon das ist in keine andere Gattung möglich. Zwar sind Homer und Phemios beide Aöden, Homer ist dies aber nicht insofern, als er von Phemios singt."

Conclusion: The future of a fiction

fictional becomes the real.[31] As the herdsmen sing their songs, they freely identify with the bucolic heroes of their own imagination, and so transform themselves in their image. In *Idyll* 7 Theocritus stages the same process in the autobiography of his young poet Simichidas, and in the *Lament for Bion* this identification of the bucolic poet with the products of his own imagination is made explicit. The first poem in Virgil's collection of bucolic poetry opens with a famous image of pastoral leisure that encapsulates this conception of bucolic poetry as imaginative freedom (*Eclogue* 1.1–2):

> Tityre, tu patulae recubans sub tegmine fagi
> silvestrem tenui Musam meditaris avena.

You, Tityrus, lying beneath the covering of spreading beech, meditate your woodland Muse on slender reed.

This poem looks as if it will begin like Theocritus' *Idyll* 1, with a contemplation of bucolic song by two accomplished musicians. Here too neither herdsman is presently engaged in music, and the verb of reflection, *meditaris*, which replaces συρίσδες, "you pipe," of *Idyll* 1, makes its contemplative character clearer still.[32] However, what develops in *Idyll* 1 into a leisurely meditation as the herdsmen compliment one another's musical skills, here immediately takes a quite different turn (1.3–5):

> nos patriae finis et dulcia linquimus arva.
> nos patriam fugimus: tu, Tityre, lentus in umbra
> formosam resonare doces Amaryllida silvas.

We are leaving the boundaries of our homeland and its sweet fields; we are exiles from our homeland; you, Tityrus, relaxing in the shade, will teach the woods to echo sweet Amaryllis.

The careful chiastic structures, brought over from *Idyll* 1, no longer express the contrasting styles of two herdsmen who inhabit the same landscape and whose only threat in the pursuit of their chosen art is the possible incursion of the god Pan, if they should awaken him with their music. Instead, this is a landscape that belongs to human landlords; it has boundaries and fields, and what one thinks of as one's home may belong to someone else tomorrow. The fictional world of *Idyll* 1 is, in a single stroke, circumscribed by a larger world of history and politics, within which its pleasant fictions are permitted to continue only at the discretion of the current owners.[33] By juxtaposing Tityrus' woodland Muse with the realities of contemporary

---

[31] Cf. Iser (1993) 22–86.   [32] Alpers (1979) 74.
[33] On Virgil's historicizing of the bucolic world, see Otis (1963) 135–36.

rural life, Virgil allows the bucolic world to manifest itself as an image of imaginative freedom under threat, while at the same time suggesting that, under such circumstances, continuing commitment to the poetics of pure fictionality in which this world originates can only be a form of self-deception; Amaryllis, we will recall, is the beloved of the goatherd of *Idyll* 3, the one character from the bucolic *Idylls* who conspicuously fails to achieve the identification with the products of his own imagination that is elsewhere the defining characteristic of the bucolic singers.

As the poem progresses, more details about the exile of the speaker Meliboeus emerge. While Tityrus has a protector in Rome, who has preserved for him the tenure of his land, Meliboeus' fields are to become the property of an "impious soldier," a "barbarian," his dispossession a result of discord amongst "the wretched citizens" (1.70–72). Once again a political register, the language of civil war, makes its appearance in the bucolic world. The threat that has hovered at the edges of the poem since its opening verses now takes on a recognizable historical shape; what threatens the herdsmen is expulsion from their land so that this property may be awarded to military veterans, just as land was in fact expropriated for such veterans in the aftermath of the battles of Philippi and Actium. How then are we to combine this pointed reference to historical reality with the equally pointed literary reference to *Idyll* 3 in the poem's opening lines? For if these verses identify the fictional herdsmen of *Eclogue* 1 as subjects of real Roman history, the initial verses pick out Tityrus as an imitator of Theocritus, and it is as an adaptor of Theocritean bucolic that Virgil himself is making his appearance as poet of the *Eclogues*.

The poem offers a series of analogues between its bucolic fiction and the world in which that fiction is published that cannot easily be worked into a single equation. If Tityrus is an imitator of Theocritus whose land was preserved for him through the agency of a powerful figure at Rome, Servius' suggestion that Tityrus is a figure of the poet, whose own land was preserved for him by some such person, seems natural enough. Yet modern scholars have pointed to the impossibility of this identification in other respects – Tityrus, at verses 27–30, is a white-haired ex-slave, and, more tellingly, his conception of bucolic song falls far short of the complex mediation of historical reality and bucolic fiction in *Eclogue* 1 itself.[34] However, it is all too easy to claim that biographical readings of the kind offered by Servius

---

[34] Cf. Putnam (1970) 64–75, who points out the impossibility of regarding Tityrus as the representation of Virgil's own poetics of bucolic, as exemplified by *Eclogue* 1 as a whole. For a recent summary of the long debate regarding the identity of Tityrus, see Martindale (1997) 116–17, who concludes that "it is because [Tityrus] in Eclogue 1 is different from Virgil (or Daphnis in Eclogue 5 from Julius Caesar) that he can be (as Servius supposed) an allegory of him." On the tradition of biographical

are an illegitimate projection from the poem itself; the poem in fact makes such projections inevitable even as it undercuts the possibility of sustaining them at length.[35]

Before returning to the question of how to read the particular kind of fictionalizing self-projection that appears in *Eclogue* 1 as compared to that of the *Idylls*, I want to look briefly at how the problem of identification this poem presents is compounded by the formal variation of the collection as a whole. The order of the poems that is consistently observed in the manuscript tradition and which is generally held to reflect an edition made by the poet himself[36] shows a clear alternation in the mode of presentation; the odd-numbered poems are dramatic, with two (*Eclogues* 1, 5, 9) or three characters (*Eclogues* 3, 7) in conversation, while the even-numbered poems are non-dramatic: they begin with a brief narrative introduction, which is followed by a monologue by a character (*Eclogue* 2), a song by Silenus in indirect discourse with embedded direct speech (*Eclogue* 6), a pair of refrain songs by characters (*Eclogue* 8), and a dramatic scene in which Gallus sings a lament (*Eclogue* 10). *Eclogue* 4 is spoken entirely by the poet, apart from the brief citation of the Fates at verse 46. While there is considerable variety in both dramatic and non-dramatic poems, Virgil has, over the course of the collection, given a consistent pattern to the diversity of form that characterizes Theocritus' bucolic poetry: poems that are purely dramatic alternate with poems that are narrated.[37]

---

allegory in the interpretation of the *Eclogues* more generally, see Van Sickle (1984) and Starr (1995). The revisionist reading of Servian allegory, firmly rejected by Rose (1942) 117–38 and Jenkyns (1998) 169–70, in Patterson (1987) 19–59 will be discussed below. Schmidt (1972) 121 rejects the biographical allegory of the ancient commentators on the *Eclogues* even as he argues for a reading of Virgil's bucolic poetry as metapoetic allegory, "poetische Poetik von Poesie" (118).

[35] Iser (2006) 78–79 discusses just this problem in relation to the allegorical identifications of Spenser's *Shepheardes Calender*. Noting that Colin Clout, the central figure, is "sometimes a poet, sometimes Spenser himself, sometimes just a shepherd, and sometimes the English people as a whole," and that the shepherdess Eliza "at different times embodies the beloved, Queen Elizabeth, and the grieving Dido," Iser suggests that the multiplicity of identifications ends up working against the independence of levels of meaning that the allegorical mode is intended to impose: "We obtain a host of semantic adumbrations that impinge on every meaning of every situation in each eclogue. Consequently, when the shepherds foreshadow certain political figures, the resemblance becomes increasingly complex, and ambiguities begin to proliferate."

[36] Coleman (1977) 18.

[37] Coleman (1977) 20–21. Van Sickle (1978) 19–20 discusses this principle of alternation among the many plans of formal and thematic variation that have been proposed for the *Eclogues*. Rumpf (1996) 203 considers it in relationship to the question of narrative framing within the poems. There is little consensus regarding the order of Theocritus' poems in the bucolic collection known to Virgil. Moreover, none of the three manuscript families, nor any papyrus, preserves the *Idylls* in an arrangement in which dramatic poems alternate with poems in other forms; see Gutzwiller (1996) 147–48, Tables I and II. It seems likely therefore that Virgil himself made a pattern of formal alteration in the *Eclogues* out of the simple variety of the *Idylls*.

However, the distinction between narrative by the poet and direct speech by his characters that such an alternation would seem to mark is suspended as the collection unfolds. *Eclogue* 2 begins with narrative: "The shepherd Corydon loved the fair Alexis." *Eclogue* 3 opens with a dialogue between Menalcas and Damoetas: "Tell me, Damoetas, whose flock is this? Is it that of Meliboeus?" The reader naturally assumes that, since *Eclogue* 2 is narration, the speaker who introduces the long speech by Corydon in *Idyll* 2 is the poet himself, while in *Eclogue* 3 the dialogue between the characters is a dramatic fiction; we do not particularly reflect on the poet who created it. In *Eclogue* 5, however, the character Menalcas offers to give to Mopsus the reed pipe "which taught me 'Corydon loved the fair Alexis,' and 'Whose flock is this? Is it that of Meliboeus?'" (5.86–87). The narrator of *Idyll* 2, we discover, was not in fact Virgil but the shepherd Menalcas, and the dramatic illusion of *Idyll* 3, to which we succumbed without thinking of its creator, was in fact authored by the same bucolic character. The moment has been noted by scholars,[38] but the unsettling effect of this sudden erasure of the difference between author and character has hardly been fully accounted for: is *Eclogue* 3, to which we responded as if it were an autonomous fictional world, in fact the creation of a character in *Eclogue* 5? If so, is a fictional world that is itself the creation of a fictional character somehow less grounded, less ontologically sturdy than a fiction that resides more immediately with the imagination of its real-world creator? Do we blame ourselves for falling victim to what is now revealed to be not a primary fiction but the fiction of a fiction? Conversely, how are we to understand this self-identification of the poet with his fictional creation, both more explicit and more fleeting than anything we have seen in Theocritus? And, finally, if Menalcas "is" Virgil in *Eclogue* 5, how are we to read him in *Eclogue* 3, in which he appears as a dramatic character? And where does this leave Tityrus? As the questions multiply, we face the same dilemma that we face in *Eclogue* 1: rather than offering the option to see the bucolic characters as instances

---

[38] Williams (1968) 323, Putnam (1970) 192, Jenkyns (1998) 155. Hardie (2002) 21, by contrast, is much more attuned to the surprise of this impossible conflation: "At the end of the poem Menalcas' 'quotation' of the openings of the second and third Eclogues breathtakingly collapses the fictional world of Virgilian shepherds into the world of the poet and his readers." See, now, the interesting discussion of the diffusion of authorial presence in the movement between author and character roles in Section 4, "Constructing Unity," of Breed (forthcoming). Samuel Beckett's *Trilogy* offers the only comparable example of retroactive reauthoring within a serial collection that I know of. In its second book, *Malone Dies* (1951), the narrator, Malone, claims to have been the author of the first, *Molloy* (1951), while in the final volume, *The Unnamable* (1953), its anonymous narrator claims to be responsible for all of Beckett's characters from Murphy to Malone. Cf. McHale (1987) 12–13, who discusses the effort on the part of Beckett's characters to imagine, and escape, their dependence on their author.

of authorial self-projection, a possibility we may freely accept or reject in Theocritus, Virgil simultaneously confronts us with both the necessity and the impossibility of this identification.

The relationship between Menalcas and the poet is explored at greater length in *Eclogue* 9, a dialogue between the tenant farmers Moeris and Lycidas. In response to Moeris' eviction from his land, Lycidas recalls his erroneous belief that "your Menalcas had saved everything with his songs" (9.10). After he has been corrected by Moeris, the two herdsmen exchange fragments of Menalcas' songs that look back over the *Eclogues* as a whole, and trace their resemblance to, and divergence from, the bucolic poetry of Theocritus. Lycidas cites a song of Menalcas that recalls *Idyll* 3 (9.23–25), and in response Moeris cites lines that address Varus and recall the theme of land appropriation in *Eclogue* 1 (9.26–29). Lycidas then echoes Simichidas' boast in *Idyll* 7 (unless this is another citation of Menalcas), that the Muses have made him too a poet, though as yet he cannot rival Varius and Cinna (9.32–36, cf. *Idyll* 7.37–41), and Moeris in reply remembers a song by Menalcas on the theme of Galateia. Finally, Lycidas recalls a song in which Menalcas had Daphnis contemplate the star of Julius Caesar (9.46–50), thereby combining the political optimism of *Eclogue* 4 with the Daphnis theme of *Eclogue* 5. Having completed half their journey, as the tomb of Bianor comes into sight (cf. *Idyll* 7.10–11), the speakers cease their exchange of songs and go on in silence.

Eclogue 9 acknowledges *Idyll* 7 as a matrix for Virgil's thought about the representation of the poet as a character within the bucolic world.[39] However, while *Idyll* 7 stages an encounter between the figure of the poet and one of his own bucolic inventions in the form of an autobiographical inspiration narrative, Menalcas, the fictional character who lays claim to authorship of *Eclogues* 2 and 3, appears only indirectly in *Eclogue* 9, in the dialogue of Lycidas and Moeris and their citations of his songs. While Moeris and Lycidas credit him with compositions that sound inescapably like the *Eclogues* themselves, he is not present for this review of Virgil's bucolic themes, having been evicted from his land. Moreover, this prospectus of bucolic poetry is a prelude to its renunciation in the last poem of the collection. In *Eclogue* 10 the narrator describes his poem as a final labor, a tribute to Gallus, who, like Daphnis, is wasting away from unrequited love (10.1–10). Yet while Gallus suffers like Daphnis, and sings like Daphnis, he remains, throughout the poem, Gallus; unlike Theocritus' Thyrsis, he does

---

[39] Cf. Williams (1968) 327: "Some of the poetic pleasure of *Eclogue* 9 resides in the riddle of its relationship to *Idyll* 7."

not become Daphnis as he sings. Nor does he, like other bucolic singers, find relief from desire in his engagement with bucolic song. By remaining himself, merely visiting the bucolic world rather than endeavoring to become one with it through song, he makes his final declaration – "love conquers all" – virtually inevitable.[40]

Among the herdsmen and pastoral divinities who visit the suffering Gallus and ask him about his love is Menalcas, and Gallus invites them all, as Arcadians, and hence true singers, to sing of it in the future (10.31–33). If we think of Menalcas here as the Menalcas of *Eclogue* 9, whom Lycidas and Moeris credit with the themes of the *Eclogues* as a whole, then this request made within the fictional world of *Eclogue* 10 is fulfiled by the very poem in which it appears. Moreover, to have fulfiled this promise in a poem worthy of Gallus' consideration will be the last act of the poet of the *Eclogues*, who closes the book by telling us that, if he has done so, then he will have sung enough in the pastoral vein (10.70–72). As Gallus fails to identify with the bucolic world, so Virgil disengages himself from it. The Menalcas of *Eclogue* 5, who claimed authorship of *Eclogues* 2 and 3, could hardly be more strongly identified with the poet himself; the Menalcas of *Eclogue* 9 gains strength as a figure of the poet by his absence from the poem, as Lycidas and Moeris identify the themes of his songs with those of the *Eclogues* themselves; the Menalcas of *Eclogue* 10, who, we are told, was one of those entreated by Gallus to sing of his love, is a minor character in the narrative, and distant from the narrative voice of the poem in which he appears.

The possibility, and the degree, of identification between Virgil and his herdsmen shift therefore as we make our way through the *Eclogues*. For Servius, Virgil's self-representation as a herdsman in the character of Tityrus is an accommodation to the necessities of patronage at a difficult moment in Rome's civic history. Theocritus, he claims, is always straightforwardly mimetic (his herdsmen are herdsmen and nothing more), but Virgil needed to thank the patrons who had saved his land and so there are moments in the *Eclogues* when the herdsmen double as figures of the poet himself. We should not look for such moments everywhere, but only in passages that deal with this issue. However, the presence of allegory is not to be deplored, since it is a sophistication (*urbanitas*) that distinguishes his poems from

---

[40] Cf. Putnam (1970) 380–81: "Hence the famous line *omnia vincit amor* is only the terse pronouncement of the predestined. The negative farewell to the woods and to the possibility of forgetting elegiac love in such a context yields to *Amor*'s expected triumph. It is the double victory of that *indignus amor* the elegist will always feel for his girl and the *insanus amor* of war and the affairs of state."

those of Theocritus.⁴¹ We would, of course, prefer to give Virgil a more universalizing intention in this transformation of his models: the poet did not introduce biographical allegory into his poems because his particular situation left him no choice but to vitiate the pure fictionality of the bucolic world with historical references; rather, he chose to do so in order to reveal the ultimate dependence of all literary fictions on the social and political circumstances in which they emerge. Nonetheless, as defenders of Servius have argued, "the principle of discontinuous allegory" in his approach to the poems recognizes that Virgil does, at moments, inescapably identify himself with his characters in a way that Theocritus does not, and that these moments make art's social and political commitments explicit.⁴²

Servius' contrast between a simple Theocritus and a complex Virgil rests upon his understanding of Tityrus as, at moments, a figure of the poet. While he does not explore the more complicated relationship between Virgil and Menalcas,⁴³ his reading anticipates modern comparisons of the two poets insofar as it recognizes, and praises, in the *Eclogues* a departure from the "semantic transparency and innocence" of mimetic representation in Theocritus, as a result of which bucolic poetry, for the first time, "becomes a metaphor for something other than itself."⁴⁴ Such a contrast ignores the fundamental role of impersonation and mimetic desire in the characterization of the herdsmen of the *Idylls*. For this doubleness makes them immediately legible as figures of their author's imagination, and it is only if they are used as a foil to the supposedly more complex characters of the *Eclogues* that their own complexity disappears. What is different about them in comparison to Virgil's herdsmen is neither their simplicity nor their realism, but the fact that, except in *Idyll* 7, their legibility as authorial self-projection is not connected to particular historical circumstances as it is in the *Eclogues*. Reading the self-fictionalizing songs of the characters of

---

⁴¹ The relevant passages are Thilo (1887), p. 2–3, 33. Cf. the discussion in Schmidt (1972) 128–30 and Patterson (1987) 32–33.
⁴² Patterson (1987) 34; cf. Martindale (1997) 119, who argues that if the poems are discontinuously allegorical, they must also be discontinuously mimetic.
⁴³ Cf. Patterson (1987) 4–5.
⁴⁴ Patterson (1987) 34, who does not perpetuate the comparison between the two poets in these terms herself. Cf. Alpers (1979) 204–209, who notes how the traditional comparison of Theocritus and Virgil so often replicates, with various degrees of explicitness and sophistication, Schiller's antithesis of naïve and sentimental poetry. Alpers is well aware of the difficulties in contrasting a naïve Theocritus with a sentimental Virgil, but thinks that the terminology of Schiller (who does not discuss Theocritus) remains valuable insofar as the poetry of Theocritus (especially the "Sorrows of Daphnis" in *Idyll* 1) "represents with remarkable directness some of the essential feelings of epic and tragic poetry." I hope that my first chapter has demonstrated how far we in fact are from such a world in *Idyll* 1, and that the discussion here demonstrates how unhelpful it is to compare Theocritus and Virgil in these terms.

the bucolic *Idylls* as analogous to those of their author is thus a possibility rather than a requirement, though the emulation of the fictional herdsman Lycidas in the autobiography of the bucolic poet Simichidas in *Idyll* 7 nudges us in this direction. The *Eclogues*, by contrast, make inescapable, though fleeting, identifications between poet and character, so that we have no alternative at those moments but to read the bucolic world as a figure of the poet's own circumstances. The question with the *Eclogues* is not, as it is with the *Idylls*, whether we should read the bucolic world in this way or not, but rather for how long, and to what extent.[45] While it is clear that Menalcas, or Tityrus, at certain moments is Virgil, what is insolubly unclear is the nature of this "is." As the *Aeneid* fuses myth with annalistic history, so the *Eclogues* fuse contemporary reality with fiction, drastically increasing both the number and the transparency of the connections between the bucolic world and the history of the poet's own times: in *Eclogue* 1 Tityrus remains within the pastoral world while Meliboeus is leaving it because his lands have been appropriated for veterans of the Roman army; Menalcas is absent from the world of *Idyll* 9 for the same reason; in *Eclogue* 10 Gallus is playing the part of Daphnis because his lover Lycoris has accompanied a Roman soldier on a military campaign. Because real historical events frequently motivate the presence or absence of a particular character within the bucolic world, this world appears to be a way of thinking about history in the guise of fiction. While Theocritus, in *Idyll* 11, uses the bucolic world as a means to investigate real-world problems, this world's ability to function as an example rests upon its crisp separation from the actual world; the power of Polyphemus' song is the allure of pure fictionality. The *Eclogues*, by contrast, fashion for this purpose a bucolic world that partially merges with the historical world, and whose legibility as an image of contemporary reality rests upon the visible presence of its author and his contemporaries within it.

The identification of poet with character negates the heuristic value of the Platonic distinction between modes of presentation that lies at the origin of Western literary criticism. If the narrator of *Eclogue* 2 turns out to be not Virgil but Menalcas, it cannot be assumed that, in a narrative poem, the poet "conceals himself nowhere," or, conversely, that, in a dramatic work, the poet himself is nowhere to be found (*Republic* 3.393b10–d1). Rather, all literature, regardless of its formal characteristics, may be read as the fictionalizing self-projection of its author's inner life. As we have seen in Hermesianax, it is already possible by the early third century BCE to read the epic poetry of Homer and Hesiod in this way, and the status

---

[45] Cf. Jenkyns (1998) 155, who notes the instability of the fictional world of the *Eclogues*.

of literature as self-expression is examined from a variety of perspectives in the work of Callimachus. It is, however, the bucolic poetry of Theocritus that poses this question in its most compelling form. By creating a world whose characters are self-evidently fictional, yet engaged in activities of poetic composition that mirror those of their author, Theocritus makes fictionality immediately legible as a form of self-projection. Moreover, by staging his characters' desire to belong to the bucolic world that, from the reader's point of view, they already inhabit, he demonstrates the recursive effect of literary fiction, the desire that it creates in its readership to belong to the worlds that it invents. This desire is thematized with particular clarity in *Idyll* 7, where the narrator Simichidas, himself a bucolic poet, concludes his autobiographical narration by attempting the imaginative gestures of the fictional shepherd Lycidas. It is celebrated in the *Lament for Bion*, where a central portion of the commemoration of the dead poet describes his successful self-assimilation to the world of his own bucolic poetry. It is given a critical turn in the *Eclogues* of Virgil and Calpurnius Siculus, who introduce themselves as characters within the fictional worlds they have created, but use this possibility to explore the limitations of a purely fictional world for the development of selfhood when confronted with the pressing demands of social and historical reality.[46] In this way, bucolic

---

[46] As in Virgil's *Eclogues*, Calpurnius Siculus' bucolic characters refer openly to contemporary events: Ornytus in *Eclogue* 1 looks forward to an era of civic peace under Nero, who has just successfully pleaded a case for the inhabitants of Troy (1.45), and Corydon in *Eclogue* 7 gives Lycotas his impressions of the vast wooden amphitheater he has witnessed at Rome (7.23–72), and of the god-like ruler in attendance (7.79–84). Corydon elsewhere discusses with Meliboeus the appropriate style in which to celebrate the present golden age and the god "who rules over peoples, cities, and toga-clad peace" (4.5–8). Under a ruler favorably disposed to song, he hopes he may rival the divine Tityrus whose pipes he has inherited (4.58–72), and Meliboeus advises him to "press the reeds which sang woods worthy of a consul" (4.76–77). This citation of Virgil's fourth *Eclogue* makes it clear that Calpurnius reads Virgil himself in the Tityrus of Virgil's first *Eclogue*, and he positions his own pastoral double as a successor to this courtly tradition: as Virgil sang of his patrons in pastoral disguise, so Calpurnius will praise Nero in the guise of Corydon. Unlike Virgil's fleeting identifications with his characters, the figure of Corydon remains stable as a figure of the poet from one poem to the next. However, as Newlands (1987) 218–31 has shown, there is more to Calpurnius' *Eclogues* than a courtly masque in which the poet addresses an appeal for patronage to Rome's current rulers. Rather, the changing fortunes of a single major character allow Calpurnius to develop a subtle but sustained critique of poetry's dependence upon courtly patronage, and of the pastoral fiction in which that dependency is figured. In particular, the ambivalence about the countryside itself that appears in Corydon's extravagant praise of the amphitheater at Rome points to the limitations of the pastoral world even as it reveals the value of the pastoral mode; the rustic poet's innocent eye allows us to once again see the city for the wonder of culture it truly is. The four *Eclogues* of Nemesianus (late third century), transmitted with the text of Calpurnius, exhibit a formal variety that ranges among the familiar types of bucolic poem, and so, at the end of the bucolic tradition, give its salient forms in miniature. However, the poems make no reference to contemporary history, and their poet does not appear in them in bucolic disguise. The two *Einsiedeln Eclogues* are too fragmentary to judge in this respect.

poetry becomes a medium in which political developments hostile to the free development of political subjects may be imagined and confronted.

This aspect of Roman bucolic poetry will particularly appeal to Renaissance pastoralists; the world of their poems offers a "counterimage" of the times in which contemporary politics can be explored in bucolic costume, and so perhaps resolved to the benefit of the society in which their bucolic fiction is published.[47] However, alongside this ability to function as a kind of critical discourse, pastoral continues to register its appeal as a literary paradise that is uniquely amenable to recreation in reality. For if its fictional world looks attractive to us, we need look no further for a plan of action than the fiction itself, as the herdsmen we encounter in its pages transform themselves before our eyes in the image of the same bucolic fiction to which we ourselves aspire. Pastoral sustains the hopes of mimetic desire more readily than other fictions, and it is as such that it finds its place in Cervantes' great reflection on this theme. For Don Quixote, acknowledging, at the end of his adventures, that the world of the chivalric romance is beyond him, appeals to Sancho with the image of a future life he has conceived in a quite different genre:

As they pursued their journey talking in this way they came to the very same spot where they had been trampled on by the bulls. Don Quixote recognised it, and said he to Sancho, "This is the meadow where we came upon those gay shepherdesses and gallant shepherds who were trying to revive and imitate the pastoral Arcadia there, an idea as novel as it was happy, in emulation whereof, if so be thou dost approve of it, Sancho, I would have ourselves turn shepherds, at any rate for the time I have to live in retirement. I will buy some ewes and everything else requisite for the pastoral calling; and, I under the name of the shepherd Quixotize and thou as the shepherd Panzino, we will roam the woods and groves and meadows singing songs here, lamenting in elegies there, drinking of the crystal waters of the springs or limpid brooks or flowing rivers. The oaks will yield us their sweet fruit with bountiful hand, the trunks of the hard cork trees a seat, the willows shade, the roses perfume, the widespread meadows carpets tinted with a thousand dyes; the clear pure air will give us breath, the moon and stars lighten the darkness of the night for us, song shall be our delight, lamenting our joy, Apollo will supply us with verses, and love with conceits whereby we shall make ourselves famed for ever, not only in this but in ages to come."[48]

---

[47] Iser (1989) 75: "This massive incursion of shepherds into the literature of the Renaissance cannot be explained simply by a humanistic predilection for a rediscovered antiquity – though this certainly played its part; of far greater significance is the fact that Arcadian fiction offered a highly efficient means of presenting contemporary problems in the reflection of their possible solutions." Patterson (1987) traces the ideological afterlife of the *Eclogues* from Petrarch to the modern period.

[48] *Don Quixote* II.67, Ormsby translation.

The knight who misses the object of his quest has failed to embody the ideal to which he aspired, but the lover whose love has been rejected has earned his admission to a world where suffering is merely the prelude to pleasurable self-invention. The names that Quixote invents get the bucolic project just right: they are fictionalizing, yet transparently so, so that the transformation of the empirical self can be recognized in its fictional double. Good cheer prevails here, because the pains its inhabitants have endured in the real world are what allow them to imagine themselves as inhabitants of a better one. Their delight in their imaginary existence outweighs the misfortunes that provoked it, so that these latter-day pastoralists are worthy successors of Theocritus and his fictional herdsmen.

Bibliography

Acosta-Hughes, B. (2002) *Polyeideia: The* Iambi *of Callimachus and the Archaic Iambic Tradition.* Berkeley and Los Angeles.
Ahrens, H. L. (ed.) (1855) *Bucolicorum Graecorum Theocriti Bionis Moschi reliquiae.* Leipzig.
Albert, W. (1988) *Das mimetische Gedicht in der Antike.* Frankfurt am Main.
Alpers, P. (1979) *The Singer of the Eclogues: A Study of Virgilian Pastoral.* Berkeley and Los Angeles.
  (1996) *What is Pastoral?* Chicago.
Arland, W. (1937) *Nachtheokritische Bukolik.* Dissertation Leipzig.
Arnott, W. G. (1996) "The preoccupations of Theocritus: Structure, illusive realism, allusive learning," in *Theocritus* [= *Hellenistica Groningana* 2], ed. M. A. Harder, R. F. Regtuit, and G. C. Wakker. Groningen: 55–70.
Ashbery, J. (1997) *The Mooring of Starting Out: The First Five Books of Poetry.* Hopewell, NJ.
Asmis, E. (1995) "Philodemus on censorship, moral utility, and formalism in poetry," in *Philodemus and Poetry*, ed. D. Obbink. Oxford: 148–77.
Bain, D. (1975) "Audience address in Greek tragedy," *Classical Quarterly* 25: 13–25.
  (1977) *Actors and Audience.* Oxford.
Bakhtin, M. M. (1981) *The Dialogic Imagination: Four Essays.* Austin.
Berger, H. Jr. (1984) "The origins of bucolic representation: Disenchantment and revision in Theocritus' seventh *Idyll*," *Classical Antiquity* 3: 1–39.
Bernsdorff, H. (forthcoming) "The idea of bucolic in the imitators of Theocritus, 3rd–1st Cent. BC," in *Greek and Latin Pastoral*, ed. M. Fantuzzi and T. D. Papanghelis. Leiden.
Bing, P. (1988) *The Well-Read Muse* [= *Hypomnemata: Untersuchungen zur Antike und zu ihren Nachleben* 90]. Göttingen.
  (1993) "The *Bios*-tradition and poets' lives in Hellenistic poetry," in *Nomodeiktes: Greek Studies in Honor of Martin Ostwald*, ed. R. M. Rosen and J. Farrell. Ann Arbor: 619–31.
  (2000) "Text or performance / text and performance: Alan Cameron's *Callimachus and His Critics*," in *La letteratura ellenistica: Problemi e prospettive di ricerca* [= *Quaderni dei seminari romani di cultura greca* 1], ed. R. Pretagostini. Rome: 139–48.
Bonesteel, M. (2000) *Henry Darger: Art and Selected Writings.* New York.

Booth, W. C. (1961) *The Rhetoric of Fiction*. Chicago.
Bowie, E. (1985) "Theocritus' seventh *Idyll*, Philetas and Longus," *Classical Quarterly* 35: 67–91.
  (1996) "Frame and framed in Theocritus Poems 6 and 7," in *Theocritus* [= *Hellenistica Groningana* 2], ed. M. A. Harder, R. F. Regtuit, and G. C. Wakker. Groningen: 91–100.
Boyd, B. W. (1995) "*Non enarrabile textum*: Ecphrastic trespass and narrative ambiguity in the *Aeneid*," *Virgilius* 41: 71–90.
Breed, B. W. (forthcoming) "Time and textuality in the book of the *Eclogues*," in *Greek and Latin Pastoral*, ed. M. Fantuzzi and T. D. Papanghelis. Leiden.
Bremer, J. M. and Furley, W. D. (eds.) (2001) *Greek Hymns*. 2 vols. Tübingen.
Brooke, A. (1971) "Theocritus' Idyll 11: A study in pastoral," *Arethusa* 4: 73–81.
Brooks, P. (1984) *Reading for the Plot: Design and Intention in Narrative*. Cambridge, MA.
  (1993) *Body Work: Objects of Desire in Modern Narrative*. Cambridge, MA.
Brown, E. L. (1981) "The Lycidas of Theocritus' Idyll 7," *Harvard Studies in Classical Philology* 85: 59–100.
Bulloch, A. W. (1984) "The future of a Hellenistic illusion: some observations on Callimachus and religion," *Museum Helveticum* 41: 209–30.
  (ed.) (1985) *Callimachus: The Fifth Hymn*. Oxford.
Burton, J. B. (1995) *Theocritus's Urban Mimes: Mobility, Gender, and Patronage*. Berkeley.
Cairns, F. (1970) "Theocritus Idyll 10," *Hermes* 98: 38–44.
  (1972) *Generic Composition in Greek and Roman Poetry*. Edinburgh.
  (1984) "Theocritus' first Idyll: The literary programme," *Wiener Studien* 97: 89–113.
Cameron, Alan. (1995) *Callimachus and His Critics*. Princeton.
Cameron, Archibald. (1963) "The Form of the *Thalysia*," in *Miscellania di studi alessandrini in memoria di Augusto Rostagni*. Turin: 291–307.
Caspers, C. L. (forthcoming) "The loves of the Greek poets: Allusions in Hermesianax fr. 7 Powell," in *Beyond the Canon* [= *Hellenistica Groningana* 8], ed. M. A. Harder, R. F. Regtuit, and G. C. Wakker. Leuven: 57–77.
Chambers, R. (1984) *Story and Situation: Narrative Seduction and the Power of Fiction*. Minneapolis.
Clay, D. (2004) *Archilochus Heros: The Cult of Poets in the Greek Polis* [= *Hellenic Studies* 6]. Washington, DC.
Coleman, R. (1977) *Virgil: Eclogues*. Cambridge.
Copley, F. O. (1956) *Exclusus Amator: A Study in Latin Love Poetry*. Baltimore.
Cozzoli, A.-T. (1994) "Dalla catarsi mimetica aristotelica all'auto-catarsi dei poeti ellenistici," *Quaderni urbinati di cultura classica* 48: 95–110.
Cremonesi, E. (1958) "Rapporti tra le origini della poesia bucolica e della poesia comica nella tradizione peripatetica," *Dioniso* 21: 109–22.
Dällenbach, L. (1989) *The Mirror in the Text*. Chicago.
Danielewicz, J. (1990) "*Deixis* in Greek choral lyric," *Quaderni urbinati di cultura classica* 34: 7–17.

De Jong, I. J. F. (1987) "The voice of anonymity: Tis-speeches in the *Iliad*," *Eranos* 85: 69–84.
Denniston, J. D. (1950) *The Greek Particles*. 2nd edn. Oxford.
Depew, M. (1993) "Mimesis and aetiology in Callimachus' Hymns," in *Callimachus* [= *Hellenistica Groningana* 1], ed. M. A. Harder, R. F. Regtuit, and G. C. Wakker. Groningen: 57–77.
De Sena, J. (1982) "Fernando Pessoa: The man who never was," in *The Man Who Never Was: Essays on Fernando Pessoa*, ed. G. Monteiro. Providence: 19–32.
Detienne, M. (1986) *The Creation of Mythology*. Chicago.
Deuse, W. (1990) "Dichtung als Heilmittel gegen die Liebe: Zum 11. Idyll Theokrits," in *Beiträge zur hellenistischen Literatur und ihrer Rezeption in Rom*, ed. P. Steinmetz. Stuttgart: 59–76.
Diggle, J. (ed.) (1994) *Euripidis fabulae*. Vol. III. Oxford.
Dolezel, L. (1988) "Mimesis and possible worlds," *Poetics Today* 9: 475–96.
    (1998) *Heterocosmica*. Baltimore.
Donnet, D. (1988) "Les ressources phoniques de la *Première Idylle* de Théocrite," *L'antiquité classique* 57: 158–75.
Dover, K. J. (ed.) (1971) *Theocritus: Select Poems*. London.
Edmunds, L. (2001) *Intertextuality and the Reading of Roman Poetry*. Baltimore.
Edquist, H. (1975) "Aspects of Theocritean otium," *Ramus* 4: 101–14.
Effe, B. (1977) *Die Genese einer literarischen Gattung: Die Bukolik* [= *Konstanzer Universitätsreden* 95]. Konstanz.
    (1978) "Die Destruktion der Tradition: Theokrits mythologische Gedichte," *Rheinisches Museum für Philologie* 121: 48–77.
Elliger, W. (1975) *Die Darstellung der Landschaft in der griechischen Dichtung*. Berlin and New York.
Erbse, H. (1965) "Dichtkunst und Medizin in Theokrits 11. Idyll," *Museum Helveticum* 22: 232–36.
Falivene, M. R. (1990) "La mimesi in Callimaco: *Inni* II, IV, V e VI," *Quaderni urbinati di cultura classica* 36: 103–28.
Fantuzzi, M. (1988) *Ricerche su Apollonio Rodio: Diacronie della dizione epica*. Rome.
    (1993a) "Il sistema letterario della poesia alessandrina nel III sec. AC," in *Lo spazio letterario della Grecia antica*, vol. I.2, ed. G. Cambiano, L. Canfora, and D. Lanza. Rome: 31–73.
    (1993b) "Preistoria di un genere letterario: A proposito degli *Inni* V e VI di Callimaco," in *Tradizione e innovazione nella cultura greca da Omero all'età ellenistica: Scritti in onore di Bruno Gentili*, ed. R. Pretagostini. Rome: 927–46.
    (1995) "Mythological paradigms in the bucolic poetry of Theocritus," *Proceedings of the Cambridge Philological Society* 41: 16–35.
    (1998) "Textual misadventures of Daphnis: The Pseudo-Theocritean *Id*. 8 and the origins of the bucolic 'manner'," in *Genre in Hellenistic Poetry* [= *Hellenistica Groningana* 3], ed. M. A. Harder, R. F. Regtuit, and G. C. Wakker. Groningen: 61–79.
    (2000) "Theocritus and the demythologizing of poetry," in *Matrices of Genre*, ed. M. Depew and D. Obbink. Cambridge, MA: 135–51.

(2004) "Theocritus and the bucolic genre," in Fantuzzi and Hunter (2004): 133–90.
(forthcoming) "Theocritus' constructive interpreters, and the creation of a bucolic reader," in *Greek and Latin Pastoral*, ed. M. Fantuzzi and T. D. Papanghelis. Leiden.
Fantuzzi, M. and Hunter, R. L. (2004) *Tradition and Innovation in Hellenistic Poetry*. Cambridge.
Felson, N. (1999) "Vicarious transport: Fictive deixis in Pindar's *Pythian* Four," *Harvard Studies in Classical Philology* 99: 1–31.
Ferrari, G. R. F. (1987) *Listening to the Cicadas: A Study of Plato's* Phaedrus. Cambridge.
Finkelberg, M. (1998) *The Birth of Literary Fiction in Ancient Greece*. Oxford.
Finnegan, R. H. (1977) *Oral Poetry*. Cambridge.
Ford, A. (2002) *The Origins of Criticism*. Princeton.
Fowler, D. (1991) "Narrate and describe: The problem of ekphrasis," *Journal of Roman Studies* 81: 25–35, reprinted in Fowler (2000): 64–85.
(2000) *Roman Constructions*. Oxford.
Fraser, P. M. (1972) *Ptolemaic Alexandria*. 3 vols. Oxford.
Freud, S. (2003) *The Uncanny*. London.
Friedländer, P. (1912) *Johannes von Gaza und Paulus Silentiarius: Kunstbeschreibungen justinianischer Zeit*. Leipzig.
Furusawa, Y. (1980) *Eros und Seelenruhe in den Thalysien Theokrits*. Würzburg.
Galbraith, M. (1995) "Deictic shift theory and the poetics of involvement in narrative," in *Deixis in Narrative*, ed. J. F. Duchan, G. A. Binder, and L. E. Hewitt. Hillsdale: 19–59.
Gallavotti, C. (1966) "Le coppe istoriate di Teocrito e di Virgilio," *Parola del passato* 21: 421–36.
(ed.) (1993) *Theocritus quique feruntur bucolici Graeci*. 3rd edn. Rome.
Genette, G. (1980) *Narrative Discourse*. Ithaca.
(1992) *The Architext: An Introduction*. Berkeley.
Giangrande, G. (1968) "Théocrite, Simichidas et les *Thalysies*," *L'antiquité classique* 37: 491–533.
(1971) "Theocritus' twelfth and fourth Idylls: A study in Hellenistic irony," *Quaderni urbinati di cultura classica* 12: 95–113.
Gill, C. (1993) "Plato on falsehood – not fiction," in *Lies and Fiction in the Ancient World*, ed. C. Gill and T. P. Wiseman. Austin: 38–87.
Girard, R. (1966) *Deceit, Desire, and the Novel*. Baltimore.
(1978) *To Double Business Bound: Essays on Literature, Mimesis, and Anthropology*. Baltimore.
Goldhill, S. (1986) "Framing and polyphony: Readings in Hellenistic poetry," *Proceedings of the Cambridge Philological Society* 32: 25–52.
(1994) "The naive and knowing eye: Ecphrasis and the culture of viewing in the Hellenistic world," in *Art and Text in Ancient Greek Culture*, ed. S. Goldhill and R. Osborne. Cambridge: 197–223.
Gow, A. S. F. (ed.) (1952) *Theocritus*. 2 vols. 2nd edn. Cambridge.

Gow, A. S. F. and Scholfield, A. F. (eds.) (1953) *Nicander: The Poems and Poetical Fragments*. Cambridge.
Guhl, C. (ed.) (1969) *Die Fragmente des Alexandrinischen Grammatikers Theon*. Hamburg.
Guillén, C. (1971) *Literature as System: Essays Towards the Theory of Literary History*. Princeton.
Gumbrecht, H. U. (2004) *Production of Presence: What Meaning Cannot Convey*. Stanford.
Gutzwiller, K. J. (1991) *Theocritus' Pastoral Analogies: The Formation of a Genre*. Madison.
  (1996) "The evidence for Theocritean poetry books," in *Theocritus* [= *Hellenistica Groningana* 2], ed. M. A. Harder, R. F. Regtuit, and G. C. Wakker. Groningen: 119–48.
  (2000) "The tragic mask of comedy: Metatheatricality in Menander," *Classical Antiquity* 19: 102–37.
Haber, J. D. (1994) *Pastoral and the Poetics of Self-Contradiction*. Cambridge.
Halliwell, S. (ed.) (1987) *The Poetics of Aristotle*. Chapel Hill.
  (1989) "Aristotle's poetics," in *The Cambridge History of Literary Criticism*, vol. 1: *Classical Criticism*, ed. G. A. Kennedy. Cambridge: 149–83.
  (2002) *The Aesthetics of Mimesis: Ancient Texts and Modern Problems*. Princeton.
Halperin, D. M. (1983) *Before Pastoral: Theocritus and the Ancient Tradition of Bucolic Poetry*. New Haven.
Hamburger, K. (1973) *The Logic of Literature*. Bloomington.
Hamburger, M. (1969) *The Truth of Poetry: Tensions in Modern Poetry from Baudelaire to the 1960s*. New York.
Hamon, P. (1981) *Introduction à l'analyse du descriptif*. Paris.
Handley, E. W. (ed.) (1965) *The Dyskolos of Menander*. London.
Harder, M. A. (1992) "Insubstantial voices: Some observations on the Hymns of Callimachus," *Classical Quarterly* 42: 384–94.
Hardie, P. (2002) *Ovid's Poetics of Illusion*. Cambridge.
Heffernan, J. A. (1993) *Museum of Words*. Chicago.
Henderson, J. (1999) *Writing Down Rome: Satire, Comedy, and Other Offences in Latin Poetry*. Oxford.
Henrichs, A. (1980) "Riper than a pear: Parian invective in Theokritos," *Zeitschrift für Papyrologie und Epigraphik* 39: 7–27.
  (1999) "Demythologizing the past, mythicizing the present: Myth, history, and the supernatural at the dawn of the Hellenistic period," in *From Myth to Reason? Studies in the Development of Greek Thought*, ed. R. Buxton. Oxford: 223–48.
Herington, J. (1985) *Poetry into Drama*. Berkeley.
Holtsmark, E. B. (1966) "Poetry as self-enlightenment: Theocritus 11," *Transactions of the American Philological Association* 97: 253–59.
Hordern, J. H. (1999) "The *Cyclops* of Philoxenus," *Classical Quarterly* 49: 445–55.
  (ed.) (2002) *The Fragments of Timotheus of Miletus*. Oxford.
  (ed.) (2004) *Sophron's Mimes: Text, Translation, and Commentary*. Oxford.

Hubbard, T. K. (1998) *The Pipes of Pan: Intertextuality and Literary Filiation in the Pastoral Tradition from Theocritus to Milton*. Ann Arbor.
Hunter, R. L. (1985) *The New Comedy of Greece and Rome*. Cambridge.
  (1992a) "Callimachus and Heraclitus," *Materiali e discussioni per l'analisi dei testi classici* 28: 113–23.
  (1992b) "Writing the god: Form and meaning in Callimachus, *Hymn to Athena*," *Materiali e discussioni per l'analisi dei testi classici* 29: 9–34.
  (1993) "The presentation of Herodas' *Mimiamboi*," *Antichthon* 27: 31–44.
  (1995) "Written in the stars: Poetry and philosophy in the *Phaenomena* of Aratus," *Arachnion* 2: 1–35.
  (1996a) *Theocritus and the Archaeology of Greek Poetry*. Cambridge.
  (1996b) "Mime and mimesis: Theocritus, Idyll 15," in *Theocritus* [= *Hellenistica Groningana* 2], ed. M. A. Harder, R. F. Regtuit, and G. C. Wakker. Groningen: 149–69.
  (1998) "Before and after epic: Theocritus (?), *Idyll* 25," in *Genre in Hellenistic Poetry* [= *Hellenistica Groningana* 3], ed. M. A. Harder, R. F. Regtuit, and G. C. Wakker. Groningen: 115–32.
  (ed.) (1999) *Theocritus: A Selection*. Cambridge.
  (2003) "Reflecting on writing and culture: Theocritus and the style of cultural change," in *Written Texts and the Rise of Literate Culture in Ancient Greece*, ed. H. Yunis. Cambridge: 213–34.
  (2004) "The aetiology of Callimachus' *Aitia*," in Fantuzzi and Hunter (2004): 42–88.
Hutcheon, L. (1980) *Narcissistic Narrative: The Metafictional Paradox*. Waterloo.
  (1988) *A Poetics of Postmodernism: History, Theory, Fiction*. London.
Hutchinson, G. (1988) *Hellenistic Poetry*. Oxford.
Iser, W. (1978) *The Act of Reading*. Baltimore.
  (1989) *Prospecting: From Reader Response to Literary Anthropology*. Baltimore.
  (1993) *The Fictive and the Imaginary*. Baltimore.
  (2006) *How to Do Theory*. Malden, MA.
Jenkyns, R. (1998) *Virgil's Experience: Nature and History*. Oxford.
Kahn, C. H. (1996) *Plato and the Socratic Dialogue*. Cambridge.
Kania, R. (2004) "The *Lament for Bion* as bucolic fiction," University of Chicago Seminar Paper: 1–22.
Kelly, S. T. (1979) "On the twelfth Idyll of Theocritus," *Helios* 7: 55–60.
  (1983) "The song of time: Theocritus' seventh Idyll," *Quaderni urbinati di cultura classica* 44: 103–15.
Köhnken, A. (1996) "Theokrits Polyphemgedichte," in *Theocritus* [= *Hellenistica Groningana* 2], ed. M. A. Harder, R. F. Regtuit, and G. C. Wakker. Groningen: 171–86.
Kossaifi, C. (2002) "L'onomastique bucolique dans les *Idylles* de Théocrite: Un poète face aux noms," *Revue des études anciennes* 104: 349–61.
Krevans, N. (1983) "Geography and the literary tradition in Theocritus 7," *Transactions of the American Philological Association* 113: 201–20.
Kripke, S. A. (1980) *Naming and Necessity*. Cambridge, MA.

Kroll, W. (1924) *Studien zum Verständnis der römischen Literatur*. Stuttgart.
Kühn, J.-H. (1958) "Die Thalysien Theokrits (id. 7)," *Hermes* 86: 40–79.
Labov, W. (1972) *Language in the Inner City: Studies in the Black English Vernacular*. Philadelphia.
Lawall, G. (1967) *Theocritus' Coan Pastorals*. Washington, DC.
Lefkowitz, M. R. (1981) *The Lives of the Greek Poets*. Baltimore.
Legrand, P.-E. (1898) *Etude sur Théocrite*. Paris.
 (ed.) (1925) *Bucoliques grecs*. 2 vols. Paris.
Lejeune, P. (1989) *On Autobiography*. Minneapolis.
Lembach, K. (1970) *Die Pflanzen bei Theokrit*. Heidelberg.
Lessing, G. E. (1962) *Laocoön*. Baltimore and London.
Levin, S. R. (1976) "Concerning what kind of speech act a poem is," in *Pragmatics of Language and Literature* [= *North Holland Studies in Theoretical Poetics* 2], ed. T. A. Van Dijk. Amsterdam: 107–41.
 (1977) *The Semantics of Metaphor*. Baltimore.
Lindsell, A. (1937) "Was Theocritus a botanist?," *Greece and Rome* 6: 78–93.
Lowe, N. J. (2000) "Comic plots and the invention of fiction," in *The Rivals of Aristophanes*, ed. D. Harvey and J. Wilkins. London: 259–72.
Lucas, D. W. (ed.) (1968) *Aristotle: Poetics*. Oxford.
MacGregor, J. M. (2002) *Henry Darger: In the Realms of the Unreal*. New York.
Manakidou, F. (1993) *Beschreibung von Kunstwerken in der hellenistischen Dichtung*. Stuttgart.
 (1996) "ΕΠΙΤΑΦΙΟΣ ΑΔΩΝΙΔΟΣ and ΕΠΙΤΑΦΙΟΣ ΒΙΩΝΟΣ: Remarks on their generic form and content," *Materiali e discussioni per l'analisi dei testi classici* 37: 27–58.
Mandel, B. J. (1980) "Full of life now," in *Autobiography: Essays Theoretical and Critical*, ed. J. Olney. Princeton: 49–72.
Manuwald, B. (1990) "Der Kyklop als Dichter: Bemerkungen zu Theokrit, *Eid.* 11," in *Beiträge zur hellenistischen Literatur und ihrer Rezeption in Rom*, ed. P. Steinmetz. Stuttgart: 77–91.
Martin, W. (1986) *Recent Theories of Narrative*. Ithaca.
Martindale, C. (1997) "Green politics: The *Eclogues*," in *The Cambridge Companion to Virgil*, ed. C. Martindale. Cambridge: 107–24.
Martinez-Bonati, F. (1981) *Fictive Discourse and the Structures of Literature*. Ithaca.
Mastromarco, G. (1984) *The Public of Herondas*. Amsterdam.
Mastronarde, D. J. (1968) "Theocritus' Idyll 13: Love and the hero," *Transactions of the American Philological Association* 99: 273–90.
McHale, B. (1987) *Postmodernist Fiction*. London.
McKay, K. J. (1962) *The Poet at Play: Kallimachos, The Bath of Pallas* [= *Mnemosyne Supplement* 6]. Leiden.
McLennan, G. R. (ed.) (1977) *Callimachus: Hymn to Zeus*. Rome.
Meijering, R. (1987) *Literary and Rhetorical Theories in Greek Scholia*. Groningen.
Meillier, C. (1993) "Théocrite, Idylle VII et autour de l'Idylle VII: ambiguïtés et contradictions de l'autobiographique," in *La componente autobiografica nella poesia greca e latina fra realtà e artificio letterario: Atti del convegno, Pisa,*

16–17 maggio 1991 [= *Biblioteca di studi antichi* 51], ed. G. Arrighetti and F. Montanari. Pisa: 101–28.
Meineke, A. (ed.) (1856) *Theocritus Bion Moschus*. Berlin.
Miles, G. B. (1977) "Characterization and the ideal of innocence in Theocritus' Idylls." *Ramus* 6: 139–64.
Momigliano, A. (1971) *The Development of Greek Biography*. Cambridge, MA.
Moran, R. (1994) "The expression of feeling in imagination," *The Philosophical Review* 103: 75–106.
Morgan, J. R. (1993) "Make-believe and make believe: The fictionality of the Greek novels," in *Lies and Fiction in the Ancient World*, ed. C. Gill and T. P. Wiseman. Austin: 175–229.
Morris, S. P. (1992) *Daidalos*. Princeton.
Murley, C. (1940) "Plato's *Phaedrus* and Theocritean pastoral," *Transactions of the American Philological Association* 71: 281–95.
Nagy, G. (1996) *Poetry as Performance*. Cambridge.
Newlands, C. (1987) "Urban pastoral: The Seventh Eclogue of Calpurnius Siculus," *Classical Antiquity* 6: 218–31.
Nickau, K. (2002) "Der Name 'Simichidas' bei Theokrit," *Hermes* 130: 389–403.
Nicosia, S. (1968) *Teocrito e l'arte figurata*. Palermo.
Nogueras, E. J. (1985) "Notes on the concept of heteronym," in *Actas do II congresso internacional de estudos Pessoanos*. Porto: 447–55.
Ogilvie, R. M. (1962) "The song of Thyrsis," *Journal of Hellenic Studies* 82: 106–10.
Olney, J. (ed.) (1980) *Autobiography: Essays Theoretical and Critical*. Princeton.
Otis, B. (1963) *Virgil: A Study in Civilized Poetry*. Oxford.
Ott, U. (1969) *Die Kunst des Gegensatzes in Theokrits Hirtengedichten* [= *Spudasmata* 22]. Hildesheim.
  (1972) "Theokrits 'Thalysien' und ihre literarischen Vorbilder," *Rheinisches Museum für Philologie* 115: 134–49.
Page, D. L. (ed.) (1975) *Epigrammata Graeca*. Oxford.
Paradiso, A. (1995) "Il motivo della voce come kosmos erotico in Saffo," in *Lo spettacolo delle voci* [= *Le rane* 14], ed. F. De Martino and A. H. Sommerstein. Bari: 103–16.
Parry, A. (1972) "Language and characterization in Homer," *Harvard Studies in Classical Philology* 76: 1–22, reprinted in Parry (1989): 301–26.
  (1989) *The Language of Achilles and Other Papers*. Oxford.
Patterson, A. (1987) *Pastoral and Ideology*. Berkeley.
Pavel, T. G. (1986) *Fictional Worlds*. Cambridge, MA.
Paz, O. (1995) "Unknown to himself," in *A Centenary Pessoa*, ed. E. Lisboa and L. C. Taylor. Manchester: 3–20.
Pearce, T. E. V. (1988) "The function of the *locus amoenus* in Theocritus' seventh Poem," *Rheinisches Museum für Philologie* 115: 277–304.
Pelling, C. (1990) "Childhood and personality in Greek biography," in *Characterization and Individuality in Greek Literature*, ed. C. Pelling. Oxford: 213–44.
Pessoa, F. (1998) *Fernando Pessoa & Co*. New York.
  (2001) *The Selected Prose of Fernando Pessoa*. New York.

Pfeiffer, R. (ed.) (1949–53) *Callimachus*. 2 vols. Oxford.
 (1968) *History of Classical Scholarship*. Oxford.
Powell, I. U. (ed.) (1925) *Collectanea Alexandrina*. Oxford.
Pretagostini, R. (1992) "Tracce di poesia orale nei carmi di Teocrito," *Aevum antiquum* 5: 67–87.
Prince, G. (1988) "The Disnarrated," *Style* 22: 1–8.
Pucci, P. (1978) "Lingering on the threshold," *Glyph* 3: 52–73.
 (1998) *The Song of the Sirens*. Lanham, MD.
Puchner, W. (1993) "Zur Raumkonzeption der Mimiamben des Herodas," *Wiener Studien* 106: 9–34.
Puelma, M. (1960) "Die Dichterbegegnung in Theokrits 'Thalysien'," *Museum Helveticum* 17: 144–64, reprinted in Puelma (1995): 217–37.
 (1995) *Labor et Lima. Kleine Schriften*. Basel.
Putnam, M. C. J. (1970) *Virgil's Pastoral Art: Studies in the Eclogues*. Princeton.
Reitzenstein, R. (1893) *Epigramm und Skolion: Ein Beitrag zur Geschichte der alexandrinischen Dichtung*. Giessen.
Robbe-Grillet, A. (1989) *For a New Novel*. Evanston.
Ronen, R. (1994) *Possible Worlds in Literary Theory*. Cambridge.
Rose, H. J. (1942) *The Eclogues of Vergil* [= *Sather Classical Lectures* 16]. Berkeley.
Rosenmeyer, T. G. (1969) *The Green Cabinet*. Berkeley.
Rossi, L. E. (1971a) "I generi letterari e le loro leggi scritte e non scritte nelle letterature classiche," *Bulletin of the London University Institute of Classical Studies* 13: 69–94.
 (1971b) "Mondo pastorale e poesia bucolica di maniera: L'idillio ottavo del corpus teocriteo," *Studi italiani di filologia classica* 43: 5–25.
 (1972) "L'*Ila* di Teocrito: Epistola poetica ed epillio," in *Studi classici in onore di Q. Cataudella*, Catania: 279–93.
 (2000) "La letteratura alessandrina e il rinnovamente dei generi letterari della tradizione," in *La letteratura ellenistica: Problemi e prospettive di ricerca* [= *Quaderni dei seminari romani di cultura greca* 1], ed. R. Pretagostini. Rome: 149–61.
Rumpf, L. (1996) *Extremus Labor: Vergils 10. Ekloge und die Poetik der Bucolica* [= *Hypomnemata: Untersuchungen zur Antike und zu ihren Nachleben* 112]. Göttingen.
Russell, D. A. (ed.) (1964) *On the Sublime*. Oxford.
Russell, D. A. and Wilson, N. G. (eds.) (1981) *Menander Rhetor*. Oxford.
Schmidt, E. A. (1972) *Poetische Reflexion: Vergils Bukolik*. Munich.
 (1987) *Bukolische Leidenschaft*. Frankfurt am Main.
Schmidt, S. J. (1976) "Towards a pragmatic interpretation of fictionality," in *Pragmatics of Language and Literature* [= *North Holland Studies in Theoretical Poetics* 2], ed. T. A. Van Dijk. Amsterdam: 161–78.
Schmiel, R. (1993) "Structure and meaning in Theocritus 11," *Mnemosyne* 46: 229–34.
Schönbeck, G. (1962) *Der locus amoenus von Homer bis Horaz*. Dissertation Heidelberg.

Seaford, R. (ed.) (1984) *Euripides: Cyclops*. Oxford.
Seeck, G. A. (1975) "Dichterische Technik in Theokrits 'Thalysien' und die Theorie der Hirtendichtung," in ΔωPHMA: *Hans Diller zum 70. Geburtstag*. Athens: 195–209.
Segal, C. (1981) *Poetry and Myth in Ancient Pastoral*. Princeton.
Seiler, M. A. (1997) ΠΟΙΗΣΙΣ ΠΟΙΗΣΕΩΣ: *Alexandrinische Dichtung κατὰ λεπτόν in strukturaler und humanethologischer Deutung* (= Beiträge zur Altertumskunde 102). Stuttgart and Leipzig.
Serrao, G. (1977) "La poetica del 'nuovo stile': Dalla mimesi aristotelica alla poetica della verità," in *Storia e civiltà dei Greci*, vol. IX: *La cultura ellenistica*, ed. L. Moretti, G. Serrao, M. Torelli, and L. Franchi dell'Orto. Milan: 200–53.
Slater, N. (1995) "The fabrication of comic illusion," in *Beyond Aristophanes: Transition and Diversity in Greek Comedy*, ed. G. Dubrov. Atlanta: 29–45.
Spofford, E. W. (1969) "Theocritus and Polyphemus," *American Journal of Philology* 90: 22–35.
Stanzel, K.-H. (1995) *Liebende Hirten: Theokrits Bukolik und die alexandrinische Poesie*. Stuttgart and Leipzig.
Starobinski, J. (1980) "The style of autobiography," in Olney (1980): 73–83.
Starr, R. J. (1995) "Virgil's seventh *Eclogue* and its readers: Biographical allegory as an interpretive strategy in antiquity and late antiquity," *Classical Philology* 90: 129–38.
Steiner, D. T. (2001) *Images in Mind: Statues in Archaic and Classical Greek Literature and Thought*. Princeton.
Steiner, G. (1989) *Real Presences*. Chicago.
Stephens, S. A. (2003) *Seeing Double: Intercultural Poetics in Ptolemaic Alexandria*. Berkeley.
Tedlock, D. (ed.) (1985) *Popol Vuh*. New York.
Thilo, G. (ed.) (1887) *Servii grammatici qui feruntur in Vergilii Bucolica et Georgica*. Leipzig.
Thomas, R. (1983) "Virgil's ecphrastic centerpieces," *Harvard Studies in Classical Philology* 87: 175–84.
  (1996) "Genre through intertextuality: Theocritus to Virgil and Propertius," in *Theocritus* [= *Hellenistica Groningana* 2], ed. M. A. Harder, R. F. Regtuit, and G. C. Wakker. Groningen: 227–46.
Van Groningen, B. A. (1959) "Quelques problèmes de la poésie bucolique grecque," *Mnemosyne* 12: 24–53.
Van Sickle, J. (1976) "Theocritus and the development of the conception of bucolic genre," *Ramus* 5: 18–44.
  (1978) *The Design of Virgil's Bucolics* [= *Filologia e critica* 24]. Rome.
  (1984) "How do we read ancient texts? Codes and critics in Virgil, Eclogue One," *Materiali e discussioni per l'analisi dei testi classici* 13: 107–28.
Vernant, J.-P. (1991) "From the 'presentification' of the invisible to the imitation of appearance," in *Mortals and Immortals: Collected Essays*, ed. F. Zeitlin. Princeton: 151–63.

Walsh, G. B. (1985) "Seeing and feeling: Representation in two poems of Theocritus," *Classical Philology* 80: 1–19.
 (1990) "Surprised by self: Audible thought in Hellenistic poetry," *Classical Philology* 85: 1–21.
Wendel, C. (1899) *De nominibus bucolicis*. Halle an der Saale.
 (ed.) (1914) *Scholia in Theocritum vetera*. Stuttgart.
 (1920) *Überlieferung und Entstehung der Theokrit-Scholien*. Berlin.
Whitaker, R. (1983) *Myth and Personal Experience in Roman Love-Elegy: A Study in Poetic Technique* [= *Hypomnemata: Untersuchungen zur Antike und zu ihren Nachleben* 76]. Göttingen.
Wiemken, H. (1972) *Der griechische Mimus*. Bremen.
Wigodsky, M. (1995) "The meaning of Ψυχαγωγία in Philodemus," in *Philodemus and Poetry*, ed. D. Obbink. Oxford: 65–68.
Wilamowitz-Moellendorf, U. von. (ed.) (1905) *Bucolici Graeci*. Oxford.
 (1906) *Die Textgeschichte der griechischen Bukoliker*. Berlin.
 (1924) *Hellenistische Dichtung in der Zeit des Kallimachos*. 2 vols. Berlin.
Wiles, D. (1991) *The Masks of Menander*. Cambridge.
 (1997) *Tragedy in Athens: Performance Space and Theatrical Meaning*. Cambridge.
Willcock, M. M. (1964) "Mythological paradeigma in the *Iliad*," *Classical Quarterly* 58: 141–54.
Williams, F. (1971) "A theophany in Theocritus," *Classical Quarterly* 21: 137–45.
 (ed.) (1978) *Callimachus: Hymn to Apollo*. Oxford.
Williams, G. (1968) *Tradition and Originality in Roman Poetry*. Oxford.
Williams, W. C. (1986–88) *Collected Poems*. 2 vols. New York.
Zanetto, G. (ed.) (1996) *Inni Omerici*. Milan.
Zanker, G. (2004) *Modes of Viewing in Hellenistic Poetry and Art*. Madison.
Zumthor, P. (1987) *La lettre et la voix*. Paris.

Index

Antimachus
  Lyde 57
Apollonius of Rhodes 84
  direct speech in 58
Aratus 14, 82
Archilochus 138, 148
Aristotle
  and fiction 6, 91
  Poetics 6–8, 12, 16, 21, 56–58, 150, 153
  Rhetoric 65
autobiography
  form of 117, 137
  poetics of 19–21, 115, 138, 141
    in bucolic poetry 149, 154
    in Callimachus 146–49, 167
    in Theocritus 149, 167
    in Theocritus scholia 150–52, 154

Callimachus
  Aetia 12, 13, 147–49
  Epigram 2 146–47
  Hecale 12, 13
  Hymn 1 (*To Zeus*) 58
  Hymn 2 (*To Apollo*) 16, 53–55
  Hymn 4 (*To Delos*) 11
  Iambi 147
  narration in 13
Calpurnius Siculus 167
Cervantes
  Don Quixote 168–69
Chambers, Ross 16, 95–96

Dällenbach, Lucien 127
Daphnis 14, 15, 17, 152
  as object of impersonation 100
  in *Idyll* 1 40–46
  in *Idyll* 6 96–97
Darger, Henry 18
  In the Realms of the Unreal 3–5

deixis
  in Callimachus 53–55
  in Euripides 51–53
  in *Idyll* 1 26–28
  in Menander 51–53
Demetrius
  On Style 51, 73
desire
  erotic 18, 100, 105, 108, 123, 140
  mimetic 18, 22, 114, 118, 127, 128, 141, 145, 165–68
didactic poetry 14
  truth claims in 14
drama
  literary 10–15, 16, 67, 92, 119
  performed 10, 50–53, 92
  dramatic mode 11, 38, 49, 53–57, 60, 72, 76, 82, 86, 114, 144
  direct speech and 13, 17, 24, 57–58, 72, 82
  fictionality and 11, 82–83

ecphrasis
  imagination and 29–40
Euripides 56
  Ion 50–51

fiction
  ancient theories of 6–9
  bucolic and pastoral 2, 14, 21, 117, 141, 160, 168
  comic 8, 13, 21
  fantastic 2, 8, 11–12, 21, 115–16
  postmodern 5, 21, 69, 142
  realist 2, 8, 12–15
fictional world 1–3, 9, 15, 17, 21, 54, 72, 81, 83, 91, 92, 118, 156, 158, 162, 167–68
  building of 28, 69, 156
  ontology of 5, 15, 20–21, 67, 70, 72, 142, 149, 154–57, 162
  presence of 4–6, 10, 11, 49, 60, 67, 72, 81, 91, 92

fictionality 9, 11, 22
    degrees of 7
    selfhood and 99–100, 109, 111–13, 115, 118, 128, 139, 142–45, 154, 158, 165–69

Genette, Gérard 59
genre 7, 9, 23, 46, 118, 150, 153
Girard, René 18, 127, 145

Heracles 82–90, 135–36
Hermesianax
    Leontion 57, 114–16, 118, 145, 148, 166
Herodas 13
    Mimiambus 4 13
        ecphrasis in 34–35
Hesiod 14
    Catalogue of Women 57, 115
    Theogony 6, 117, 131, 137–39, 141, 148, 157
    Works and Days 82, 85
Homer 6, 8, 72
    Longinus on 58, 114
    Muses in 135
    mythological examples in 65
    Odyssey 121–22, 137
    representation of performance in 47–48
    rhapsodic performance of 49
    scholia to 7–8, 59
    Shield of Achilles in 38
Homeric Hymns 53, 58

imagination
    and identification in bucolic song 68, 93–94, 118, 128, 130, 140, 144, 150, 158–59, 162
    in dramatic performance 50–53
    in *Idyll* 1 27–28, 31–36, 40, 46
    in *Idyll* 3 63
    in *Idyll* 7 135, 140
    in *Idyll* 11 72–73, 76–77
    in *Idyll* 12 105, 107
impersonation 46, 67, 93–94, 96–100, 111, 144–45, 152, 165
inspiration 141–43, 148–49
intertextuality 3, 9

Lament for Bion 21, 155–58
    fictional world of 156–57
    history in 156–58
    presence of poet in 155–58
Longinus
    On the Sublime 58–59, 114, 148
Lycidas 17–20, 87, 117, 120–28, 139–40, 154

Menander 8, 56
    Dyskolos 51–53
metafiction 21

mime 2, 11, 13, 54, 118
mimesis 2, 8, 9, 18, 21, 49, 57, 111, 164–65
mise en abyme 38, 64, 126–27
Munatius 21, 153–54
myth 1–3, 6, 8, 11–12, 14–15
    in *Idyll* 3 65–66
    in *Lament for Bion* 156

Nicander 14, 82
non-fiction 11, 14, 82

orality 46–47
    imagination and 46–47

Palaikastro Hymn
    mimesis in 49, 56
performance
    of tragedy and New Comedy 50
    representation of in bucolic poems 41–42, 44–48, 67, 80, 98, 124
Pessoa, Fernando 20–21, 119
    heteronym and autobiography in 20, 141–44
Phanocles
    Erotes 57
Pindar 6
Plato
    Ion 49
    Phaedrus 118, 127, 139
    Republic 16, 55–56, 82, 90, 111–13, 166
Polyphemus 14–17, 68–82, 154
    bucolic imagination of 79
    comic tradition and 70–71
    in *Idyll* 6 96–100
    in *Idyll* 7 135–36

Robbe-Grillet, Alain 39

Sophron 13, 118

Theocritus
    Idyll 1 14–17, 123, 126–27, 131, 140, 151, 155, 159
        dialogue in 25–28
        ecphrasis in 28–40, 45–48
        song in 40–48
    Idyll 2 62, 110
    Idyll 3 16–18, 60–67, 110, 129, 136, 151, 153, 160
        deixis in 61
        theatricality in 61–63, 67
        fictional world of 62–64
        myth in 65–66
    Idyll 4 151
    Idyll 5 17, 22, 131
    Idyll 6 17, 76, 94–100, 152
        framing in 94
        interpreting dramatic situation of 95, 98–99

Index

  Polyphemus in 95–96
  impersonation in 96–100
Idyll 7 17–19, 87, 111, 116–45, 151, 153, 157
  and Virgil's *Eclogues* 163, 166
  as autobiography 116–18, 138–45, 167
  description in 132–34
  fiction in 123
  heteronyms in 144–45
  history in 117
  imagination in 124–26, 135, 140–41
  inspiration in 117, 119, 139, 141
  Lycidas in 117, 120–28, 139, 144, 145
  miniaturization in 126–27
  mythical examples in 134–36
  presence of poet in 145, 154
  Simichidas in 118, 128–38
  unique form of 119, 136
Idyll 8 22, 100, 152
Idyll 9 22, 100, 151
Idyll 10 74–76, 87
Idyll 11 16, 67–82, 109, 152, 166
  framing in 68, 72–73, 78
  naming in 69
  fictional revisionism and 69–71
  imaginary vision in 77, 79, 80–82
Idyll 12 18, 22, 100–11, 129, 154
  comparisons in 101–03
    temporality in 103–04, 106–07
    fantasy in 107–08
    speaker of 109–10
    world of 109–10
Idyll 13 16, 22, 82–90
  framing in 82
  narrative distance in 83, 89–90
  representation of speech in 86–88
Idyll 14 13
Idyll 15 13
  ecphrasis in 34–35
Idyll 16 121
Idyll 22 58
Idyll 24 11–12
Idyll 27 100
scholia to 21, 24, 29–31, 33, 59, 150–54
Theon 153
truth and falsehood
  in early Greek poetry 6

Virgil
  Aeneid 137, 166
  Eclogues 22, 150, 159–66
    form of 161–62
    history in 159–60, 166
    presence of poet in 160–67
    Servius on 160, 164–65

Printed in Great Britain
by Amazon.co.uk, Ltd.,
Marston Gate.